Latino
Political
Power

LATINOS:
EXPLORING DIVERSITY AND CHANGE

Latino Political Power

Kim Geron

LYNNE
RIENNER
PUBLISHERS

BOULDER
LONDON

Published in the United States of America in 2005 by
Lynne Rienner Publishers, Inc.
1800 30th Street, Boulder, Colorado 80301
www.rienner.com

and in the United Kingdom by
Lynne Rienner Publishers, Inc.
3 Henrietta Street, Covent Garden, London WC2E 8LU

Library of Congress Cataloging-in-Publication Data
Geron, Kim, 1951–
  Latino political power / Kim Geron.
      p. cm.—(Latinos, exploring diversity and change)
  Includes bibliographical references and index.
  ISBN 1-58826-000-3 (hardcover : alk. paper)
  ISBN 1-58826-321-5 (pbk. : alk. paper)
  1. Hispanic Americans—Politics and government—20th century.   2. Hispanic
Americans—Politics and government—21st century.   3. Power (Social
sciences)—United States—History—20th century.   4. Power (Social
sciences)—United States—History—21st century.   5. Political
participation—United States—History—20th century.   6. Political
participation—United States—History—21st century.   I. Title.   II. Series.
  E184.S75G47   2005
  320.973'089'68—dc22
                                                                          2004029654

British Cataloguing in Publication Data
A Cataloguing in Publication record for this book
is available from the British Library.

Printed and bound in the United States of America

       The paper used in this publication meets the requirements
  ∞   of the American National Standard for Permanence of
       Paper for Printed Library Materials Z39.48-1992.

       5   4   3   2   1

Contents

Tables

1

Pathways to Incorporation

In 1963, an electoral nonviolent revolution took place in the south Texas town of Crystal City. While no shots were fired, the impact of what took place has reverberated for more than forty years. Fed up with the domination of an entrenched Anglo leadership that controlled the politics of the local schools, city council, and economic affairs of the town, an alliance formed between the Political Association of Spanish-Speaking Organizations (PASSO) and the Teamsters Union to change local politics. Led by Juan Cornejo, a local leader of the cannery workers' division of Teamsters, a dedicated group of Mexican American political activists organized to topple the entrenched Anglo political leaders and replace them with five Mexican American city council members.[1] This bold action, long overdue in a town with a 75 percent Mexican population, launched the contemporary movement for political incorporation by Mexican Americans and other Latinos throughout the United States. This book introduces the reader to the efforts of countless numbers of Latinos who have sought to fully participate in the U.S. political system at its most basic level, as voters, political participants, candidates for office, and officeholders.

A largely untold story in American politics is the ascension of Latinos to elected office nationwide. In the early years of the twenty-first century there are Latino elected officials at the local, state, and federal level; many have achieved elected office fairly recently due to changing political structures, demographics, and Latinos' growing awareness of the importance of holding political power. Although there is uneven progress in the extent of office holding from state to state and community to community, Latinos have established considerable influence statewide in several key Electoral College states, including California, Florida, and Texas. Latinos are also the dominant influence in numerous large cities, such as Miami and San Antonio, and have growing influence in other cities such as New York, Los Angeles, Chicago, and San Jose.

1

Yet Latinos in political office are not a new phenomenon in the United States. Spanish and Mexican settlers arrived in the late 1500s and established settlements and governed themselves in the northern New Mexico area beginning in the early 1600s under the sovereignty of Spain and Mexico.[2] After the United States annexed the northern half of Mexico in 1848, following the war between the United States and Mexico, the New Mexico region became a U.S. territory. The Hispano descendants continued to govern themselves until New Mexico became a state in 1912. Mexicans who remained in the Southwest region of the United States following the annexation of northern Mexico became U.S. citizens; over the next 100 years some of them were elected to political office, including city council and mayor, U.S. senator, U.S. House of Representatives member, and governor. Outside of New Mexico, however, only a handful of Latinos were elected to office; by and large Latinos remained marginalized in the U.S. electoral arena. This began to change in the 1960s.

This book is a comparative analysis of the diversity of Latino politics. It explores the political struggles of Mexican Americans, Puerto Ricans, Cubans, Dominicans, Salvadorans, Colombians, and other Latinos in rural, suburban, and urban areas of the United States to make a transition from marginalized descendants of the Spanish conquest and indigenous peoples, to immigrants and political refugees, and to officeholders and decision makers. While the media have begun to focus on the growing significance of the Latino vote for presidential elections, the development of Latino political efforts at the state and local levels has not received much coverage. The aim of this book is to explain one facet of a larger story of the Latino political experience—the efforts of Latinos to obtain political power, particularly at the local level, where the forces of opposition to their efforts at achieving political equality have been most virulent.

The purpose of this book is twofold: (1) to describe the transition of Latinos from disenfranchised outsiders to political leaders and policymakers at the local level and, increasingly, at the statewide level, and (2) to observe the relationships they hold with their ethnic communities as candidates and as elected officials. I examine to what degree Latino elected officials are sensitive to ethnic community concerns and whether they deliver policy benefits to their communities. This book highlights how Latinos have achieved political empowerment and how they have provided leadership in office. After obtaining elected office, not all Latinos act the same. Some are more responsive to ethnic community needs; others are more attentive to concerns of the larger communities they serve; still others straddle ethnic community needs and universal needs in their policymaking priorities. This chapter begins with a discussion of key terms used in the text, including the racialization process of Latinos; then the underrepresentation of Latinos in politics is briefly reviewed. Next, an exploration of the growing impact Latinos are having on electoral power in the twenty-first century provides a look into contemporary Latino politics. This is followed by a discussion of the concepts explored in the text, including representation and political incorporation.

What is Latino politics? A discussion of the terms used in this text must by necessity begin with a definition of *politics*. Politics is the study of who gets what, when, and how. The *who* are the participants in politics, including voters, interest groups, political parties, and elected and appointed government officials. The *what* are the public policies produced by the political system in areas such as education, health care, and national defense. *When* and *how* refer to the dynamics of the political process, including campaigns for office and elections, implementation of legislation, and decisions made by the courts.[3]

In this book, the term *Latino* is used to refer to all individuals originally from Spanish-speaking regions of Latin America and the Caribbean. *Latino* does not refer to a specific race of people, rather it is inclusive of indigenous, white, black, Asian, and mixed-race people. As Marcelo Suarez-Orozco and Mariela Paez note, "The Latino population is a highly heterogeneous population that defies easy generalizations."[4] The term *Latino politics* will be used to refer to the broad array of efforts by Latinos in politics, whether they are joint efforts by several national-origin groups working together in one group or political activity or the efforts simply of one national-origin group.

The term *Hispanic* is used by the U.S. government, and some who self-identify themselves, to include anyone from a Spanish-speaking region, including Spain. This term will be used sparingly, except where it refers to a governmental designation or in those instances where this is the chosen self-designation. While *Hispanic* is controversial in some quarters, in a recent survey conducted by the Pew Hispanic Center, it was preferred over other such terms.[5]

Mexican American and *Chicano* are used to refer to people of Mexican descent raised in the United States. The term *Chicano* became popular among Mexican American political activists in the late 1960s as a means of political self-definition, and it retains popularity today. Others from a Spanish-origin population apply terms such as *Hispano*, *Spanish American*, and *Latin* to their heritage. *Tejanos* and *Californios* are used to refer to Mexicans who lived in what is now the U.S. Southwest before its annexation in 1848. Where possible, the word or term used in previous research or in a group or person's self-identification is used. *White* and *Anglo* are used to refer to non-Latino Caucasians, and *black* and *African American* are used to refer to residents of the United States with an African heritage. People from the Caribbean islands are referred to by their country of origin; similarly, persons from Central and South America are referred to by their country of origin.

In spite of the diversity among Latinos, a common political legacy has been formed by their collective experiences and identity. This is not to say each distinct national-origin group does not have unique political as well as other characteristics, but the dominant U.S. political system has racialized Spanish-speaking peoples from throughout the hemisphere into a broad category known by labels such as *Latino, Hispanic,* and *Hispanic American.* In other circumstances, multiple national-origin groups of Latinos are racially lumped into one predominant group such as Mexican, Puerto Rican, or Cuban by those outside the Latino community, such as government agencies, the English-speaking media, and the public. In both instances, this has the effect of diluting national distinctions, and many Latinos find such dilution problematic.

Racialization is "the construction of racially unequal social hierarchies characterized by dominant and subordinate social relations between groups."[6] One form racialization takes is the U.S. government's use of racial and ethnic categories for census enumeration and apportionment for political representation. After each ten-year census, federal, state, and local governments redivide political boundaries based in part on broad racial and group categories, including Hispanic. This process groups together all persons with Spanish-speaking origins and countries. The lumping of peoples from throughout the Americas into one category masks important political and social differences among Latinos, such as the influence of homeland politics, national-origin distinctions, party affiliation, citizenship status, and ideological beliefs. On the positive side, the commonality of a panethnic designation has brought Latinos together to work for shared political goals including civil rights, redistricting of electoral boundaries, support for bilingual education, and equal opportunity.

Still, despite efforts at cooperation among Latino ethnic groups and the growth of panethnic organizations, in the present period there is no political agenda adhered to by all Latinos. The heterogeneity of political views among the major ethnic groups, the lack of an identifiable national leader (or leaders) who could unite all Latinos around a common program, and a high percentage of new immigrants in the Latino community with strong ties to their country of origin make political unity difficult in the short run. While Latinos tend to agree on some social issues such as support for bilingual education, they are not united in their views on other issues, such as immigration—particularly undocumented immigrants. In 2004, 60 percent of registered Latinos believed undocumented immigrants help the economy, while more than 30 percent said these immigrants hurt the economy by driving down wages.[7] This disharmony does not permit the development of a political agenda that would unite Latinos nationally. Instead, the presence

of Democrat and Republican Latinos in Congress and in several state legislatures reflects political and more fundamental ideological differences and
has resulted in distinct Latino caucuses based on party affiliation at the
state and federal levels.

Nevertheless, as racial minorities in the United States, the majority of
Latinos find themselves in barrios with poor educational institutions, where
crime and drugs are prevalent, and where politically they have been disenfranchised until very recently. This book makes the case that the Latino
community in the twenty-first century has developed common political
experiences, whether they live in Lawrence, Massachusetts; Orlando,
Florida; Brownsville, Texas; Cicero, Illinois; Pueblo, Colorado; or
Oakland, California, and these similar experiences cross state lines and
regional particularities. Today, a typical group experience of Latinos,
whether they are American born or immigrant, involves participating in
efforts to achieve political incorporation at the local level and beyond. In
some instances, Latinos join together as Latinos, not simply as an alliance
of national-origin Latinos. Other times there is a go-it-alone attitude, with
an emphasis on national-origin compatriots. This is both a unique and not
so unique experience: like African Americans and other racial minorities,
Latinos have learned they need to join together to increase their opportunities for advancement, yet at times there is only limited cooperation among
Latino national-origin groups. Nevertheless, there is some evidence that a
distinct brand of politics known as Latino politics has emerged in the
United States. Time will tell whether it becomes established as a distinctive
form of politics or becomes more similar to the political activities of other
groups.

■ The Underrepresentation of Latinos

Historically, the domination of politics and economics by Anglos was
almost universal in the United States. There were virtually no nonwhite
elected officials until the 1950s, except in New Mexico and a few local
areas. The emergence of the modern Latino civil rights and nationalist
movements in the 1960s and 1970s forced open the political process to an
ethnic group previously disenfranchised.[8] Latinos used a variety of methods to gain entrance to institutions that had previously excluded them, "but
underrepresentation remained the rule."[9] Inequalities in employment,
unequal access to education, limited opportunities for social advancement,
and a cultural bias that privileged the language, customs, and values of
whites were difficult to overcome. According to pluralist theory, an important theory in the study of U.S. politics, power is dispersed in society somewhat equally among various groups and institutions; thus no one group

dominates the full policy agenda in American politics. However, the experiences of racial minorities, including Latinos, reveal continuing major disparities between whites and nonwhites in the political sphere and other aspects of society. Conventional pluralism is unable to explain why racial minorities have little power in our society despite the growth of interest groups focused on equality. The theory of two-tiered pluralism more accurately describes the system's formal political inclusion of minorities with whites while minorities remain marginalized with few avenues for full participation and equality.[10]

The political legacy of discrimination and marginalization of minority groups is manifested in underrepresentation in elected offices. According to one author, "When marginalized groups are chronically underrepresented in legislative bodies, citizens who are members of those groups are not fairly represented."[11] The extent of electoral empowerment of racial minorities can be viewed as a measure of whether the U.S. political system can be categorized as just: "Equal access to decision making is therefore defined as an equal opportunity to influence the policy-making process. Such a situation has two elements: a realistic opportunity to participate on the basis of self-defined interests and a continuous opportunity to hold representatives accountable to community-based interests."[12]

To gain access to the electoral process, Latinos have used grassroots activism, legal challenges, and group protest.[13] The passage of the Voting Rights Act in 1965, the extension of voting rights legislation to language minorities in 1975, the elimination of structural barriers to participation, and the creation of single-member districts eliminated many formal barriers to inclusion.

These legal and structural changes, combined with group mobilization efforts, have enabled Latinos to hold elected office in locations, and in numbers, not previously possible. In 1973, a few years after the passage of the Voting Rights Act, there were only 1,280 Spanish-surnamed officials in the six largest Latino-population states.[14] The growth of Latino political efforts in the post–civil rights era of the 1980s and 1990s is evident in the numbers of Latinos who hold elective office at all levels of government. In 2004, there were 4,853 Latino elected officials, 29 percent of them Latinas (see Table 1.1).

Yet the total number of Latino elected officials (LEOs) is still woefully discrepant with Latinos' percentage of population. The 4,853 LEOs listed in Table 1.1 represented less than 1 percent of the nation's 513,200 elected officials,[15] while the Latino population had risen from 9 to 12.5 percent between 1990 and 2000.[16] By comparison, there were 9,101 African Americans in office in 2001,[17] and African Americans were also 12.5 percent of the total population in 2000. Thus the number of African American elected officials is nearly double the number of LEOs for a comparable

Table 1.1   Total Latino Elected Officials, 2004

Level of Office	Number of Males	Number (and Percentage) of Latinas	Total
U.S. representative	15	7 (47)	22
State officials	7	3 (43)	10
State senators	41	20 (49)	61
State representatives	119	41 (34)	160
County officials	307	167 (54)	474
Municipal officials	1,188	397 (33)	1,585
Judicial/law enforcement	488	150 (31)	638
Education/school boards[a]	1,118	605 (54)	1,723
Special districts	143	37 (26)	180
Total	3,426	1,427 (29)	4,853

Source: National Directory of Latino Elected Officials (2004).
Note: a. Does not include Chicago local school council members.

minority population. While the number of African American elected officials still falls far short of their percentage of the population, their larger number relative to LEOs reflects several factors, including the long struggle to obtain the right to vote in the South and a high rate of U.S. citizenship, which has enabled more African Americans to participate in the voting process and vote for an African American candidate.[18]

The imbalance in the number of LEOs relative to the Latino percentage of the population reflects a combination of factors, including the legacy of exclusion and structural barriers faced by Latino candidates for office, low participation rates in politics among Latino groups, and a high percentage of immigrants who are not yet engaged in politics. Latino elected officials are concentrated in nine states, including three of the four largest states in the country (see Table 1.2). These nine states represented 82 percent of the

Table 1.2   LEOs in Selected States, 2003

State	Total
Arizona	363
California	987
Florida	91
Colorado	149
New York	89
Texas	1,967
New Mexico	634
Illinois[a]	78
New Jersey	76
Total	4,434

Source: NALEO Education Fund (2003).
Note: a. The number of officials from Illinois does not include local school site councils.

Latino population and accounted for more than 96 percent of Latino elected officials in 2003. In California, New Mexico, and Texas, LEOs represented 75 percent of all Latinos elected in the United States.[19]

■ The Impact of Latinos in Recent Electoral Campaigns

While historically Latinos have enjoyed very limited electoral success, this is beginning to change. The growth and presence of Latinos in electoral politics is evident in recent high-profile electoral campaigns in the Southwest and other areas in the United States. In 2001, in New York, Los Angeles, and Houston—three of the four largest U.S. cities—Latino politicians mounted well-funded, credible challenges for the office of mayor. In 2002, Latino candidates in Texas and New Mexico sought the governorship and ran highly competitive campaigns. The unsuccessful campaign of Tony Sanchez in Texas and the successful campaign of Bill Richardson in New Mexico (both were Democrats) illustrate the difficulties and the opportunities for Latinos to achieve statewide elected office. In November 2004, two Latino candidates, Mel Martinez from Florida and Ken Salazar from Colorado, made political history by becoming the first Latinos elected to serve in the U.S. Senate in nearly thirty years. Also, "John Salazar, the brother of U.S. Senator elect Ken Salazar, became the first Latino elected to the U.S. House of Representatives from the State of Colorado, bringing the total number of Latinos in Congress to 27."[20]

Tony Sanchez's race took place within a highly racialized atmosphere in Texas. Sanchez was attempting to defeat incumbent Rick Perry, who had been elected after George W. Bush was elected president. Sanchez, a wealthy south Texas oilman, spent millions of his own money in the attempt to win elected office. He had never held elected office previously and ran against an established politician. Sanchez did very well in heavily Mexican districts and did poorly among white voters. According to an exit poll, 85 percent of Latino voters voted for him.[21] Bill Richardson, meanwhile, was successful in New Mexico, where Latinos make up more than 40 percent of the population. Richardson had name recognition and had been previously elected to a high-level office. His opponent was also Mexican American, so racial dynamics were less apparent in the outcome of this race.

In the 2001 mayoral races, racial dynamics and locations of certain contests in the Northeast, South, and Southwest illustrate the growing strength of, and problems confronting, Latino politics nationally. Latino politicians ran historic campaigns for mayor and nearly won their elections in three of America's largest cities and were successful in numerous other cities. New York City uses a partisan election format: candidates compete in party primaries first and then compete with the opposing party candidates in the general election. If no candidate in the primary election receives 50 percent of the vote, then a runoff election is held between the two top vote getters. Fernando Ferrer, a seasoned Puerto Rican political veteran, was the leading vote getter in the Democratic Party primary but was defeated in a tight runoff by Mark Green, a liberal white candidate. Ferrer's defeat came despite his having built a coalition of African Americans and Latinos. While Latinos and blacks together make up 51.5 percent of New York City's population, they make up a much smaller percentage of the voters. While Ferrer won 70 percent of African American votes, he only gained 20 percent of white votes, and he failed to mobilize enough Latino voters to the polls. In the primary runoff, white ethnic voters, whose votes were originally divided between three white candidates, voted en masse for Green. In the runoff, Latinos and African Americans were angry that Green had wooed white voters with racial code words in his final campaign ads, implying that Ferrer could not be trusted and criticizing his connection to Al Sharpton, a well-known African American community activist (and presidential candidate in 2004).

After the Green victory, his campaign was unable to smooth over the problems with Ferrer and Sharpton. Many Latino and black voters responded by either switching allegiances or sitting out the general election. In the general election, Republican candidate Michael Bloomberg defeated Mark Green. In a city with a 4:1 Democratic Party registered-voter lead over Republican voters, the impact of race was undeniable in the final vote outcome.

Los Angeles uses a nonpartisan election format for mayor, and the first candidate to receive 50 percent of the vote wins. If no candidate gains 50 percent of the vote, a runoff election is held between the top two candidates. Antonio Villaraigosa, a popular Mexican American former State Assembly member who rose quickly to become the speaker of the California State Assembly, built a broad coalition of Latinos, labor, and liberals to become the top vote getter in the general election. He was defeated in the runoff, however, to James Hahn, a white liberal who had served as the Los Angeles City attorney for twenty years.

While Villaraigosa was successful in establishing a broad left-liberal coalition, Hahn won by carrying mainstream and conservative white voters from the San Fernando Valley area of Los Angeles and a decisive 80 percent of the black vote. Two very important, perhaps decisive, factors were Hahn's extensive family ties to the black community (his father was a long-time county supervisor and had mentored many African Americans who rose to become senior leaders in the area) and some questionable ads that marred the campaign. Latino leaders charged that Hahn trafficked in racial stereotypes with a last-minute campaign ad that criticized Villaraigosa for supporting amnesty for a drug dealer and linked his image to the use of crack cocaine and drug dealing. In a city with a Latino population of 48 percent, Villaraigosa lost 54–46 percent in the runoff election.

In Houston, the mayor's election is a two-stage process. The general election involves multiple candidates, as there are no party primaries. Candidates are not formally labeled by party affiliation. If no one candidate obtains a majority of the votes, a runoff between the two highest voter getters is held. In 2001, Orlando Sanchez, a Cuban American Republican at-large member of the city council, was one of two top vote getters in the general election. In the runoff, Sanchez put together a campaign that combined a heavy focus on Latinos and white conservative voters. He stressed cultural and linguistic pride and fiscal conservatism. Well-known African American incumbent mayor Lee Brown narrowly defeated him.[22]

These big-city mayoral campaigns, along with the Southwest governor's races, the U.S. senatorial campaigns, and the growing number and influence of Latino voters, signal the arrival of Latino politics on the national scene. The Villaraigosa campaign took place in the city with the largest number of Latinos, primarily of Mexican descent, in the country. Latinos make up nearly the majority of the population of Los Angeles and are on the cusp of leading a dramatic transition to a new Los Angeles in the twenty-first century, where Latinos will numerically dominate but have yet to achieve political leadership. In New York City, the 2001 mayoral campaign was overshadowed by the terrorist attack on September 11. Nevertheless, the Ferrer campaign also broke new ground in big-city politics, particularly in the Northeast, home to large numbers of Puerto Ricans, Dominicans, and other new immigrant Latino voters. With 27 percent of the New York City population, the Latino community has a significant number of voters. The Sanchez campaign for governor of Texas was significant because it demonstrated the ability of a wealthy individual of Mexican descent to fund a major campaign for office in the second-largest state in the country. The Richardson electoral victory in New Mexico reestablished the importance of Latinos in a state that contains the highest percentage of Latino voters in the country. The Martinez and Salazar campaigns for U.S. Senate broke new ground in demonstrating the statewide appeal of credible, well-funded Latino candidates from both political parties.

With much less national publicity, Latinos were successful in retaining or winning the office of mayor in Albuquerque, Austin, El Paso, Miami, and San Antonio in 2001. San Antonio is America's ninth largest city, and of the ten largest cities, it is the only one with a majority Latino population. San Antonio is also a historic center of Mexican American politics. Ed Garza's campaign enabled a Mexican American to win the mayor's office, which had not been held by a Mexican American since Henry Cisneros's terms (1981–1989).

Meanwhile, in hundreds of cities, counties, school districts, and state capitols around the country, Latinos continued their steady march toward political empowerment as they won election to office or were returned as incumbents. In Connecticut in 2001, Eddie Perez became the first Puerto Rican elected mayor of Hartford, the state capital, after fashioning a multiethnic coalition. Perez, a community activist, won election in a city with a 40 percent Latino population and signaled the growing influence of Latinos in the Northeast region.[23]

Latinos in the United States are still searching for means to increase their political clout. While they recently became the nation's largest minority group, they are not a homogenous political voting block; this diversity represents a challenge for both major parties. In addition to their voting behavior, the attainment of political power by Latinos is tied to a number of factors including their economic resources, demographics in electoral districts, and influence in political parties. There are also issues of social class and racial identity, the role of grassroots organizing, and the use of various electoral strategies to achieve power. All of these need to be considered to determine their usefulness as explanatory factors in a study of Latinos politics and political representation.

■ Latinos and Representation in Government

Political representation has been the focus of the struggle for political equality by people of color, women, and others historically disadvantaged. *Political representation* refers to a prescribed relationship between elected officials and constituents. There are different dimensions of representation: formal, descriptive, symbolic, and substantive.[24] Descriptive representation for people of color matches the race, ethnicity, or national origin of the representative and his or her constituents.[25] As one author states, "Voters want to see someone who looks like them in office. Black voters tend to support black candidates and Hispanic voters tend to support Hispanic candidates."[26] The highest form of representation is substantive representation, where a representative acts in the interests of the represented, in a manner responsive to them.[27] The main component of substantive representation is policy responsiveness: "there should be meaningful connection between the representative and the represented."[28]

Descriptive representation, in which the representative reflects the social composition of the people he or she represents, is still an important goal to achieve in many Latino communities. Once elected, Latino officeholders need to bring both symbolic and material benefits to the Latino community.[29] Symbolic representation is important because Latino elected officials become role models to a community that has had few visible political leaders. Yet symbolism is not enough; the majority of Latinos remain impoverished, with many social problems that need to be addressed.

Economic resources are needed to provide affordable housing, expand youth services, improve the quality of education, and build recreational facilities. The structural inequalities in America severely limit what politicians can do to erase fundamental problems of inequality and poverty. Nevertheless, under certain circumstances some Latino officials have taken action to direct resources to address longstanding problems in the Latino community. Such actions need to be analyzed. Of course, Latino politicians do not exist in a vacuum; LEOs have also prioritized universal issues such as economic development, fiscal accountability, crime reduction, environmental cleanup, and traffic congestion reduction. While these types of issues are concerns within Latino communities, the benefits of new policies are not specifically directed at the elected official's own community.

In a democracy there are limits to what an individual representative can accomplish for his or her constituents, since competing interests and priorities vie for the attention of lawmakers in all levels of government. Particularly for minority legislators, ascending to elected office has not always substantively benefited the constituents who helped put them into office.[30] Some argue that minority legislators and executives have only begun to achieve political power after many years of exclusion; they are still a minority of the elected officials at the federal level and in state capitols and have limited resources at the local level to solve basic inequalities.[31]

■ Latinos and Political Incorporation Theory

To move from disenfranchisement to political power, Latinos have used a variety of methods. To explain the process of achieving and retaining political power, I use political incorporation theory. The theory of political incorporation is a central idea in the study of politics; when a group is politically incorporated, it has opportunities to influence public policy.[32] According to Rufus Browning, Dale Marshall, and David Tabb, political incorporation explains local "movements demanding the power of political equality and their ability to achieve it."[33] *Political incorporation* is a widely used term to measure the extent to which group interests are effectively represented in policymaking in government.[34] At the lowest level, a group is not represented at all: there are no elected officials from the group, and the group does not participate in the governing coalition that controls political decision making through its use of resources. At the next level, racial minorities have formal representation in a governing body, but the government body is dominated by a coalition resistant to minority group interests.

The highest form of incorporation is when racial minorities have an equal or a leading role in a dominant coalition that is strongly committed to minority group interests.

For Latinos, the achievement of political incorporation has been uneven; there is wide divergence in the levels of incorporation at the local, state, and national levels. Because the history of political movements of Latinos to achieve incorporation has unfolded differently in state and local contexts, patterns of mobilization have also evolved differently. In some situations, Latinos were until recently completely excluded from access to government. In other situations, they were partially included in a governing coalition as junior partners in political party or business-centered slates. Under certain circumstances, they achieved an equal or dominant role without the use of a biracial coalition; an example is the achievement of Cubans in Miami.[35]

Groups seek to obtain political objectives in several ways. Groups can petition or pressure government from the outside (the interest group strategy) or they may seek to achieve representation and a position of power or authority by electing members of the group to office (the electoral strategy). Each of these approaches is pursued depending on the circumstances that exist. The protest strategy is usually employed when a group has been excluded and seeks to use group pressure to win appointments to positions, program funds, and increased hiring of members of the group. The electoral strategy is used when a group is sufficiently large to win office by itself or with allies in a coalition.[36]

■ Pathways to Political Incorporation

I have modified these two forms of mobilization to include other pathways to incorporation. There are at least four distinct pathways to political incorporation: (1) demand/protest, (2) nonconfrontational political evolution, (3) legal challenges to structural barriers, and (4) coalition politics.

The first pathway, demand/protest, includes violent and nonviolent protests (sit-ins, demonstrations, boycotts) and also includes more traditional tactics such as mass mobilization at city meetings and exchanges with city officials.[37] A second pathway is a more gradual political evolution without demand and protest; instead, individuals in the Latino community are cultivated by political elites to run for office, usually as probusiness candidates and as alternatives to more grassroots candidates. A third pathway is the use of legal challenges, usually voting-rights lawsuits that challenge redistricting and reapportionment plans and that lead to restructuring the electoral system. Latinos have used the legal approach nationally in many communities to overturn discriminatory political structures and create single-member districts.

The fourth pathway is the use of coalition politics. Browning, Marshall, and Tabb discuss the critical importance of biracial coalitions of minorities and liberal whites to achieve political incorporation for minorities where the minority group is not a majority of the local population. I view the coalition pathway as including other possibilities depending on the situation, such as African American and Latino coalition efforts in cities like Pomona, California, in 1987 and New York City in 2001. It can also include Latino-labor alliances, such as in the 2001 mayor's race in Los Angeles.

These pathways are not mutually exclusive; each may include aspects of other pathways to achieve political incorporation. Latino political incorporation efforts have historically used all of them in small towns, medium-sized cities, major urban centers, and state houses of government.

What can reasonably be expected in a democratic society as a result of the incorporation of previously disenfranchised groups? One school of thought holds that there are limits to what local officials can accomplish, given the fiscal limitations of local government in this era of global capital mobility and decreased federal and state assistance.[38] Others argue that while there are indeed limits to what public bodies can accomplish in an era of globalization and fiscal conservatism, this does not mean that local government has no ability to redirect resources.[39] The general fund portion of any budget can be directed to address problems including inequalities; however, the level of resources will depend on the structural limitations of available funds. Furthermore, city leaders do not simply respond to a cost-benefit analysis of the prospect of economic advancement and political empowerment of racial groups. Poor and working-class people sometimes exercise power when they mobilize in mass defiance, breaking the rules that have restricted their participation in the institutions of a densely interdependent society.[40] At times resources are redirected to confront systemic problems. Many of the antipoverty programs of the 1960s arose in response to the riots in urban communities by racial minorities.

In addition to the structural arguments about achieving political power, there is the historical argument that the deeply embedded character of race relations and the history of racial antagonisms on an individual and institutional level have limited full participation by people of color in the economic, political, and cultural arenas of our society. The weight of this economic, political, and cultural domination has forced Latinos to try to overcome the legacy of exclusion, or condescension by Anglo politicians. The various outcomes of those efforts are important to document and compare.

As historical barriers to political inclusion have come down, Latino electoral efforts have blossomed; however, not enough is known about the consequences of these changes. Obviously, not all electoral efforts begin in the same way or seek to achieve the same objectives or accomplish the same goals. These distinctions in the empowerment of Latinos reflect basic differences in political conditions and the individual philosophies of candidates regarding the role of government. Both internal dynamics within ethnic communities and forces external to the Latino community influence its political development.

In short, this book examines Latina and Latino efforts to overcome discriminatory barriers, seek political office, and establish policy priorities once in elected office. It explores how LEOs address the challenges of limited resources and conflicting interests that confront all elected officials, while maintaining ties to the Latino community. In particular, this text explores the role of Latinas, immigrants, and ethnic-specific and panethnic Latino politics.

■ Research and Data Sources

The research for this book is based on primary and secondary sources. Archival research, survey data, in-depth interviews, and ethnographic methods were used to gather materials. In 1997–98, I conducted forty semi-structured interviews with a cross-section of community leaders and activists in Watsonville and Salinas, California, and observed firsthand how Latino politics operated in these two communities. I lived and worked there and took part in local politics as a participant observer, gaining insights from the politicians, government officials, and business and community activists. Subsequently, I have continued to study these two cities and observe the unfolding of Latino power.

A mail survey was completed by a random sample of 112 Latino elected officials in 2000–2001. I also conducted forty-four in-person interviews with Latino elected officials during the summer and fall of 2001 in several major sites of Latino political activities in eight states, to observe the dynamics of contemporary Latino politics in local communities; I also conducted archival research in public libraries, universities, and local governments in those areas.[41] I also spoke with scholars and activists in many of the cities to draw on their insights about how Latino politics operates in different contexts. Subsequently, I have continued to interview elected officials and study more recent political developments in several cities and counties.

I have also attended a variety of national conferences and meetings of organizations involved with Latino politics, including the National Association of Latino Elected and Appointed Officials and the Southwest Voter Registration Fund (SWREF). A detailed review of articles, books, dissertations, and studies about Latino politics was completed as part of this research. This combination of research methodologies and sources has produced a study that combines the practical experiences of electoral politics with analytical observations about Latino politics.

■ Organization of the Book

This is an introductory text about Latinos in American politics. Its purpose is to provide an overview of historical and current efforts by Latinos to achieve political power. While there are many books written on the Latino experience, and several have been written on Latino politics, this book discusses in detail the strategies and methods Latinos have used to achieve political power. Furthermore, it tracks what happened once Latinos achieved political incorporation in various political contexts. The electoral arena is not the only, nor even the main, vehicle that Latinos have used to achieve equal treatment under the law, end discrimination in schools, housing, and jobs, oppose racist stereotyping, and create positive images of themselves. Nevertheless, a study of the broad range of efforts by Latinos to influence and participate in the electoral system provides a means to explore the progress made to achieve representation.

We are now ready to explore the history and development of Latino politics and its contemporary features. The book is divided into two sections. The first section (Chapters 2–5) examines the history of efforts to achieve political power by Latinos. The second section (Chapters 6–8) analyzes political incorporation efforts and explores the views of Latino elected officials.

Chapter 2 details the history of Latino politics in this country from the 1800s to the 1940s. It chronicles the turmoil of the U.S. annexation of the Southwest and the subsequent political activities of Mexican Americans, as well as those of Puerto Ricans in New York.

Chapter 3 examines the modern era of Latino politics, from the 1950s to the 1970s, when Latinos went from being outsiders to, for the first time, holding office in significant numbers.

Chapter 4 explores the mainstreaming of Latino politics. It continues the political history of Latinos between 1994 and 2001, giving attention to the emergence of new political voices.

Chapter 5 provides a national overview of the demographics and political behavior of Latinos. The chapter also includes an analysis of Latino elected officials at the congressional, state, and local levels and offers a critical look at the interrelationship between Latino candidate types and demographically distinct electoral districts. The chapter concludes with an assessment of the current state of Latino politics and the challenges facing Latino politicians as they extend their influence.

Chapter 6 uses case studies to explore political incorporation strategies and effectiveness of Latinos in the cities of Miami, San Antonio, and Los Angeles.

Chapter 7 highlights the efforts of Chicanos to win and hold office and build an effective local governing coalition in the medium-sized city of Salinas, California.

Chapter 8 examines the views and policy behavior of Latino state and local elected officials nationally and how they perceive their policy priorities.

Chapter 9 summarizes contemporary Latino politics. It draws conclusions from the case studies of Latino political incorporation efforts and looks ahead to future avenues of research.

This book will not explain all facets of Latino politics. A study of Latino grassroots efforts to influence the political process by opposing anti-immigrant laws, fighting discrimination in communities and workplaces, and obtaining quality health care and education lies beyond the scope of this book. These struggles, many of them at the local level, produce the seeds of change that create community leaders. Some of these activists run for office, oftentimes successfully, other times not. *Latino Political Power* seeks to explain the history of political activism that has led to electoral empowerment efforts by Latinos. It is my intent to add to the understanding of Latino politics as part of the broader political process unfolding in the twenty-first century.

■ Notes

1. J. S. Shockley (1974); A. Navarro (1998).
2. In 1680, a mass revolt by the Pueblo Indians forced the Spanish settlers to flee; it took more than a decade for Spain to reestablish its colonial outposts. See M. G. Gonzales (1999).
3. T. R. Dye (2001), p. 1.
4. M. Suárez-Orozco and M. Páez (2002).
5. Pew Hispanic Center and Kaiser Family Foundation (2002b).
6. M. Marrable (2004).
7. Pew Hispanic Center and Kaiser Family Foundation (2004).
8. J. Jennings and M. Rivera (1984); L. Estrada et al. (1988); A. Torres and J. E. Velasquez (1998); C. Munoz (1989).
9. J. Gomez Quiñones (1990).
10. R. Hero (1992).
11. M. S. Williams (1998), p. 3.
12. L. Guinier (1995), p. 24.
13. J. Jennings and M. Rivera (1984); J. Regalado and G. Martinez (1991); A. Navarro (2000).
14. F. Lemus (1973).
15. U.S. Bureau of the Census (1992).

16. U.S. Bureau of the Census (2001b).

17. D. Bositis (2003).

18. The situation is changing as the African Diaspora draws immigrants to the United States; African and Caribbean immigrants of African descent cannot vote until they become U.S. citizens. See D. Fears (2002).

19. National Association of Latino Elected Officials (2003).

20. National Association of Latino Elected Officials (2004).

21. William C. Velásquez Institute (2002).

22. In 2003 Sanchez ran again for mayor of Houston and again was defeated in the runoff, this time by Bill White, an Anglo Democrat. Sanchez received the majority of conservative votes and won a plurality of Latino votes but trailed White among moderate and liberal voters, particularly African Americans, who voted overwhelmingly for the Democratic candidate.

23. E. M. Weiss (2001).

24. H. Pitkin (1967), pp. 11–12.

25. C. Swain (1993), p. 5.

26. C. Menifield (2001b).

27. H. Pitkin (1967), p. 209.

28. K. J. Whitby (1997), p. 7.

29. K. Geron (1998).

30. A. Reed (1995); R. Smith (1990b); J. Regalado (1998).

31. F. Matos Rodríguez (2003); R. Browning, D. Marshall, and D. Tabb (2003), pp. 377–78.

32. A. Stinchcombe (1987).

33. R. Browning, D. Marshall, and D. Tabb (1994).

34. R. Browning, D. Marshall, and D. Tabb (1997), p. 9.

35. D. Moreno (1996).

36. R. Browning, D. Marshall, and D. Tabb (1997), p. 10.

37. R. Browning, D. Marshall, and D. Tabb (1984), p. 78.

38. P. Peterson (1981).

39. S. S. Fainstein et al. (1983); C. Stone and H. Saunders (1987); C. Stone (1989).

40. F. P. Piven and R. A. Cloward (1977).

41. Information on the mail survey is provided in Chapter 8. A list of all interviews conducted can be found in the reference section at the end of the book.

2

Latino Politics
Before World War II

In the 1960s, Latino group efforts gained national prominence with the development of the Chicano movement in the Southwest, the Puerto Rican movement in the Northeast and Midwest, and the arrival of thousands of Cuban refugees to south Florida. While the 1960s was a landmark decade for U.S. Latinos in their political growth and maturation, the seeds of these group efforts had been planted in the colonization and conquest of the Americas by European powers.[1] This chapter explores Latino politics in the United States before the 1940s, focusing on the efforts of Mexicans and later Puerto Ricans to participate in political activities and achieve political incorporation in government. Both of these Latino ethnic groups were visible political activists before World War II. Unfortunately, their group efforts were usually met with exclusion, and their efforts to achieve political empowerment were largely stymied. Other Latino immigrants, such as Cuban émigrés who came during Cuba's war of independence from Spain in 1868, will not be addressed in this chapter but will be discussed later in the book.

People of Spanish-speaking ancestry were active in territorial and pre-annexation politics long before becoming U.S. citizens. Mexicans and Spanish settlers governed themselves for hundreds of years in parts of the Southwest. The indigenous population also had sophisticated forms of government throughout the Americas. After the United States acquired Florida from Spain in 1819, the Florida territory was created, and the first Latino, Joseph Marion Hernandez, was elected as a delegate to the U.S. Congress.[2] Mexico's independence from Spain in 1821 produced a change in governmental structure in the northern territories, as the Mexican government installed new leadership there. However, within twenty-five years Mexico's largest territory, Texas, was occupied by Anglo settlers and annexed by the U.S. government. In 1846, Mexico was invaded by the U.S. military and was forced to surrender after Mexico City was surrounded by troops entering from the north and by a seaborne invasion from Vera Cruz, Mexico. The troops that landed in Vera Cruz marched to the capitol using a route similar to the one traveled by Spanish conqueror, Hernán Cortés, centuries before. After strong resistance, the war would claim 50,000 Mexican lives. Mexico subsequently sold 947,570 square miles of land, almost half its national territory, to the United States. This vast region included only 1 percent of Mexico's population at the time.[3]

Following the end of the Mexican-American War in 1848, the Mexicans who decided to remain in the United States became U.S. citizens, and those who held public office continued to serve where they were allowed to do so. After the creation of the New Mexico Territory in 1850, José Manuel Gallegos was elected as delegate to the U.S. Congress in 1852, the second Latino so elected.[4] Gallegos's election started a succession of Hispanos who served as New Mexico's delegates during its sixty-two years of territorial status.[5] In 1877 a Republican, Romualdo Pacheco, was elected to serve as the first Latino member of Congress from the State of California.

In California, the original Mexican settlers, known as the Californios, governed what was called Alta California before it became a state in 1850. After statehood, in areas where there were numerically more Mexicans than Anglos, the Californios continued to hold state and local elected offices in the nineteenth century.[6] Eventually, as demographics changed and the Anglo American population grew in the West, Mexicans found it extremely difficult to be elected to office, except in New Mexico, where Spanish and Mexican descendants remained the majority population until the middle of the twentieth century. In parts of south Texas, Mexicans remained the majority population, and a few Mexican Americans held elected and appointed positions, but the local party bosses tightly controlled them.[7]

The first half of the twentieth century did not produce many more Latinos elected to the U.S. Congress; two were elected to the House from Louisiana, and three House representatives were elected from New Mexico, including Dennis Chavez in 1930. Chavez went on to serve in the U.S. Senate from 1935 to 1962, one of only three Latinos elected to the Senate until the 2004 election, when two new Hispanic senators were elected— Ken Salazar, Colorado, and Mel Martinez, Florida. The other two senators previously elected were Octaviano Lazzarola and Joseph M. Montoya, both from New Mexico.[8]

While the election of Mexican Americans to federal offices was limited to only two states until the 1960s, throughout the Southwest region they have held public office in territories and states since 1848, when northern Mexico became a territorial part of the United States. Other Latino groups were active in politics before 1960, although without as much electoral success.

The participation of Latinos in the U.S. political process is tied to a number of factors, including the status of Mexicans before the U.S. annexation of the Southwest in 1848, the colonization of Puerto Rico and its impact on migration, the time and location of arrival of subsequent immigrants and political refugees, and the structure of local, state, and federal governments that existed when they arrived. This chapter will focus on the period beginning with the annexation of Mexican lands: the struggle to retain political power in the Southwest during the nineteenth century and the formation of labor and middle-class organizations in the first decades of the twentieth century leading up to World War II. Besides Mexican Americans, the other Latino group with sustained political activity before the 1950s was Puerto Ricans, and they will also be discussed later in this chapter.

While there is some overlap among the different Latino groups in the times of arrival and the growth of political participation, there has been uneven progress due to differences in political experience, class composition of Latino ethnic groups, and levels of participation. Early political activities of Mexican Americans and Puerto Rican migrants will be discussed as they set a context for the post–World War II era of Latino politics. There is no agreement as to when Latino politics commenced in the United States. For example, some scholars of Mexican American politics highlight a period of Chicano politics that began in the 1930s, which one author has dubbed "the Mexican American Generation."[9] Scholars of Puerto Rican politics in the United States also point to early political organizing efforts that preceded World War II.[10] Other scholars begin their exploration of Latino politics in the preannexation period in the Southwest, when Spanish and Mexican settlers built communities and practiced colonial and independent governance in New Mexico.[11]

This book will focus primarily on the efforts of Latinos to achieve political empowerment in the twentieth century, since this is when contemporary Latino groups began to engage in politics in the United States. However, for Mexican Americans the story begins much earlier and requires an analysis to establish the context for understanding contemporary Mexican American politics and the politics of other Latino communities.

■ Mexican and Mexican American Politics Before 1950

Beginning in the 1600s, when Spanish and Mexican explorers settled in northern Mexico and staked their claim to what is now known as the Southwest of the United States, they established missions and settlements with a form of colonial government. Since Mexico remained a colony of Spain until 1821, the descendants of these explorers, along with new inhabitants from Mexico, governed their territories, intermarried with the indigenous population, and carried out economic activities in what is now Texas, Colorado, New Mexico, Arizona, and California.[12] While there were numerous settlements, the total numbers of settlers were quite small, and usually they did not live more than a few hundred miles north of the modern Mexican border. According to Carey McWilliams, before the arrival of white settlers, there were 5,000 Mexicans in Texas, 60,000 in New Mexico, and another 7,500 in California.[13] These settlers were virtually on their own, isolated from both Spanish and Mexican society, and often were vulnerable to attacks by Native Americans.

When Mexico achieved its independence from Spain in 1821, independent forms of government that reflected Spanish roots emerged in its northern territories. Tejanos, or Mexican Texans, were Mexican residents who lived in the province known as Texas. The form of government in Texas before annexation was the *ayuntamiento*, or city council, which had been introduced in the early eighteenth century by the Spanish. After formal recognition by the Spanish government, elections were held for various local offices. Following Mexico's independence from Spain, the Mexican government of Texas continued the implementation and development of the *ayuntamiento* form of government.[14] Despite harsh natural conditions, many of the settlements throughout the Southwest survived and the settlers continued to conquer and Hispanize the Native American tribes they encountered. They governed themselves in south Texas even as increasing numbers of Anglo settlers moved into the territory in the 1820s.[15] This brief period of Mexican rule was shattered in the 1830s, as Anglo settlers in Texas declared their independence from Mexico.

Nevertheless, the strong presence of an electoral structure instituted by the Spanish enabled the widespread election of Mexicans throughout south Texas area. In the city of San Antonio, between 1837 and 1847, fifty-seven of the fifty-eight aldermen were Spanish surnamed.[16] However, among many of the Anglo settlers there were strong anti-Mexican sentiments. In 1845, Anglos tried to exclude Tejanos from voting at the Texas constitutional convention.[17] The ability of Tejanos to influence elections was greatest in the urban areas near the border with Mexico. In rural areas, Tejano political power came to be almost nonexistent as Anglo *patrones* (bosses) gained dominance. The patron controlled the votes of the *peones* who worked the land and manipulated them for his own interests.[18] Members of some wealthy Mexican families in the south Texas region operated as "lesser bosses . . . who entered the political arena to maintain and defend their traditional status."[19] The hand of the Anglo boss was always evident. Mexicans' ability to have any sway in political affairs was contingent on the presence of a large Mexican electorate.[20]

In California, the period before annexation and statehood was characterized by political isolation from Spain and Mexico and domination by the Catholic Church. However, following Mexican independence from Spain in 1821, a new generation of California-born Mexican politicians arose. The original landowning elites in California, the Californios, began to participate in politics; some became delegates to the Mexican Congress, while others served as provincial governors, judges, mayors, and representatives in town councils in California.[21]

The United States and Mexico went to war in 1846 for a variety of reasons, including the annexation of Texas by the United States. The war lasted until 1848 and resulted in the annexation of the remaining territory of northern Mexico. The Treaty of Guadalupe Hidalgo ended the war, and as a result, the U.S. obtained sovereignty over half of Mexico's land. Under the threat of occupation by U.S. troops, and struggling with internal weaknesses in its newly independent institutions, the Mexican government ceded the area now known as the Southwest for $15 million.[22] The original Mexican inhabitants were guaranteed U.S. citizenship rights and protection of language, laws, and religion. In practice, however, the treaty was largely ignored, along with most of its guarantees.

■ After Annexation: 1848–1900

Following the conquest, annexation, and sale of Mexican lands, Mexicans used various methods to adapt to the changed conditions. The Southwest was no longer the northern outpost of Mexican society; instead, it was part of a new frontier controlled by the United States. Drawn by the discovery of gold in California, more than 200,000 European settlers arrived within a few years, along with miners recruited from Mexico and China. One method of adapting to the new political realities was accommodation; the alternative was to resist the occupation of Mexicans' historic lands. Mexican Americans employed both methods.

Gaining U.S. citizenship enabled members of the educated and landowner classes of the original inhabitants from Mexico to hold political positions, and several were elected to office in the Southwest states following the Mexican-American War. This segment of the Mexican American community sought to hold on to some form of power and leadership through accommodation with the U.S. government and alliances with those in power. Some became members of local political machines that answered to the more powerful Anglos. In the territories of New Mexico and Arizona and the states of Texas, California, and Colorado there were numerous Mexican American elected officials, including city and county officials, district judges, and marshals, who accommodated themselves to the Anglo power structure. As the Anglo population grew with continued migration into the region, the Mexican community's influence declined everywhere in the Southwest except for New Mexico.

The Hispano New Mexicans had resided in this territory since the late 1500s. They outnumbered the Anglo population in the territory and used their political skills to gain many major political positions before statehood in 1912. Throughout the territorial period they elected Mexican American delegates to Congress as well as to both state houses and local offices: "This pattern of incumbency allowed the nuevomexicanos to thwart the kind of political domination that befell Mexicanos in other parts of the Southwest."[23]

In those other areas, the decline in Mexican American political influence occurred quite dramatically. In San Antonio, a Mexican settlement long before the Mexican-American War, there was a rapid decrease in office holding by Mexican Americans between 1848 and 1866. During this period, no more than one or two Mexican representatives were elected at any one time. By the period 1895–1904, there were no Mexican representatives elected from this city.[24] Only in a few locations in south Texas and northern New Mexico, where Mexicans remained the majority population until the mid-twentieth century, did they continue to hold significant political offices. Anglo settlers eventually became the majority population, and Mexicans found it difficult to retain electoral positions at state and local levels.

While some Mexican Americans accepted the new political reality of the Southwest, others used resistance and revolted against the occupation of their land by white settlers and the U.S. government. In 1877, the El Paso Salt War erupted after Anglos attempted to privatize the salt beds that belonged to the Mexican community on both sides of the U.S.-Mexico border. For generations the people of the El Paso Valley and those across the river in Mexico had relied on these salt deposits for their livelihood. When an Anglo businessman attempted to lay claim to the salt beds, years of bitter conflict arose between Anglos and the Mexican inhabitants on both sides of the border. Eventually, after numerous violent conflicts, the Texas Rangers and Anglos seized the salt beds.[25]

In New Mexico, Hispanos organized the Gorras Blancas, or White Caps, named for the masks they wore when carrying out night raids on large Anglo landowners in San Miguel County. Hispanos were the dominant population, having lived and self-governed in this county for almost 100 years. The Mexicano majority felt threatened by a sudden and rapid growth in the Anglo population in the 1880s, and the Gorras Blancas responded by cutting the fences of the large Anglo landowners. The Gorras Blancas waged a two-year guerrilla war against the invasion of their homeland by the Anglo outsiders, who sought to change the economic structure of New Mexico: "Striving for ethnic solidarity and touched by egalitarian and anticapitalistic ideology, the White Cap movement gave dramatic proof of Mexican American discontent with the Anglo territorial regime."[26] Local Hispano elected officials in various towns in the county and a community newspaper sought to defend the poor working-class groups that carried out these actions of militant defense of Mexicano land.[27]

The oppositional actions precipitated the formation of El Partido del Pueblo Unido, a new county political party that brought together middle-class and working-class Hispanos. This political organization challenged the existing parties and sought to build a broad Hispano united front against encroachment by Anglos. Unfortunately, politicians bogged down the party, and the members of the working-class base returned to their homes and towns. Thus what had begun as an opposition movement evolved into a political effort that operated within the existing political structure of the day.[28] There were also numerous rebels who organized resistance among Mexicans, both north and south of the U.S.-Mexico border, including Juan Cortina in Texas and Tuburcio Vasquez in California.[29]

The process of California's annexation and statehood left the Mexican population weakened politically but numerically still a visible presence, particularly in southern California. The Spanish-speaking population had a numerical majority until the 1870s and played an active role in local politics. While there was no strong patron class, as in New Mexico and parts of Texas, Anglos and Mexicans cooperated and clashed in the political arena, and political parties arose and competed for voters in the Mexican communities. In Los Angeles and Santa Barbara counties, the Mexican community took a prominent part in elections, with numerous members holding elected office. However, no Californios had statewide stature in the period immediately following statehood. Most politicos were locally based and were limited to those with "wealth, family connections, landownership, or the backing of a bloc of 'Spanish-speaking' voters."[30] They served in a wide variety of capacities, including jurors, judges, party delegates, city council members, mayors, assemblymen, and senators. This period of electoral success changed dramatically as the century came to a close.

By the end of the nineteenth century, as the Anglo population continued to grow and the capitalist economic system expanded in the Southwest, Anglos consolidated their hold on political institutions and elected offices. In the areas where Mexican and Spanish descendants were the dominant population, such as counties in south Texas, northern New Mexico, and southern Colorado, Anglo politicians formed alliances with Mexican American politicos. For example, in rural south Texas "the overwhelming majority were Mexican Americans who worked as ranch hands, farm laborers, sharecroppers, and small ranchers and farmers. Because of the survival of the patron-peon relationships, the large landowners were able to deliver the votes of their lower-class Mexican American employees and neighbors."[31]

In places where Mexicans were not the majority population, they faced more difficulties participating in politics. Devices were employed that limited their participation, including the poll tax and white-only primaries in Texas. The poll tax was used in Southern states to exclude black and Mexicans by requiring persons to pay a tax in order to vote. The white-only primary allowed only whites to participate in primaries and effectively disenfranchised Mexican Americans in local elections. In Dimmit County, Texas, this practice was introduced in 1914 and lasted for several years.[32]

Some Mexican American communities sought to build their political influence by forming political slates to achieve electoral representation and get rid of the political boss system of patronage and control.[33] In many locations, Mexican Americans served on city councils or as county judges, commissioners, and officers of the law.[34] In other locations, where the Mexican American elite was weak, collaboration with Anglo bankers, lawyers, merchants, and politicians was minimal, and the conquest of the political landscape occurred quietly.[35] Overall, levels of political incorporation of Mexican Americans were uneven. In communities where they had the numbers and political status and opportunity, they achieved strong political incorporation; however, in most communities they had weak or nonexistent political representation. Their efforts would grow in the coming decades.

■ The Working Class and the Middle Class Organize: 1900 to the 1930s

In the first thirty years of the twentieth century, Mexican Americans in the Southwest were unable to make major political gains. They were limited by restrictive electoral practices, such as the white primary and the poll tax, and were outnumbered by the rapid growth of the Anglo population, which quickly dominated the economic resources and gained political control in most areas. Large numbers of new immigrants from Mexico, economic and political refugees who arrived during and after the Mexican Revolution (1910–20), greatly increased the numbers of Mexicans but did not increase their political power. In a pattern that would continue for most of the twentieth century, the growing Mexican population was limited politically by its youthfulness, immigrant status, poor educational opportunities, and institutional barriers.

Denied full political participation, Mexicans were drawn into and heavily influenced by the labor movement. Mexican workers played a key role in building the infrastructure and wealth of the Southwest. Mexican labor helped develop agriculture, mining, construction, and the railroads.[36]

Mexican workers were relegated to the lowest-paying and dirtiest jobs; many joined unions and became leaders of labor struggles in the Southwest and Midwest regions.[37] Unfortunately, anti-Mexican sentiments that emerged in the 1920s, as part of restrictive legislation embodied in the Quota Acts of 1921 and 1924, continued to grow. When the Great Depression began in 1929, an intense period of repatriation to Mexico began, involving the indiscriminate removal of hundreds of thousands of Mexican nationals and U.S. citizens of Mexican descent; this lasted until 1935.[38]

Still, Mexican Americans began to achieve limited political progress in the 1930s. In the Southwest, Mexican Americans had been elected to several state legislatures by the end of the 1930s. In New Mexico, Hispanos achieved highly visible representation in the state legislature and at the local level, and Dennis Chavez was elected to the U.S. Senate in 1935.[39] Chavez was a Democrat, while most Hispanos were Republicans. The 1930s saw the electoral dominance of the Democratic Party in New Mexico. Previously, Anglo voters had been divided between the Republican and Democrat parties, which enabled Hispanos, who were overwhelmingly Republican, to divide the Anglo vote and retain elected offices. Eventually, Hispano voters increasingly registered with the Democratic Party. In those years, the Democrats controlled the U.S. presidency and the Congress, and through patronage power they controlled jobs and resources. The party built a federal machine and an army of civil service workers and appointed officeholders at the state level. Democrats' control of state jobs influenced Hispanos to switch allegiance, and Chavez became the new patron in New Mexico politics.[40] The establishment of this type of Hispano political power was similar to the building of local political machines by Irish and other European ethnics in the nineteenth century in the United States.

An early transmission belt for the organization of the Mexican and Mexican American community was mutual aid associations. These associations, called *mutualistas*, combined resources of Mexican immigrants to provide funeral and insurance benefits to members. They also provided a forum for community discussion and were an important form of social life in the community. Some of the mutual aid societies were clearly political and were concerned with social action. One of the best examples of this trend was the La Alianza Hispano-Americana, which formed in Arizona and spread throughout the Southwest. Other mutualistas were involved in militant labor actions in the 1930s.[41]

Another significant political development among Mexican Americans in the pre–World War II era was the formation of several civil rights organizations. The most prominent among the many groups that were formed during the Depression was the League of United American Citizens (LULAC).

It was founded in 1929 in Corpus Christi, Texas. This organization grew out of an earlier organization known as the Orden de Hijos de America, founded in 1921. Representing middle-class Mexican Americans, LULAC fought to integrate its people into the social and economic mainstream. The focus of LULAC was on U.S. citizens and gaining participation in the political process.

The emergence of LULAC and other civil rights groups exemplified a new generation of Mexican American leadership. Almost all of their initial actions were geared toward becoming more integrated into the American system: "Unlike the older generation of Mexican-American politicos who subordinated themselves to Anglo political machines, purchased the Mexican-American vote, and literally herded Mexican Americans to the polls, those involved in the 'new politics' hoped to cleanse Mexican-American politics by stressing nonpartisan civic action and avoidance of machine politics."[42] In the 1930s, although officially nonpolitical, LULAC took up campaigns for educational equality, such as an effort to end school segregation in Del Rio, Texas, in 1931. They also protested job discrimination by city governments and businesses and campaigned for political candidates, not as LULAC but as members of the Democratic Party or of ethnic clubs. Throughout the 1930s, the organization mounted organizing drives to set up local councils throughout Texas and eventually throughout the Southwest. These local councils agitated for an end to segregated schools, inferior educational facilities, and segregated public accommodations in swimming pools, lodging, restaurants, and hospitals.[43] Besides discrimination in public accommodations, LULAC opposed job discrimination in various forms. It opposed discrimination in Works Progress Administration jobs during the Depression and the exclusion of Mexican Americans from skilled positions in many industries in the Southwest.[44]

Despite the prohibition against participating in electoral politics mandated in the LULAC constitution, LULAC members were allowed to take part in politics, but they were expected to do so in a nonpartisan fashion. This did not stop LULAC activists from registering to vote and supporting candidates who would benefit the Mexican American community. Although LULAC rules prohibited councils from operating as political clubs, individual LULAC members participated in political campaigns and ran for office, and many were successful at the local level beginning in the 1930s.[45] However, the group forbade public officials from holding membership in LULAC.

Other political groups that formed in the 1930s included the Mexican American Movement (MAM), which grew out of a YMCA youth conference held in California in 1934. Seeking to raise up Chicano leadership in education, social work, and business, MAM created a leadership institute to train young people. It declined after World War II but left a legacy of youth-directed activities for social change.[46] Another organization was El Congreso Nacional del Pueblo de Habla Española (National Congress of Spanish Speaking Peoples); the Congreso espoused radical working-class politics and included Puerto Ricans from New York, Cubans from Tampa, Florida, and elected officials from New Mexico. The purpose of this group was to promote working-class causes.[47]

Political incorporation of Mexican Americans continued to grow in this period as they developed more sophisticated forms of political organization. By the end of the 1930s, there were several distinct trends of political activity: traditional mutual aid clubs and associations, middle-class organizations, and multiethnic working-class radical resistance. Each of these trends would continue to flourish following World War II; however, most radical resistance was limited during the 1950s due to heavy political repression by law enforcement agencies and the threat of deportation for immigrant activists.

■ Mexican Americans in the World War II Era

During World War II, the Mexican and Mexican American community focused on different political objectives. The Mexican American generation was preoccupied with supporting the U.S. war effort. While most LULAC chapters became inactive, the LULAC organization continued to agitate for fairness and equality in the military and in defense-related jobs. Mexican Americans waged numerous battles against discrimination and racial violence at home during the war; race riots in Los Angeles between white sailors and young Mexican Americans, for example, were known as the Zoot Suit Riots.[48]

For Mexican immigrants during World War II, the U.S. government, under pressure from agricultural interests, started an official guest worker program, known initially as the Emergency Labor Program and eventually as the Bracero Program. This program launched a legally sanctioned seasonal workforce of Mexican workers into the United States. The politics of the program involved negotiations between the U.S. government and the Mexican government. It lasted until 1964, when new farming techniques and growing opposition by organized labor and Chicano groups ended it. The conclusion of World War II did not bring an end to the problems of discrimination and second-class treatment of Mexican Americans; in many respects the disparity between Anglos and Mexicans was only heightened.

■ Puerto Rican Political Activities Before the 1950s

The other major Latino group that actively participated in sustained, organized political activities before the 1960s was Puerto Ricans. Significant Puerto Rican migration to the United States began around 1900. Before then, there was a small immigrant community based in New York that included political exiles and sought Puerto Rican independence from Spain.[49] Following the Spanish-American War in 1898, when the United States invaded the former Spanish colony and declared it a U.S. protectorate, Puerto Rican migration to the United States grew. There were only 3,000 Puerto Ricans stateside in 1910. The first migrants settled primarily in New York City, although some seasonal contract agricultural laborers worked in California, Connecticut, Florida, New Jersey, Illinois, and Hawaii. After Puerto Rico became a U.S. colony, the desire of Puerto Ricans to become an independent nation did not subside:

> Congress repeatedly turned down petitions by Puerto Rican leaders for full self-rule and eventually statehood for the island. . . . In response, the Puerto Rican House of Delegates asked Washington to cede the island its independence. Congress responded with the Jones Act in 1917 imposing U.S. citizenship on all Puerto Ricans over the unanimous objection of their House of Delegates.[50]

Although Puerto Ricans involuntarily became U.S. citizens through the Jones Act of 1917, literacy tests and other obstacles prevented them from registering and voting in large numbers until the 1960s.[51]

While more Puerto Ricans migrated to New York and other locations stateside to work, politically their influence was fairly weak. Although technically they were U.S. citizens, in practice they were not encouraged to register to vote, nor were they inclined to do so, as many viewed their time on the mainland as temporary. Most Puerto Rican workers sought to earn enough money to eventually return to Puerto Rico. The main forms of organization were mutual aid societies and labor associations.

One key vehicle for pre–World War II organizing in New York City was Puerto Rican cigar makers. Cigar makers were a critical part of the local economy. In response to being excluded from the main union, the Cigar Makers' International Union, Puerto Ricans formed their own union, Trabajadores Amalgamados de la Industria del Tabaco, also known as the Spanish Auxiliary. They led militant strikes in 1919 against the cigar manufacturers. The cigar makers played an important role in setting a militant standard and helped develop political influence for the Puerto Rican community by inspiring Puerto Ricans to organize in political and community groups.[52]

In the 1930s, the Republican Party showed some interest in the Puerto Rican community. Republican support helped elect the first Puerto Rican to office when Oscar Garcia Rivera won the East Harlem Assembly seat in 1937. His election was part of a reform movement to topple the Tammany Hall Democratic Party political machine, which had held control of New York politics since the nineteenth century.[53] Garcia Rivera was a radical, and he won with the support of Republicans, the American Labor Party, and other groups. However, Puerto Ricans were primarily Democrats, and the party continued to organize them. By 1936, the Puerto Rican Division of the Democratic National Committee included "150 advisory committee members, 12 New York City coordinators, a 21 member ladies committee and honorary membership of U.S. Senators Robert F. Wagner and Dennis Chavez from New Mexico."[54]

The 1930s were filled with political protests involving Puerto Ricans. Puerto Ricans supported the International Brigade that went to Spain to fight the Fascists. The growing movement for independence also drew the support of many mainland Puerto Ricans. In 1935 a non-Latino, Vito Marcantonio, was elected East Harlem's congressman. Marcantonio called for the independence of Puerto Rico and took part in organizing a march in August 1936 in support of independence; it drew 10,000 people.

During the 1930s and 1940s, electoral politics on the mainland continued to develop. One estimate is that there were 30,000 Puerto Ricans registered to vote in New York City by 1940 and that 80 percent voted for Franklin D. Roosevelt for president that year.[55] However, these numbers did not yet translate into political incorporation. While Puerto Ricans had the legal right to vote, they did not yet have the political organization and resources nor the political capability to build effective Puerto Rican political machines capable of electing their own to office. This would take more time. Meanwhile, the Puerto Rican population continued to grow and become more integrated into U.S. society.

Puerto Ricans, like Mexican Americans, enlisted in large numbers during World War II. During the war 62,000 Puerto Ricans entered the military; the 65th Infantry was made up mostly of Puerto Ricans. They would later gain recognition for their actions in Korea. In the 1940s, Puerto Rican migration to the United States continued to grow, from 90,000 between the late 1800s and 1944 to 150,000 by 1950.[56]

■ Conclusion

The legacy of Latino political contributions to America before World War II is immense, beginning with the establishment of various forms of government before the U.S. government's annexation of northern Mexico.

In the postannexation period, Mexican Americans, where they were allowed to fully participate, won elections for territory, state, and federal government offices. Where they were excluded, they mounted campaigns for inclusion and used many tactics to become equal participants in the political system. In most cases they were rebuffed, but they did not give up and by the 1940s were beginning to win electoral office in a few locations. In other places, they were starting to open up the closed and discriminatory political system. To win electoral office and retain these positions required organization, resources, a get-out-the-vote operation, and electable candidates. All were in short supply before World War II because of the closed political environment of most local communities. In most cases, Latinos did not have the numbers, and voters and candidates alike faced discriminatory barriers that prevented significant political advancement in the late 1930s. Most Puerto Rican and Mexican American efforts to achieve political incorporation were limited in scope and duration, yet they were important building blocks in the decades-long struggle of Latinos to achieve political power. These early efforts would not reap rewards until the 1960s.

■ Notes

1. R. Griswold del Castillo and A. De León (1996), pp. 1–13; J. Gonzalez (2000), pp. 3–26.
2. M. Vigil (1987), pp. 5–6.
3. M. G. Gonzales (1999), pp. 77, 79.
4. Ibid., p. 6.
5. Ibid., p. 9.
6. L. Pitt (1998).
7. E. Anders (1982).
8. U.S. Library of Congress (n.d.).
9. M. T. Garcia (1989).
10. V. Sánchez Korrol (1994), pp. 172–203.
11. M. Vigil (1985), p. 16.
12. Ibid., pp. 12–13.
13. C. McWilliams (1990).
14. Ibid., p. 32.
15. A. Tijerina (1994).
16. D. Montejano (1987), p. 40.
17. Ibid., p. 39.
18. R. Brischetto et al. (1994), p. 234.
19. D. Montejano (1987), p. 40.
20. Ibid.
21. L. Pitt (1998), pp. 4–5.
22. R. Griswold del Castillo (1990). Also, the Gadsden Purchase of 1853 resulted in the sale of the remaining portion of the Southwest, including parts of Arizona and New Mexico, to the United States.

23. R. Griswold del Castillo and A. De León (1996), p. 33.
24. D. Montejano (1987), p. 40.
25. M. Romero (1985), pp. 119–143.
26. R. Rosenbaum (1981), p. 99.
27. Ibid., pp. 99–109.
28. Ibid., pp. 138–139.
29. R. Acuña (1988).
30. L. Pitt (1998), p. 137.
31. E. Anders (1982), p. 6.
32. D. Montejano (1987), p. 144.
33. R. Griswold del Castillo and A. De León (1996), p. 49.
34. Ibid., p. 50.
35. Foley, Mota, Post, and Lozano (1988), p. 2.
36. R. Acuña (1988), p. 141.
37. Ibid., pp. 178–84.
38. M. G. Gonzales (1999), p. 148.
39. R. Griswold and A. De Leon (1996); J. Gomez Quiñones (1990).
40. R. Acuña (1988), pp. 241–242.
41. R. Garcia (1983).
42. M. T. Garcia (1989), pp. 28–29.
43. Ibid., p. 48.
44. Ibid., p. 51.
45. Ibid., pp. 41–42.
46. A. Navarro (1995), p. 50.
47. R. Acuña (1988), p. 238.
48. G. J. Sanchez (1993), p. 267.
49. A. Falcon (1984), p. 19.
50. J. Gonzalez (2000), p. 62.
51. V. E. Sánchez Korral (1994), p. 183.
52. J. R. Sanchez (2000), pp. 30–31.
53. Ibid., p. 33.
54. A. Falcon (1984), p. 33.
55. Ibid., p. 38.
56. Ibid., p. 35.

3

The Emergence
of New Voices

Following World War II, the entire global political situation changed dramatically, and so did the fortunes of Latinos in the United States and Latin Americans throughout the hemisphere. The political behavior and the demographic composition of the U.S. Latino population were dramatically transformed. This transformation took place in the context of two global factors: Competition between the United States and the Soviet Union for political domination and the expansion of economic globalization.

After the war, the defeat of German Nazism, Italian Fascism, and Japanese military aggression rapidly evolved into a global conflict between the two major economic and political blocs headed by the United States and the Soviet Union. The conflict between these "superpowers" overshadowed everything as both sides sought to gain political dominance throughout the world. The struggle between the superpowers spilled into every nation, including those of Latin America, and had a profound impact on U.S. foreign policy.

The international political conflict occurred just as economic globalization entered a new stage. Following World War II, the United States emerged with its industrial base intact and was unchallenged as the world's dominant economic power. Europe and Japan had to rebuild their infrastructures and reestablish their industrial capacity. By the 1960s, U.S.-based companies faced greater competition as transnational corporations challenged their economic control over resources and markets. Faced with declining profits and rising taxes to cover expanding social services, U.S. companies began to relocate some of their activities, first to less developed regions within the country—the South and Southwest, where wages and unionization rates were lower—and then overseas to less developed nations.

Globalization marked a new stage of the world economy. Capital investments from European and Northern American countries were already active in the less developed world, primarily in extraction of raw materials.

35

During the 1960s, international capital began to shift manufacturing to the developing countries, where wages were dramatically lower than in the developed world.[1] Developed countries began to experience deindustrialization as manufacturing industries moved abroad and service industries expanded.[2]

These two interrelated political and economic developments provided the external context to the rapid growth of Latino politics in this era. In the turmoil and conflict that erupted internationally, a window of opportunity emerged in the 1960s that enabled Latino and other social movements to emerge and grow.

Four distinct developments in the 1950s–1980s dramatically changed the landscape of Latino politics. Each of them was connected to the U.S. government's foreign and domestic policies: first, U.S. involvement in the internal politics of Cuba and the Dominican Republic and subsequent agreements to accept large numbers of Caribbean-based Spanish-speaking political refugees; second, a 1965 change in U.S. immigration policy that enabled large numbers of Latin Americans to immigrate to this country; third, the rise of protest movements around the world; fourth, the eruption of long-standing internal conflicts in Central America in the late 1970s and early 1980s, leading to a new wave of political refugees fleeing to the United States.

The protest era of the 1960s was defined by the Vietnam War, the African American civil rights movement, and independence movements in the developing world. The struggles of Latinos in this country for civil rights, quality education, and political power reflected the militant tenor of the times and help create a rich resistance to domination and exploitation that would spread nationwide. Beginning in the 1950s and 1960s, Latinos began to more aggressively pursue electoral office in more locations in the Southwest and elsewhere. Their efforts to overcome discrimination and win elected office were aided by the street protests of the late 1960s and 1970s. Political incorporation for Latinos was beginning to become a reality for a growing segment of the community. During this period, then, Latinos went from being perpetual outsiders to enjoying symbolic and in some cases more substantive representation.

■ Roots of the Chicano Movement, 1950–1964

After World War II ended, Latino politics grew and developed in the context of an international Cold War dynamic that influenced how politics were framed. As thousands of Mexican Americans and Puerto Ricans returned from the war, their contribution to the worldwide fight against fascism and for democracy came up against the economic and political reality of a segregated society. Mexican Americans continued to work in low-wage jobs and live in segregated housing in barrios throughout the Southwest, and in growing numbers in the Midwest, where their labor was required in the postwar economic boom. As the only major industrial power to emerge from the war unscathed, the United States quickly rebounded and used the Bracero Program to keep wages low throughout the Southwest, particularly among farmworkers. As one United Farm Workers (UFW) leader said: "When I got out of the Army, I went back into the fields. I had left for the Army from the labor camp near Los Baños and I was getting 85 cents an hour then. When I got back, the wage was down to 75 cents an hour, but the Braceros were getting 90 cents. That is when I led my first strike (1947). We didn't get very far."[3] On the international front, the United States stepped up its direct involvement in the affairs of other nations as U.S. relations with the Soviet Union worsened. This included increasing U.S. influence in Latin America.

In 1947 a funeral home in Three Rivers, Texas, refused to bury a Mexican American war veteran, Felix Longoria. In 1948 Hector Garcia and a group of concerned Mexican American veterans from Corpus Christi responded by founding the America G.I. Forum, a veterans' organization dedicated to combating discrimination and improving the status of Mexican Americans in Texas. They succeeded in having Longoria buried in Arlington Cemetery in Washington, D.C. By 1949, the G.I. Forum had established over 100 forums in Texas. Although it was officially nonpartisan, the organization's members were encouraged to participate in politics. In the 1950s, when other groups were intimidated by anticommunist hysteria and cold war politics, the leadership of the Forum used patriotic symbols and its members' veteran status to combat charges that the organization was advocating leftist programs.

While middle-class Mexican Americans were beginning to develop their political influence, the plight of Mexican immigrants grew worse. The cold war exacerbated anti-immigrant sentiments. The growth of the Bracero Program and increasing numbers of undocumented workers fueled a public backlash; one highly publicized action in 1954, Operation Wetback, led to the deportation of more than 1 million Mexicans, including many who were U.S. citizens.[4] This was the second major mass deportation of Mexicans; during the 1930s, 400,000–500,000 Mexicans, many of whom were U.S. citizens, were forcibly removed by the U.S. government. The cold war atmosphere also had a chilling effect on labor organizing efforts. Under the McCarren-Nixon Internal Security Act of 1950, immigrants found guilty of subversive activities could be deported; Mexican labor organizers were deported as part of this crackdown.[5]

The massive deportation of Mexicans, combined with the cold war view that any criticisms of policies of the U.S. government were communist inspired, greatly affected the political climate for Mexican Americans in the 1950s. Nevertheless, Mexican Americans continued to struggle for equal rights and political empowerment.

One group that formed in 1960 openly admitted the political nature of its activities. The Mexican American Political Association (MAPA) was founded as a statewide organization in California by leaders who recognized the need for an organization solely dedicated to advancing the political interests of Mexican Americans in California. These leaders had lost faith in the Democratic Party's commitment to fight for the cause of Mexican Americans. They were upset that when Edward Roybal ran for lieutenant governor of the state in 1954, he had received only token support from the Democratic Party. In 1958, when Henry Lopez ran for state treasurer, he also received little financial support from the state Democratic Party leaders, and went down to defeat in the midst of an otherwise strong Democratic landslide.[6] These and other actions prompted the formation of MAPA in 1960 at a convention in Fresno.[7] MAPA worked within the Democratic Party but took direct political action independently. Its emergence signaled a new direction of militant political action by Mexican Americans who had grown weary of being disrespected and underestimated by Democratic leaders in California. MAPA grew into an important force, particularly in California politics.

In addition to the formation of political groups, individuals continued to seek electoral office in the Southwest. Four Mexican American political leaders, from three different states, can serve as exemplars: U.S. Senator Dennis Chavez, New Mexico; Congressman Edward Roybal, Los Angeles; Henry B. González, San Antonio, Texas; and Mayor Raymond Telles, El Paso, Texas. Each of these politicians created political space for himself in the local and state conditions within which he operated in the 1940s, 1950s, and 1960s.

Edward Roybal, born in Albuquerque, New Mexico, moved to Boyle Heights in East Los Angeles when he was young. He served in the army during World War II. Following the war, he immediately got involved in local politics. In 1947, Roybal was a thirty-seven-year-old social worker. He made an unsuccessful attempt to win a Los Angeles City Council seat. Following this attempt, he cofounded the Community Service Organization (CSO), the mandate of which was to carry out community action, voter registration, and improve voter participation. Roybal immediately began running for the same city council seat he had sought previously. His message transcended ethnicity and appealed to a majority of residents in the Ninth Council District: all residents deserved a fair share of city services and benefits. He backed up his campaign platform with his own record of service to the community, and civil rights and social justice, including opposition to discrimination in all forms.[8] After a grassroots voter registration drive and get-out-the vote effort by the CSO, Roybal won a seat on the Los Angeles

City Council, which he held until 1962, when he won a seat in the U.S. Congress. Roybal's victory in 1951 for city council was a grassroots effort that included strong labor support, as well as other minority and ethnic groups including Jewish, African American, and Asian American. While the Latino percentage of his district remained around 34 percent, he continued to receive support from other ethnic communities that resided in his district as well as from business associations.

The CSO played an influential role for many years in the Mexican American community and provided a place to train community activists. By the early 1960s, there were thirty-four chapters in California and 10,000 dues-paying members. Most of the CSO chapters were in farmworker communities in California. The CSO registered a half million Mexican American voters, offered citizenship classes, and helped thousands of people to become naturalized U.S. citizens. More important, it provided the Mexican American community in California with a sense of power and a voice to exert pressure on city hall, the school board, and county government.[9]

Many CSO leaders came out of the labor movement, while others, once trained as CSO organizers, went into the labor movement. The CSO worked closely with Fred Ross, a community organizer for the Industrial Areas Foundation (IAF). The IAF is a network of community organizations started by organizer Saul Alinsky in Chicago in the 1940s, dedicated to organizing poor people to fight for basic services in their communities.[10] Ross was later to come into contact with a farmworker in a poor San Jose, California, barrio known as Sal Si Puedes. Ross convinced this man to become an organizer for CSO in the 1950s. The new CSO organizer went on to build a movement for farmworkers, eventually known as the United Farm Workers of America (UFW). The name of this humble community activist was Cesar Chavez.

Chavez's message as a CSO organizer to farmworkers in the 1950s was that the only way they would solve their basic problems—poverty wages, labor contractor abuses, and the lack of unemployment insurance—was to get organized. Gilbert Padilla, a UFW vice president, said of Chavez's vision: "He was talking about how some day the people should have some sort of representation in the political structure. And we were thinking that if we could get someone elected, then we could get some laws that would help farm workers."[11] The CSO's efforts to organize the barrios in the 1950s paid off with large numbers of new voters. Chavez worked with other farmworker activists, including Dolores Huerta (a Chicana community organizer) and Larry Itliong and Philip Vera Cruz (veteran Filipino farmworker organizers). The UFW was an important vehicle for farmworkers and for Chicano political empowerment in the Southwest.

In San Antonio, the Mexican community became more politically active in the postwar period as their numbers grew. Mexican American voter turnout increased from 55 percent in 1948 to 69 percent in 1956, to 87 percent in 1964.[12] The leading politico of this era in the San Antonio area was Henry B. González. González was active for many years in community affairs. After an unsuccessful run for state representative in 1950, he won a seat on the city council in 1953. In 1956 he won a seat on the state senate, and in 1961 he won a special election for the U.S. Congress, where he served until 1998. González was an independent voice during his tenure on the San Antonio City Council and fought to desegregate public facilities. As a state senator, he carried out a filibuster against segregationist bills in the legislature in 1957.[13]

In El Paso during the 1940s and 1950s, the Mexican population swelled with new arrivals from Mexico. Most Mexicans lived in abject poverty in El Segundo District, located near the border with Juárez, Mexico. El Paso, like San Antonio, was located near military installations. An important political victory for Mexican Americans took place in 1957. A veteran of the Korean War, Raymond Telles, ran for mayor of El Paso in 1957. Telles was a conservative who ran primarily as an American and against strong opposition from the business community, whose members did not believe a Mexican was qualified to be mayor. Telles won with the support of 90 percent of eligible Mexican voters, demonstrating that the Mexican community would participate in politics if given a reason to do so.[14]

In New Mexico, the post–World War II era saw growth of the Anglo population and a corresponding decline in the percentage of Hispano population. This brought dramatic changes in the culture, economics, and politics of the state. In 1848, immediately following the Mexican-American War, over 80 percent of the Spanish-speaking people in the Southwest had resided in New Mexico. Up to World War II, the state's Spanish-surnamed population remained the majority population in the Rio Grande Valley and was influential in both parties.[15] While northern New Mexico continued to reflect the influence of more than 350 years of continuous Spanish, Mexican, and Pueblo Indian culture and political institutions, in southeastern New Mexico the political conditions were more similar to those of neighboring Texas. Most of the Mexican Americans in this region were recent immigrants from Mexico, entering an Anglo-dominated economic and political system that kept them in a subordinate position.[16]

With more Anglos coming to the state, U.S. Senator Dennis Chavez (D) found it more difficult to hold on to his seat as the state grew increasingly conservative and Republican. He championed liberal causes throughout his service, including the 1944 introduction of the Fair Employment Practice Bill, designed to prohibit discrimination in employment on the basis of race, creed, or national origin. Twenty years later his pioneering efforts led to the passage of the 1964 Civil Rights Act.[17] Chavez was reelected five times, in hotly competitive races. He fought to open the political process to more Mexican Americans.

■ The Viva Kennedy Movement

In 1960, the establishment of Viva Kennedy clubs across the country marked the first attempt by Latinos to influence the outcome of U.S. presidential elections and the beginning of a more militant push for equal rights among Chicanos. The Viva Kennedy movement arose out of efforts by middle-class Mexican American leaders and organizations to gain more visible and effective participation in Democratic Party politics and that year's presidential campaign. While there had been other efforts after the war to woo Latinos to support Democrat and Republican presidential candidates, before this there had been no systematic, nationally coordinated efforts. Viva Kennedy clubs spread throughout the Southwest and in other parts of the country. Many local G.I. Forum groups temporarily shifted their agenda to transform into Viva Kennedy clubs.[18] The Viva Kennedy clubs brought Latinos together as Puerto Ricans, Cubans, and others from South and Central America joined.

In different states and regions, the form of the Viva Kennedy Clubs reflected the political organization of Latinos at that time. In California the organizing was led by MAPA and CSO members, with Congressman Roybal playing a key role as these organizations functioned separately from the presidential campaign. In Arizona, La Alianza Hispano-Americana and Mexican American–dominated local unions and branches of the International Union of Mine, Mill, and Smelter Workers were the key political forces. In New Mexico, Senator Dennis Chavez led the campaign. In the Midwest, there were active Viva Kennedy organizations in Indiana, Illinois, and other states. In Texas, numerous local groups and individuals worked on the campaign, which connected national politics with local communities and "crystallized a new Mexican American politics."[19]

Following the victory of the Kennedy campaign in 1960, there were great expectations that finally Mexican Americans would be appointed to high posts in the Kennedy administration, something that had not occurred under previous administrations. Leaders of the Viva Kennedy campaign also attempted to transform the campaign efforts into a political coalition, composed of leaders of the established organizations—G.I. Forum, MAPA, the League of United American Citizens (LULAC), and eighteen other Spanish-speaking organizations. They decided to call themselves the Political Association of Spanish-Speaking Organizations (PASSO). From its inception, PASSO members held different points of view on how aggressively to pursue a political agenda. PASSO never got off the ground as a nationwide organization; instead, each of the groups went back to continuing its own activities. The Texas-based group would keep the name for a few years, but its activities remained focused in Texas.

■ The Campaign for "Los Cinco" in Crystal City, Texas

In 1962–1963, PASSO became involved in Crystal City, Texas, to help elect a slate of Mexican Americans to the city council. Crystal City, unlike many communities in south Texas, was not a product of Spanish settlement. It had incorporated as a city in 1910 and was principally an agricultural town with a high percentage of Mexicano workers. While Mexicans made up more than 70 percent of the population by the late 1950s, Crystal City's city council, school board, and the Zavala County Court of commissioners were "all Gringos. Segregation continued in public and private facilities."[20]

While these conditions were common throughout the Southwest at the time, in Crystal City a series of discriminatory actions by the Anglo minority sparked an electoral revolt of the Mexican American community. These actions included a land scandal that involved blatant discrimination against Chicano war veterans, denial of entrance into a predominantly Anglo private school of a prominent Mexicano minister's son, and mobilization of the Anglo population to defeat a Mexican American candidate for school board in 1960.

In late 1962, Juan Cornejo, a Teamsters leader, formed an alliance with the newly created chapter of PASSO to raise funds for a poll tax drive. Throughout Texas at the time, all citizens who wanted to vote were required to pay a poll tax of $1.75. This severely hampered the political organizing efforts of poor Mexican and African Americans. After successfully completing the poll tax drive, raising funds for those who did not have the money to pay the tax, the coalition needed to run a slate of candidates. They found five Mexican Americans to run for city council; one was Cornejo himself. Through a grassroots campaign that relied heavily on the working-class base of Teamster cannery workers and agricultural workers, "Los Cinco" won the election.

The decision to actively participate in the Crystal City elections was controversial in PASSO, as some conservative members felt that the organization was becoming too involved in ethnic politics. For the more militant members of PASSO, Crystal City represented an important breakthrough in Mexican American politics. The election of Los Cinco showed that "hard work, good planning and coalition politics, could bring positive results at the ballot box and make it possible for Mexican Americans to control their own destiny."[21]

In the aftermath of the electoral victory, however, the new Mexican

American officeholders and the community found it extremely difficult to maintain the unity they had exhibited during the campaign. The coalition between the Teamsters and PASSO broke up, and a slate put forward by PASSO was defeated in the next election cycle, in 1965, by an Anglo–Mexican American coalition. Nevertheless, Los Cinco made some changes that helped improve the quality of life for Mexican Americans in Crystal City. This included securing funds for street pavement and other infrastructure improvements in the barrio.[22] Their election signaled the beginning of the end of the system of segregated politics in Texas. On a practical and symbolic level, the Crystal City electoral challenge was an important statement of the potential for Latino political power and was a harbinger of other political uprisings of Chicanos in the Southwest and Latinos in other parts of the United States.

■ The Rise of the Chicano Movement in the 1960s

The 1960s were a dramatic period for the nation's oldest and largest Latino ethnic group: Mexican Americans. The effort to elect Mexican Americans to the city council in Crystal City, Texas, was soon followed by other organizing efforts in the Southwest, including electoral campaigns, labor organizing, student organizing, community struggles for access to services, and attempts to end discrimination in jobs and housing. There were efforts that directly challenged the two-party political system and capitalism. There were numerous nontraditional organizing projects in various parts of the Southwest that changed the image of Mexican Americans in society and raised Chicanos' expectations about their right and ability to achieve sweeping political changes.

The political leaders who launched these organizing projects responded to local conditions of poverty, neglect, and discrimination by the larger society. In a short overview, it is not possible to discuss all of the organizing efforts. My focus will be on several projects that significantly contributed to Latinos' efforts to achieve political power.

❏ *Building a Movement of Farmworkers*

In California, while Chicano community activists were active in numerous organizing efforts in the early 1960s, the most impressive campaigns erupted not in urban centers but in the agricultural fields. The Bracero Program, which imported seasonal workers from Mexico and other Latin American nations beginning in 1942, undercut farmworkers' wages and weakened working conditions. Farmworkers were excluded from the protections afforded other private-sector workers by the National Labor

Relations Act of 1935.[23] In 1965, two separate organizing efforts joined forces to take on the agribusinesses that had for decades kept wages low and working conditions oppressive. The catalyst was a strike of mainly Filipino grape pickers in Delano by the Agricultural Workers Organizing Committee, led by Larry Itliong. Cesar Chavez's National Farm Workers Association soon joined this strike, and together these two organizations launched a strike that eventually developed into a national boycott of grapes. In 1966, these two unions merged into one organization, the United Farm Workers Organizing Committee. In 1972, it would change its name to the United Farm Workers of America (UFW).[24] The strike ushered in a new era of militant labor struggles by workers of color and mobilized strong community support in the Chicano community and the civil rights movement. The UFW, led by Chavez and Dolores Huerta, would build an international presence and support for many labor and civil rights, as well as prolabor candidates for office. The UFW maintained close ties with the liberal wing of the Democratic Party and viewed itself as a labor organization; however, it was also known for supporting numerous broader Chicano causes and advocating for peace and justice.[25]

In Texas, another state with a large farmworker presence, organizing agricultural workers was problematic. Texas is a "right-to-work" state, which means workplaces are open shops where unions have only limited rights. Workers can choose not to be part of a union; this weakens unions' effectiveness. Organizing of workers into unions in this antilabor environment was extremely difficult. The long border with Mexico made the importation of cheap labor easy for employers. Decisions handed down by hostile local courts and actions of the antilabor Texas Rangers also greatly hampered organizing efforts.[26]

In 1966, however, a strike by farmworkers against eight growers in Starr County, south Texas, for a minimum wage became a catalyst for the emerging Chicano movement.[27] Chicanos from all over the state joined in a farmworker-led march from Rio Grande City to the state capitol in Austin. Well-known civil rights groups, including LULAC, G.I. Forum, and PASSO, supported the marchers.[28] The march concluded with a huge rally of 10,000 people in Austin, attended by Cesar Chavez and other political leaders. The march and the support it received spurred other forms of community organizing among Mexican Americans in Texas.

❏ Community and Land Struggles in the Southwest

Another significant struggle involved efforts to reclaim or to retain land and water rights in northern New Mexico, an area with a strong historical presence of Hispanos. One organization, Alianza Federal de Pueblos Libres, was organized in 1962 by Reies López Tijerina. The Alianza powerfully symbolized the issue of historical sovereignty for Mexican and Indian people. As one author states: "The Alianza was formed to reclaim for descendants of land grantees, both Mexican and Indian, hundreds of thousands of acres of Spanish and Mexican government land grants dating from before the takeover by the United States" following the end of the Mexican-American War in 1848.[29] It grew from a moderate pressure group into a militant organization that held demonstrations and used more aggressive tactics, including taking over the Tierra Amarillo courthouse in 1967.[30] While the Alianza's actions did not result in the return of lands to the original descendants, the issues of land, rural poverty, and governmental control were introduced and provided many in the Chicano movement and other movements with an awareness that Mexicans had a rightful claim to land and political power that predated modern political realities. The Alianza was a catalytic agent that helped spur the development of the Chicano movement in New Mexico and throughout the Southwest.

A third node of political organizing during this period was the Crusade for Justice organization, formed in Denver, Colorado, under the leadership of Rodolfo "Corky" Gonzalez, a former Democratic Party activist. In 1966, the Crusade was born as a civil rights organization. It focused on building alternative institutions, fighting Denver's poor educational system, and opposing the war in Vietnam. It successfully hosted two national youth liberation conferences, which helped galvanize an upsurge in Chicano youth organizing in colleges and secondary schools throughout the Southwest.[31]

❑ *The Texas Chicano Student*
  Movement and La Raza Unida Party

Political activities among Latinos in south Texas increased as the energy and enthusiasm that grew out of Crystal City spread to other communities in the region. In 1967, a group of Chicano student activists at St. Mary's University in San Antonio formed the Mexican American Youth Organization (MAYO). MAYO, like the United Mexican American Students (UMAS) in California and other student groups in the late 1960s, was born out of a combination of ethnic pride and a desire to be activists for Chicano power.[32] One of MAYO's first actions was a 1969 campaign to elect Chicanos to the city council in San Antonio. The students helped form the Committee for Barrio Betterment, challenged the status quo, and offered alternative candidates. Soon they also launched the Winter Garden Project in other communities in south Texas.

In one of many actions in this era, in 1969 Chicano high school students walked out of their classes to protest racist practices, including a discriminatory process for selecting high school cheerleaders in Crystal City. Working with MAYO organizers, they called a boycott of elementary, junior high, and high schools; it lasted for more than one month. The students won most of their demands. This was one of thirty-nine boycotts organized by MAYO between 1967 and 1970.[33]

The success of this well-planned boycott and other organizing efforts culminated in the formation in 1970 of a new organization, La Raza Unida Party (LRUP). The party's launch was a bold call to action by Chicano activists to build a political party that would challenge the hegemony of the two-party system. LRUP viewed itself as an alternative to the dominant parties, an organization that could give voice to Chicanos' desire for self-determination of their political destiny. Initially focusing on south Texas, LRUP ran candidates for city, county, and school boards in Crystal City and other towns. It was successful in winning city council and school board majorities and mayoral positions in several small towns, defeating the Democratic Party, the dominant political power in the region.[34]

By the summer of 1972, the concept of an independent political party for *la raza* caught on in other communities. LRUP expanded its organizing base to various counties where Mexicans were the majority population; it held a Texas state convention that was attended by delegates from twenty-five counties. A young attorney, Ramsey Muñiz, ran for Texas governor and garnered 219,000 votes, or 6.4 percent. Other LRUP candidates for statewide office fared poorly; at this juncture the strength of LRUP was evident mainly in local communities in south Texas.[35]

The idea for a third party was not unique to Texas; Chicano activists in California, Colorado, New Mexico, and Arizona also formed organizing committees of the LRUP. In 1972, a national conference of the LRUP brought together representatives from eighteen states. The conference resolved not to endorse either of the two major party candidates for U.S. president; however, differences regarding organizing strategies and ideology went largely unresolved. In some areas LRUP was a pressure group, while in others it sought to function as a political party and post candidates for electoral office. LRUP activists continued to organize throughout the region and in the Midwest during the 1970s. The party failed to grow substantially, though, as it competed with the Democratic Party for voters and fought internal battles over the strategies and tactics for building the movement.

Outside of south Texas, the LRUP model of achieving political dominance at the local level faced numerous obstacles. Local LRUP chapters in northern and southern California were active in organizing around community issues and also began to participate in local politics. In East Los Angeles, LRUP activist Raul Ruiz ran against Richard Alatorre, a Mexican American Democrat, in the Forty-eighth Assembly District in 1971. Ruiz's candidacy generated enough support to split the Mexican American vote and contributed to a white Republican winning office in a Mexican-majority district.[36] LRUP had proved that it could compete in electoral contests outside of Texas, yet here the result was to deny a Mexican American candidate the opportunity to win a valuable state representative seat at a time when Latinos had no representation in state government.

Significantly, LRUP and other Chicano activists provided leadership to a campaign to incorporate East Los Angeles area into a city. This area housed the largest concentration of Mexicans in the state, but without incorporation, residents had virtually no political representation. The County Board of Supervisors of Los Angeles were all Anglos who paid little attention to the needs of the Mexican American community. In 1974, a community campaign to win incorporation and gain community control was defeated by conservative community elements, who argued that incorporation would mean higher taxes for residents and would result in inferior services, including law enforcement. The forces opposed to incorporation also raised the specter of militants taking over and turning East Los Angeles into a radical Chicano city composed of poor, undocumented workers with rampant crime and no tax base.[37] The incorporation defeat marked a turning point for LRUP in California, and it slowly declined in influence and attraction for Chicano activists, who joined other political groups.

According to one knowledgeable participant, a number of external factors led to LRUP's demise by the late 1970s and early 1980s, including the end of the protest era of the 1960s and 1970s, Democrat Party co-optation, the system of two-party financing that makes it extremely difficult to raise sufficient funds to run credible campaigns, and restrictive electoral structures, such as winner-take-all systems. Also there was the "incessant political, judicial, ideological, social, and physical pounding" by those who sought to maintain the status quo.[38]

Certain internal factors also weakened LRUP, including disagreements over ideology, lack of unified political organizing strategy, and limited funds.[39] Yet while LRUP was not successful in achieving electoral victories, except in south Texas and to a small degree in New Mexico, it provided an important vehicle for dissatisfied Chicanos of this period to engage in political action: "The Raza Unida Party inspired a whole generation of Mexican Americans to participate in the electoral process on a scale never before attempted."[40]

❑ *Seeking New Means to Build the Movement*

In California, despite the problems with building the LRUP, the UFW continued to organize among farmworkers in the 1970s, including the three-year lettuce strike and boycott in the Salinas Valley. There were other important organizing efforts during the period that played a role in shaping the politics and orientation of the Chicano movement. In Los Angeles, Chicano high school and middle school students protested the lack of quality education in their schools by conducting mass walkouts. "Blowouts" by more than 10,000 Chicano students highlighted the unequal, poor-quality, and racist education in East Los Angeles in 1968.[41] This was followed by the largest Chicano anti–Vietnam War march, on August 29, 1970. This event, called the Chicano Moratorium against the War, drew over 20,000 people to East Los Angeles.[42] The police savagely attacked the peaceful event and killed three people, including famed *Los Angeles Times* news reporter Ruben Salazar.[43]

Community groups focused on Mexican workers made important contributions to the Mexican American community's understanding of economics and class-based analysis during this period. A progressive organization that functioned in the Mexican community was Centro de Acción Social Autónoma–Hermandad General de Trabajadores (CASA-HGT). Established in 1968 by veteran Mexican American community activists and labor organizers Bert Corona and Soledad Alatorre in Los Angeles, CASA was a mutual aid organization to provide services to undocumented Mexican workers. By 1970 CASA had expanded to include autonomous local affiliates in other California cities and in Texas, Colorado, Washington, and Illinois, and provided immigration counseling and notary and legal assistance to undocumented workers.[44] In 1973, CASA helped to establish the National Coalition for Fair Immigration Laws and Practices, which sought to promote a positive view of immigration from Mexico. Later, in the 1970s, CASA disbanded as a national group, having made important contributions to the debate about a more humane immigration policy, the need to view the U.S.-Mexico border as an artificial barrier, and the critical role of Mexican workers in the U.S. economy.[45]

Another organization that was influential in the Southwest was the August 29th Movement. This organization was formed out of several local collectives, including several in California. The August 29th Movement was predominantly Chicano but also included non-Chicanos. The political orientation was Marxist, and the stated principal task was to build a revolutionary party to overthrow the capitalist system. It actively participated in labor, land, community, and student campaigns, advocating self-determination for Chicanos in the Southwest.[46] The significance of leftist groups such as the August 29th Movement was their focus on an economic analysis of U.S. capitalism and the central role of U.S. workers, combined with the call for political power for Chicanos.

The formation and development of such social movement organizations in the 1960s came about because there was a vacuum of political leadership within the Mexican American community. Chicanos were effectively excluded from the political process in most places. In 1970, virtually no Latinos were elected to office. In Los Angeles, there were no Chicanos on the city council or the county board of supervisors. After Edward Roybal left the council in 1962 to join the U.S. Congress, no other Latino was elected. The situation was not much better in other Southwest states. At the state legislature level, Chicanos were significantly underrepresented compared to the size of their population (see Table 3.1).

❏ *A Campaign to Win a*
   Chicano Majority in Parlier, California

While there were only a small number of Latino elected officials in 1970, there was a strong potential for local political control by Chicanos in many communities, such as in Crystal City. The process of Chicano empowerment was tested in Parlier, California, a rural town of fewer than 2,000 people in the San Joaquin Valley. Parlier's residents in 1970 were 85 percent Spanish surnamed, primarily farmworkers; it was a traditional farm town, with the major industry and employers tied to agriculture. The town's political and economic elites were Anglo and to a lesser degree Japanese American farmers. From 1921 to 1972, there was only one Spanish-surnamed elected official. In 1971, the city council passed over a Mexican American who was an eighteen-year veteran of the police force in favor of a less-experienced Anglo officer for the position of Parlier police chief. When the council was challenged by the Chicano community to rescind its decision, it refused. After a year of protests and boycotts of local businesses by the Mexican community, and two recall petitions that were thrown out due to technicalities, a voter registration drive was launched and a slate of Chicano candidates put forward. After sixteen months of continuous struggle, the Chicano majority won all electoral positions; they "were now in control of local government and could now pursue policies which would bring about important changes to the community of Parlier."[47]

The previously unorganized Chicano community was brought together by a grassroots organization, the Parlier Fact Finding Committee, that

Table 3.1 Chicano Electoral Representation, 1970

State	Total Number of Legislators	Number of Chicano Legislators	Percentage of Chicano Legislators	Chicano Percentage of Total Population
Arizona	90	11	11.1	18.8
California	118	5	4.2	15.5
Colorado	100	4	4	13
New Mexico	112	32	34	40.1
Texas	181	10	5.5	18.4

Source: F. C. Garcia and R. O. de la Garza (1977), p. 107.

sought to involve the entire community. After taking power, the new council's views were reflected in the Parlier General Plan, 1973: "What's really unique about Parlier is that the City Council represents our majority population: Mexican-American. This is the only place in California where this has ever happened in American history: majority Mexican-Americans voted minority Anglo Americans out of elected authority."[48] Before the 1970s, four rural communities and one urban community in California had elected Chicano-majority city councils. After the Parlier decision, five other towns established Chicano-majority city councils.[49] The Parlier struggle was echoed in other California communities in the following decades, as Chicanos used various paths to achieve electoral power. The Parlier campaign was similar to the Crystal City struggle: in both places Mexican Americans organized themselves and launched political empowerment efforts to unseat intransigent Anglo officials. They sought political incorporation into the local political system to have an equal voice in their government. These were the opening salvos in a broader movement for political inclusion by Mexican Americans.

■ Puerto Rican Politics in the United States in the 1940s and 1950s

Following World War II, "Operation Bootstrap" was launched, an economic development plan by the U.S. government to industrialize Puerto Rico. It resulted in displacing tens of thousands of farmworkers, who then migrated to the United States to seek postwar jobs. Puerto Rican migrants fanned out to many states to work in low-wage jobs in agriculture, manufacturing, and service industries.

The Puerto Rican government sought to oversee the employment and adjustment experience of migrants by the creation of the "Migration Division—or Office of the Commonwealth as it came to be known."[50] It not only served as a clearinghouse for migrants but also represented the interests of Puerto Ricans on the mainland. During the 1950s and 1960s, however, the existence of the Commonwealth office hindered the development of Puerto Rican politics in the United States, for many assumed that "political leaders, patrons, were unnecessary so long as Puerto Ricans were represented by the Commonwealth Office."[51]

The relative calm of the Puerto Rican migration was shattered in 1954, when five Puerto Rican nationalists, led by Lolita Lebron, opened fire in the gallery of the U.S. House of Representatives, shouting, "Long live a free Puerto Rico." Five Congressmen were wounded in the assault. This violent action placed the question of Puerto Rico's colonial status on the world agenda. It followed a United Nations vote on a U.S. motion declaring that the issue of Puerto Rico "was an internal matter for the United States."[52] The attack on Congress was the Puerto Rican independistas' response, a stark reminder that the question of independence for Puerto Rico was never far from the surface during this period. The five were imprisoned for twenty-five years and were pardoned by President Jimmy Carter after a long campaign by the Puerto Rican community for their release.

Meanwhile, Puerto Ricans continued to find they were not welcomed by either of the political parties even though they were eligible to vote. The 1950s were marked by limited economic and political progress for Puerto Ricans. In New York City, the Democratic Party and the Tammany Hall machine had been on the decline since the 1930s, when the government, not the party, began to provide social services for the needy. By the 1950s, the Democratic machine had little to offer the newcomers for their votes. In the chill of cold war tensions and anticommunism, Puerto Ricans were viewed by the establishment as troublesome. The city's Democratic Party was primarily made up of white ethnics who had no use for poor, nonwhite workers.[53]

■ Puerto Rican Politics in the 1960s

Before the 1960s, many in the Puerto Rican community viewed U.S. politics only in the context of issues pertinent to Puerto Rico. As noted earlier, many had been enticed to come to the mainland to provide cheap labor in the wake of Operation Bootstrap. The priority for working-class Puerto Ricans was not the achievement of political power but rather jobs and economic rewards. Many sought to earn enough to return to the island; however, as the number of Puerto Ricans grew, they became a substantial population in several cities. More than 1 million Puerto Ricans came to the United States between 1946 and 1964, but most found only low-paying manufacturing and service jobs.[54] The new migrants were forced to live in urban ghettos in overcrowded and dilapidated housing. These socioeconomic conditions were to spawn militant actions by Puerto Ricans in the late 1960s and 1970s.

In the early 1960s, groups such as the Puerto Rican Day Parade Committee, the Congress of Puerto Rican Hometowns, and an educational group know as ASPIRA developed in New York to build cultural and social networks and develop leadership. These social service organizations "offered a springboard from which several Puerto Rican activists would later enter into the political arena."[55] ASPIRA, founded by Antonia Pantoja, continues to provide services to the Puerto Rican community today in the field of youth leadership development.

A spontaneous action signaled the frustration many Puerto Ricans felt in the face of years of poverty, police harassment, and racism in major urban centers. In 1966, in the Division Street neighborhood of Chicago, a white policeman shot a Puerto Rican man; for the next few nights the Puerto Rican community protested against police brutality. They also looted neighborhood businesses, leaving some fifty buildings destroyed and causing millions of dollars in damages.[56] Underlying the actions of the rioters were severe socioeconomic problems that existed in many Puerto Rican colonias in the United States.

The difficulties faced by most new migrants may have had an impact on the migration to the United States from Puerto Rico. During this period migration slowed dramatically as work opportunities became more limited; in the 1950s there had been a high of 480,000 migrants, but that fell to 222,000 in the 1960s and only 41,000 in the 1970s.[57]

■ Accommodation and Confrontation in the Puerto Rican Movement

Despite slowing migration, political activities increased in the 1960s. Two political trends emerged in the Puerto Rican community in this decade: the first was to work within the system and seek positions in electoral politics, and the second involved militant confrontational politics that challenged the political system. The first trend was represented by Herman Badillo, who emerged in the 1960s as a reformer in the Democratic Party. He was elected to borough president of the Bronx in 1965 and became the first Puerto Rican elected to Congress in 1970. He also ran for New York City mayor unsuccessfully several times. He even joined the administration of New York mayor Ed Koch in 1977. Other notables active during this period included Gilberto Gerena Valentin, a longtime labor and community activist who moved to the United States in the 1930s, worked as a union organizer, and headed a division of New York City's Human Rights Commission under Mayor John Lindsay in 1966.[58] He also served on the New York City Council in the 1970s. A third figure who emerged was Ramon Velez, who rose from the antipoverty programs of the 1960s to control various ethnic groups and antipoverty funds and organizations in the South Bronx.[59] These three leaders would battle for political influence throughout the 1970s and 1980s.

In 1970, there were no Puerto Rican city council members and only a handful of state representatives. By 1978, there were three in the New York City Council and seven state representatives and senators, along with one member of Congress. Yet Puerto Ricans were still woefully underrepresented. In fact, until redistricting in the 1990s, Puerto Ricans focused on achieving representation. During the 1990s, Puerto Rican representation finally reached parity with the community's share of the electorate. By 2000, twenty-one of the twenty-three Latino elected officials in office in New York City were of Puerto Rican origin, and the other two were Dominican.[60]

■ Formation of Militant Puerto Rican Organizations

While these leaders operated within the political system, the Black Power and antiwar movements and the struggle for Puerto Rican independence from the United States contributed to the development of a more radical and confrontational style of Puerto Rican politics. Three main groups emerged within this trend: the Movimiento Pro Independencia (MPI), which later changed its name to the Puerto Rican Socialist Party (PSP); the Young Lords Party, which later became the Puerto Rican Revolutionary Workers Organization (PRRWO); and El Comité–Movimiento de Izquierda Nacional Puertorriqueño (MINP).

While the population center of the Puerto Rican community was in New York City, the Young Lords formed out of a Puerto Rican youth group in Chicago. The Young Lords actually arose out of the Chicago Lords, a street gang that had begun in the 1950s. A leader of the Chicago Lords, Jose "Cha Cha" Jimenez, became politicized while incarcerated, and when he got out of jail he organized the Young Lords Organization to protest urban renewal in the Puerto Rican community.[61] In 1969, Puerto Rican community activists in New York City formed a second chapter of the Young Lords. In 1970, the elements in New York split from the Chicago organization and formed the Young Lords Party. Its politics combined emphasis on social justice stateside and support for independence for Puerto Rico.[62] Its members included youth who had grown up in Puerto Rico and others who had grown up in the United States. In 1969 the Lords led protests in East Harlem over infrequent garbage pickups, and they occupied a church, where they set up a free breakfast program, day care center, and health clinic. In 1970, the Young Lords occupied Lincoln Hospital in the South Bronx to expose the inadequate health care it provided to community residents.[63]

The PSP likewise attempted to organize for both Puerto Rican independence and the social and political struggles of Puerto Ricans in the United States. It had its roots in Puerto Rico, where the group known as Movimiento Pro Independencia (MPI) formed. A chapter was established in 1964 in East Harlem, composed essentially of first-generation Puerto Ricans. Later it would expand to include second-generation activists and would serve as a bridge organization between Puerto Ricans residing in the United States and those living in Puerto Rico.[64] In addition to leading the campaign for independence for Puerto Rico, this organization participated in organizing migrant workers and other campaigns for democratic rights in this country.

El Comité began in early 1970 when a group of residents on the west side of Manhattan took over a storefront to oppose the city's plans to displace local residents and businesses in order to make room for new high-rise developments. El Comité was composed mostly of Puerto Ricans but also included other Latinos; its leader, Federico Lora, was a Dominican. El Comité initially supported bilingual education and community control. Later it evolved into a consciously leftist organization and sought to build support for socialism in the United States.

By the late 1970s each of these organizations experienced internal difficulties, and they all eventually dissolved. However, in the late 1960s and early 1970s they represented an important new trend in the Puerto Rican community of seeking to resist capitalist exploitation and U.S. imperialism. The Puerto Rican radical community created new forms of collective identity and built strong ties to the labor movement and the new left movement that arose during this period. Together with Marxists and other leftist forces in the Chicano movement, the radical Puerto Rican leftist forces represented an important alternative to mainstream machine politics during the 1960s.

■ Cuban Political Refugees, Dominicans, and Central Americans

The 1960s introduced a new wave of immigrants from the Caribbean Islands into the U.S. political structure: Cubans and Dominicans. While people from both nations had migrated in small numbers before this time, mass migration began in the 1960s due to internal political dynamics that produced large numbers of political refugees.

In Cuba, a popular uprising led by Fidel Castro in 1959 defeated the Fulgencio Batista government; the business elites that had supported the government responded by fleeing. Many from the middle and upper classes found their way to the United States in the 1960s and 1970s. They brought with them a complex mix of entrepreneurial, political, and technical skills. The U.S. government, which had strongly backed the Batista government, provided assistance in the form of the Cuban Adjustment Act of 1966. The refugees became eligible for public assistance in the form of Medicaid and food stamps. They received business credits and start-up loans. There were also numerous connections between U.S. and Cuban businesses, particularly those owned by Cuban Jews, that enabled a relatively smooth economic transition for a segment of the Cuban refugees.[65]

Many of this first wave of refugees were highly educated, often in U.S. universities. At the time of their arrival, 36 percent of the refugees had at least completed high school, and 12.5 percent had completed four years of college or more. One-quarter of the refugees were professionals or attorneys, and another 12 percent had held managerial or executive positions.[66] Many in this first wave were also members of the Cuban political establishment and had important political skills that would be utilized as they entered the U.S. political arena. The U.S. government generally welcomed this segment of the Cuban Diaspora. According to one author, "Much of the economic health of the Cuban exile community was facilitated by U.S. government grants extended to émigrés in the context of the cold war."[67]

Subsequent waves of Cuban refugees were not so warmly welcomed. For example, in 1980 a new wave of Cubans, more than 124,000 in a few months, arrived suddenly and with no advance warning.[68] The "Marielitos," as they came to be known, were named for the place most of them had left in Cuba. They were a mixed group of unemployed workers, and some were criminals released from Cuba's prisons. This group, unlike earlier arrivals, was perceived as an economic burden, and upon arrival in south Florida; many of them found it extremely difficult to find work in Miami. They were vilified in the media as troublemakers, criminals, and opportunists.[69] Many of them were held in U.S. jails for long periods. The chaotic handling of the Marielitos by the U.S. government and their economic and social impact on south Florida fueled a new period of anti-immigrant sentiments in the region.[70]

■ The Arrival of Dominicans and Their Emergence in U.S. Politics

Dominicans began their mass exodus to the United States in the mid-1960s. For thirty-one years, the Domincan Republic was ruled by Rafael L. Trujillo, who had installed himself as president and been a ruthless dictator. In 1961, he was assassinated and in 1963 a progressive leader, Juan Bosch, was elected. Several months later, Bosch was removed from office by a coup d'état ogranized by an alliance of military officers and big-business interests.[71] In response, a military faction allied with the popular forces attempted to reinstate Bosch. The U.S. government sent in 40,000 troops to prevent what they feared was another communist revolution (as had occurred earlier in Cuba). To ease political tensions in the country and remove potential opposition forces, the U.S. government allowed antigovernment foes to enter the United States to weaken the opposition and help stabilize the Domincan political scene. Many of these people went to New York City.[72] President Lyndon Johnson feared that the revolt would lead to a Castro-style revolution. The U.S. military occupation marked the beginning of a thirty-year period of political instability in the Dominican Republic. To defuse the postelection crisis, U.S. officials hastily facilitated a mass exodus of pro-Bosch supporters. Many Dominican leftists came to New York as political exiles.[73] However, unlike Cuban refugees, the Dominicans were not classified as political refugees, and they received no federal assistance upon arrival. Many of the Dominicans who arrived in the U.S. in the 1960s had skills similar to those of the Cubans. They were generally highly educated and politically conscious; some had economic resources and started up small businesses in New York City. Subsequently, however, large numbers of undocumented and working-class immigrants, faced with limited avenues for advancement, have kept Dominicans one of the poorest Latino groups on average in the United States. The average per capita household income for Dominicans was $11,065 in 1999, with higher rates of unemployment than the national average.[74] Dominicans had a poverty rate of 27.5 percent, the highest among all Latino groups.[75]

Their main destination was the Washington Heights area of Upper Manhattan. More than 400,000 Dominicans legally migrated to the United States between 1961 and the mid-1980s. There were 332,713 Dominicans living in New York City in 1990, according to the census. If one takes account of the large number of undocumented Dominicans, the population was above half a million. The intensity of politics in the Dominican Republic, the political skills of many of those who left their homeland, and the high concentration of Dominicans in one area of the city with limited political visibility led to the development of numerous grassroots political organizations.

The first political efforts centered on issues of concern in the homeland. In the 1960s, a number of autonomous, voluntary ethnic associations were established that did not run candidates but helped local Democratic candidates through leafleting and voter mobilization.[76] As the new political exiles arrived, the ethnic associations began to take on a new character that reflected their needs and interests. In the 1970s, the various associations combined businessmen who could obtain funding from city agencies and younger U.S.-educated Dominicans who became active in New York politics. Dominicans were rallied to support and vote for Democratic candidates.[77]

By the 1980s, Dominicans were actively participating in party politics and educational reform in Washington Heights. The Dominican Day Parade grew in size, indicating the growth of the community's presence, with over 100,000 in attendance by 1983. That year Dominicans organized to gain representation in the city's antipoverty bureaucracy, including the Community Development Agency and its locally elected advisory group, known as the Area Policy Boards. Until then, no Dominicans had served on a policy board. As a result of these organizing efforts, significant increases in funding for Dominican groups in Washington Heights were gained.

In addition, the lack of decent public education in New York City led Dominican community activists to form parents' and teachers' groups and enter into mainstream politics to address their concerns, running for local school boards and other positions.[78] The 1980s also witnessed a significant increase in Dominican participation in New York City school board politics. The school boards are decentralized and democratically elected and allow noncitizens to vote. Several Dominican community organizations focused on gaining control of their local educational institutions. The movement of parents and community activists to address school overcrowding and substandard education led to the election of teacher and community activist Guillermo Linares in 1983 to the Washington Heights area Community School Board (at the time it was one of thirty-two decentralized school boards in New York City). Linares relied heavily on parents and community residents to win the election, both citizen and noncitizen alike.[79]

In 1991, after pressure from the Dominican and Puerto Rican communities and Puerto Rican elected officials, a redrawing of New York City's electoral maps created a Dominican-majority city council district in Upper Manhattan.[80] After a highly competitive race, Guillermo Linares emerged as the first Dominican to be elected to the city council. In 1992, the redistricting of the New York State Assembly created a strong majority-Latino district in northern Manhattan, with a 78 percent Latino population. Longtime incumbent Brian Murtaugh ran and won election that year, however, defeating a Dominican and a Puerto Rican candidate.[81]

In 1996, Adriano Espaillat defeated Murtaugh in the Democratic primary and won the general election. The campaign focused on representation and national origins, and Espaillat stressed his ability, given his Dominican origin, to better represent the district's residents.[82] The 1980s and 1990s saw the Dominican community grow numerically and politically. They now compete with other ethnic and racial groups for political influence and have gained a limited level of political incorporation in the country's largest city. By 2000, the U.S. Dominican population was estimated at 579,000, an increase of 240,000 since 1990. Dominicans are now nearly 27 percent of the Latino population, up from 19 percent in 1990, while Puerto Ricans have declined from 48 to 38 percent (830,000) of all Latinos.

An example of the level of political interest in politics in the Dominican community was when New York City Council member Linares was termed out of office in 2001. There were eight candidates for this position, reflecting the diversity of political viewpoints and allegiances within the community. The winner was Miguel Martinez, who was president of a political club associated with Assembly member Espaillat. Other candidates had ties to Linares and other political alliances in the Dominican community. Also elected in 2001 in Brooklyn was another Dominican, Diana Reyna, a former aide to Assemblyman Vito Lopez. Both incumbents won reelection in 2003, with many of the same rivals running against them—an indication that differences remain in the Dominican and larger Latino community over who can best represent the Latino community throughout the city.

Dominicans have also been elected to state and local offices in several other states. In Lawrence, Massachusetts, a former mill town that still receives new immigrants as it did in the nineteenth century, two Dominicans and two Puerto Ricans sit on the city council in 2005. A Puerto Rican and a Dominican ran for mayor of Lawrence in 2001, and the Puerto Rican candidate, Isabel Melendez, nearly won.[83] In a city with 60 percent Latino population and 38 percent Latino voters, this election is a portent of the future as Latinos seek to become politically incorporated in towns not historically known for being centers of Latino culture and politics. In the neighboring state of Rhode Island, there are three Dominicans elected to office from the Providence area: State Senator Juan Pichardo, State Assembly representative Grace Diaz, and Providence City Council member Miguel Luna in 2004.

In Atlantic City, New Jersey, Ramone "Tito" Rosario was elected to the city council in 2000 and became the state's first Dominican city council member. Rosario is emblematic of Dominicans who arrived in New York City and then moved to other locations to start businesses and establish roots. He was born in the Dominican Republic and came at a young age to the United States with his parents. There is now also a Dominican city commissioner in Union City and another city council member in Trenton, New Jersey. These and other Dominicans have been elected to office since the mid-1990s, reflecting the newness of this community's efforts to win electoral office.

The Dominican population has grown rapidly. According to the 2000 census, the Dominican American population had spread to numerous cities and communities beyond New York City. Table 3.2 lists the top ten cities with numbers of Dominican residents. An important issue for Dominicans and other Latinos was the 2000 census undercount of Latinos in the United States. The wording of the census questionnaire required all Latinos other than Mexicans, Cubans, and Puerto Ricans to write in another Hispanic category, but no examples of other categories were offered to orient respondents as had been given in 1990. For this reason an unprecedented number of Dominicans and other Latino groups gave no specific information on

Table 3.2 Top Ten Cities with Dominican Population, 2000

	Mumford 2000	Census 2000
1. New York, NY, PMSA	602,714	424,847
2. Miami, FL, PMSA	53,940	36,454
3. Bergen-Passaic, NJ, PMSA	50,080	36,360
4. Jersey City, NJ, PMSA	39,926	27709
5. Boston, MA-NH, PMSA	37,637	25,057
6. Nassau-Suffolk, NY, PMSA	30,394	21,071
7. Lawrence, MA-NH, PMSA	26,601	19,055
8. Providence-Fall River-Warwick, RI-MA, MSA	25,357	17,965
9. Newark, NJ, PMSA	22,995	15,457
10. Middlesex-Somerset-Hunterdon, NJ, PMSA	20,906	15,467

Source: Lewis Mumford Center, SUNY, Albany (2001).

their ethnic origin, so that 6.2 million, or 17.6 percent, were counted as "other Hispanics"—a far larger number than previously recorded. Most of them were new immigrant Latinos, with the result that many distinct Latino groups were undercounted. The Lewis Mumford Center, using 1998 and 2000 Current Population Survey data, estimates that the Dominican population was on average significantly higher than what was counted in the 2000 census. Table 3.2 shows where Dominicans are concentrated and the size of the undercount in the top ten cities with a significant Dominican population.[81]

Dominican migration and incorporation into the United States has been limited by both economic and racialized discrimination. While Dominicans do not necessarily define themselves as black, the dominant racial ideologies in the United States tend to treat them as such. Thus Dominicans have faced the intense stereotyping, prejudice, and discrimination "to which all people of African origin are subjected."[84] According to one author, Dominicans' migration to the United States at some point in the 1980s "gained enough economic and political weight in the life of the island to speak about a transnational community."[85] The Dominican migration includes participation in both the Dominican Republic and U.S. politics. The Dominican American community is a large contributor to various political parties and candidates in national Dominican elections.[86] New York State politicians regularly visit the island nation to maintain political relationships. Dual citizenship has been a hotly debated topic since the early 1990s.

Overcoming the extreme poverty in the Dominican Republic that fuels emigration will require continued financial and other assistance from the overseas Dominican community. The electoral fortunes of Dominicans in the United States will continue to be closely connected politically and financially to their home country for many years to come.

■ **Central Americans Begin to Organize**

One of the diverse forms of Latino politics that developed in California during the 1960s and 1970s occurred in San Francisco. The Mission District became a center for a growing influx of new immigrants from Central and South America and Mexico. New immigrants found a community that was run down, with poor schools and limited resources. In the 1960s, as Latino communities experienced political awakening, community and student activism grew. Latino students were involved with the Third World Strike at San Francisco State College in 1968–1969, which led to the establishment of ethnic studies programs in colleges around the nation. On May 1, 1969, a confrontation between Latino immigrant youth and the police led to the killing of a San Francisco police officer.[87] All of the community youths charged with murder were from Central American countries. The Oakland/San Francisco area had "substantial numbers of Latinos from various parts of Latin America who did not identify as Chicano or Mexicano."[88] A campaign to free the seven youths, some of whom were student activists, was launched with rallies and community fundraisers. The organizing efforts led to the formation of a grassroots political organization known as Los Siete de la Raza. The Los Siete organization started a free breakfast program, modeled after the Black Panther Party's program. It also established a free clinic and other community services and produced a newspaper known as *Basta Ya*.[89] After eighteen months and a highly charged trial, the Latino community successfully rallied to win the freedom of the youths. Many of those who became involved in Los Siete continued their activism in later efforts to organize labor and community struggles.

As internal conflicts in El Salvador and Guatemala heated up in the late 1970s and early 1980s, hundreds of thousands of political refugees fled north. Many Central Americans, victims of torture and abuse in their homelands, became active in efforts to build solidarity with the peoples of Central American countries.[90] They also built new organizations to meet the needs of the immigrant community. Especially as the civil wars came to an end in the 1990s, many Central Americans focused their efforts on obtaining legal status in this country. In Los Angeles, organizations such as the Central American Refugee Center (CARECEN), El Rescate, and the Guatemalan Information Center provided a range of services, including legal counseling for those seeking asylum. Efforts to win political asylum for those who were victims of the brutal civil wars in Central America have continued into the twenty-first century.[91] One organization that continues to offer assistance to immigrants and refugees is the Coalition for Humane Immigrant Rights of Los Angeles (CHIRLA), a nonprofit established in 1986 to "advance the human and civil rights of immigrants and refugees in Los Angeles."[92]

Salvadorans began to participate in U.S. electoral politics. Oscar Rios, for example, became the first Latino elected in district elections in Watsonville, California, in 1989. Rios was born in El Salvador and moved to the United States at a young age; he was a labor organizer at the time of his election. California State Senator Liz Figueroa, the first Latina elected to the State Assembly and Senate from northern California, represents the Tenth District—the vicinity of the city of Fremont in the San Francisco Bay area. The daughter of Salvadoran parents, she was a small business owner before joining the state legislature in 1994. In the state of Maryland, Ana Sol Gutierrez, a Salvadoran American, was elected to the state's House of Delegates in 2003. Her new position followed her election to the Montgomery County School Board in 1990, after first organizing people to register to vote in her community. Gutierrez's election represents the beginning of a wider presence by Salvadorans in the area. In Washington, D.C., there are 135,000 Salvadorans, who constitute the nation's second-largest Salvadoran community after Los Angeles. Salvadorans are beginning to register to vote and be courted by local candidates for office. Their numbers will grow as the second generation comes of age and begins to participate in local politics.

■ Conclusion

At the beginning of the 1960s, Latino politics were at a takeoff point. While organized political activity was still extremely limited in most areas with substantial Latino populations, the pioneers of Latino politics were already positioned within the political system to represent at least the Mexican American segment of the community on a national level. The formation of Viva Kennedy Clubs marked a new effort to unite Latinos. However, without organizational resources and political will on the part of all participants, these efforts were not sustained through the 1960s. Puerto Ricans' political influence, with very few elected officials, was limited to the New York City area. Restrictive electoral structures and limited numbers of voters had kept Latinos heavily dependent on others if they were to obtain policy benefits from the system. The impoverished conditions of Mexican and Puerto Rican colonias led to explosions of protest and demands in the 1960s. Other Latinos had not yet made their political presence felt in this country.

This would all change as new immigrants and political refugee groups arrived from Latin America, built ethnic enclaves, and began to participate in politics. In four decades, 1960–2000, Latinos went from being viewed as insignificant and marginalized to being considered politically important, with leaders emerging from immigrant communities. Yet political incorporation was uneven in Latino communities nationwide. Members of some immigrant communities were relatively new to the United States and not in a position to mount political efforts, while others who had arrived only recently were already becoming major political actors in their communities. Where Latinos built political organization, developed electoral candidates, and raised the necessary economic resources to be competitive with Anglos and others, they were able to become politically viable and win public office.

This period represents a significant advance from the 1940s, when political incorporation efforts were still only nascent. The next chapter discusses the use of legal mechanisms to change electoral structures that had inhibited Latino political incorporation; it goes on to survey biracial coalitional politics, grassroots organizing efforts of Latinas, nonelectoral community organizing, and the rise of immigrant politics in the Latino community.

■ Notes

1. P. Ong, E. Bonacich, and L. Cheng (1994), pp. 8–9.
2. B. Bluestone and B. Harrison (1982).
3. R. Taylor (1975), pp. 88–89.
4. M. G. Gonzales (1999), p. 177.
5. R. Griswold del Castillo and A. De León (1996), p. 106.
6. M. T. Garcia (1994), pp. 195–96.
7. Ibid., pp. 197–203.
8. K. Underwood (1997a), p. 4.
9. R. Taylor (1975), pp. 84–86.
10. Industrial Areas Foundation, www.industrialareasfoundation.org.
11. R. Taylor (1975), p. 90.
12. R. Acuña (1988), p. 283.
13. R. Rosales (2000), pp. 71–72.
14. M. T. Garcia (1989), pp. 113–144.
15. F. C. Garcia (1974b), p. 179.
16. Ibid.
17. M. Vigil (1996), p. 28.
18. I. M. Garcia (2000), p. 53.
19. Ibid., pp. 88–103.
20. A. Navarro (1998), p. 20.
21. I. M. Garcia (2000), p. 150.
22. A. Navarro (1998), p. 47.
23. W. B. Gould (1993), pp. 34–35.
24. United Farm Workers of America (n.d.).
25. J. Gomez Quiñones (1990), pp. 105–107.
26. J. Gomez Quiñones (1994), p. 254.
27. D. Montejano (1987), p. 284.
28. R. Acuña (1988), p. 328.

29. J. Gomez Quiñones (1990), p. 115.
30. A. Navarro (2000), p. 178.
31. Ibid., pp. 80–94.
32. A. Navarro (1995), p. 53.
33. Ibid. p. 117.
34. A. Navarro (2000), pp. 31–33.
35. Ibid., p. 50.
36. Ibid., pp.140–144.
37. Ibid., p. 165.
38. I. M. Garcia (1989), p. 226.
39. A. Navarro (2000), pp. 272–282.
40. I. M. Garcia (1989), p. 231.
41. R. Acuña (1988), p. 336.
42. C. Munoz (1989), p. 86.
43. Ibid., pp. 173–174.
44. D. Gutiérrez (1995), pp. 190–191.
45. M. T. Garcia (1994).
46. C. Muñoz (1989), p. 94; J. Gomez Quiñones (1990), p. 152.
47. A. Sosa Riddell and R. Aguallo (1979), p. 11.
48. Ibid., p. 19.
49. P. C. Takash and J. Avila (1989).
50. V. E. Sánchez Korrol (1994), p. 225.
51. J. Jennings (1977), p. 77.
52. Libertad (1994).
53. S. Baver (1984), p. 45.
54. M. E. Perez y Gonzalez (2000), p. 64.
55. S. Baver (1984), p. 46.
56. F. Padilla (1987), pp. 145–146.
57. F. Bean and M. Tienda (1985), p. 105.
58. S. Baver (1984), p. 47.
59. Ibid., p. 48.
60. A. Falcon (2003).
61. I. Morales (1998), p. 212.
62. M. Abramson and Young Lords Party (1971).
63. S. Baver (1984), p. 49.
64. J. Velázquez (1998), pp. 49–51.
65. Interview with Jose Smith, Miami Beach City Council member, July 11, 2001.
66. R. R. Fagen, R. A. Brody, and T. J. O'Leary (1968), p. 19.
67. M. de Los Angeles Torres (1999).
68. M. C. Garcia (1996), p. 68.
69. Ibid., p. 72.
70. Cuban American electoral efforts will be more fully explored in subsequent chapters.
71. J. Gonzalez (2000), p. 118.
72. P. Levitt (2001), p. 42.
73. H. Jordan (1997), p. 38.
74. R. Hernández and F. L. Rivera-Batiz (2003).
75. U.S. Bureau of the Census (2004).
76. E. Georges (1984).
77. H. Jordan (1997), p. 38.

78. Interview with New York City Council member G. Linares, July 16, 2001.
79. Ibid.
80. H. Jordan (1997), p. 40.
81. P. Graham (1998), p. 55.
82. Ibid.
83. C. Cole (2001).
81. Lewis Mumford Center (2001).
84. J. Duany (1998), pp. 148–149.
85. J. Izigsohn et al. (1999).
86. M. Jones-Correa (2001).
87. M. Heins (1972), pp. 142–143.
88. A. Navarro (2000), p. 136.
89. M. Heins (1972), p. 162. The Black Panther Party sought to unite black and brown political organizing efforts; it offered the new Latino group part of its newspaper for a bilingual issue in 1969, and the added section was called *Basta Ya.*
90. In Nicaragua a popular struggle led by the Sandinista National Liberation Front to topple longtime dictator Anastasio Somoza took place over many years. In 1979, the Sandinistas were successful. The conflict had major repercussions in the United States, as many Nicaraguans fled their country during the turmoil. Many Nicaraguans went to the Miami area and San Francisco. Today there is a population of political refugees who fled during the Somoza regime and another wave of persons who fled later to protect their economic assets.
91. N. Chinchilla, N. Hamilton, and J. Loucky (1993), p. 71.
92. Coalition for Humane Immigrant Rights in Los Angeles (n.d.).

4

Into the Mainstream

B efore the electoral pathway for Latinos could open fully, changes needed to take place in the political structures that had historically restricted
their ability to achieve elected office. Racialized voting and gerrymandered
districts were major obstacles to the election of Latinos in most places.
Efforts began in the late 1960s to challenge the inequalities in electoral
structures that disadvantaged Latinos. As these structural barriers have
come down, political incorporation efforts have blossomed, and grassroots
efforts to elect Latinos to office have grown. This chapter explores the
growth of Latino legal organizations and their role in changing the rules to
level the playing field in the electoral arena so that Latino voters would
have a fair chance to elect someone of their own choosing and Latino candidates would have an equal opportunity to seek political office. We will
also explore efforts to build national and local "rainbow" political coalitions and other grassroots organizing efforts, the emergence of strong
Latina leaders and community organizations, and finally the development
of new Latino political voices in the 1990s.

■ Political, Legal, and
Organizational Challenges to Exclusion

In 1968, a new civil rights organization was founded, the Mexican
American Legal Defense Fund (MALDEF). This organization was the idea
of Texas attorney Pete Tijerina. It was modeled on the National Association
for the Advancement of Colored People's Legal Defense Fund and was initially funded by the Ford Foundation, the nonprofit arm of Ford Motor
Corporation.[1] While initially viewed with suspicion because of its financial
support from corporate America, MALDEF would soon prove critical in
the struggle to advance the voting rights of Latinos.

By the mid-1970s, many of the groups that had emerged in the late 1960s were in decline due to internal conflicts, inexperience, massive police interference in their activities, and the changing external context. Meanwhile, several other developments would dramatically change the options and potential for Latino political incorporation. By 1975, many of the inhibitors to voting as well as districting practices that had proved negative to the election of Latinos were beginning to be addressed.[2] For example, in 1970, in a landmark decision, *Garza* v. *Smith*, MALDEF won its challenge to Texas election laws that had enabled voting officials to assist physically handicapped voters but had not permitted assistance to voters who were not proficient in English. The argument in *Garza* foreshadowed the broadening of the Voting Rights Act to Texas. In 1975, the Voting Rights Act was extended to states and counties that had historically failed to provide multilingual election materials.[3]

The elimination of barriers to registration and voting often did not result in the election of minority candidates, however, even in locations with large numbers of minorities. Several structural roadblocks remained: multimember districts (including at-large elections), racial gerrymandering, and malapportionment.[4] These barriers diluted minority voting strength, as racial voting among Anglos combined with certain election rules prevented a cohesive bloc of minority voters from electing candidates of their choice. After the extension of the Voting Rights Act in 1975, numerous vote-dilution legal cases produced some form of single-member districts election in most major Texas cities, including Houston, San Antonio, and Dallas. The high level of litigation is illustrated by the fact that between 1975 and 1990 the Justice Department brought 131 objections to voting procedures in the state of Texas alone.[5] As electoral rules and structures were changed, the number of elected minority officials seeking office grew, and their election to office increased.

As a result of Texas voting litigation, in 1982 Congress amended the Voting Rights Act by clarifying that at-large elections that produced a discriminatory result were sufficient proof of minority vote dilution. This change in the law meant that discriminatory intent need not be shown; only the results of an at-large electoral system were needed to substantiate a claim. Legal challenges were also used in other states where Latinos had historically been unable to elect their own candidates. Legal challenges remain an important weapon in determining electoral opportunities for Latinos.

❏ *Puerto Ricans and Voting Rights*

While Mexican Americans were beginning to build successful legal and mobilization strategies to achieve electoral office, Puerto Ricans built civil rights and advocacy groups. Among the new organizations that formed was the National Puerto Rican Coalition (1977), an umbrella advocacy organization that continues to provide a public forum to express the views of the Puerto Rican community. In 1981, the National Congress for Puerto Rican Rights was founded by former Young Lords party members and others involved in progressive Puerto Rican politics. The Institute for Puerto Rican Policy, a research and policy think tank, was founded by Angelo Falcon during this period.[6] These organizations advocated for the rights of Puerto Ricans, and they also worked with the Puerto Rican Legal Defense and Education Fund (PRLDEF), a civil rights advocacy group similar to MALDEF, which was founded in the 1970s.

The Puerto Rican Legal Defense and Education Fund filed several voting rights suits. In New York City, the PRLDEF stopped the 1981 municipal elections and forced the federal courts to eliminate the proposed district boundaries.[7] The redrawn council districts opened up electoral opportunities for Puerto Ricans and produced several more independent Puerto Rican officials in addition to the the candidates backed by local machine politics.

In Chicago, MALDEF and PRLDEF, a group of black voters, and the Republican Party joined together to challenge the state of Illinois's legislative assembly district lines. The suit was settled out of court, and the resultant redistricting map enabled Jose Berrios to be elected in 1982—the first Puerto Rican elected to the state assembly of Illinois.[8] The redistricting map of the Chicago city council districts was challenged in 1982. Voting rights law was used by civil rights attorneys to apply pressure to change the jurisdiction of long-standing machine aldermen.[9] Following both the 1990 and 2000 censuses, Puerto Ricans continued to propose district lines that would allow fair representation of Puerto Ricans. The PRLDEF developed a strategy in 2000 to open up the redistricting process to the Latino community. Working in eight states on the East Coast, they created the Latino Voting Rights Project to educate Latino communities about the legal and political aspects of redistricting at the local, state, and congressional levels.[10]

❑ *Increasing the Voting Potential of Mexican Americans*

In addition to attempts to reform political structures through legal pressure, in 1974 William Velásquez, a former MAYO student activist, founded the Southwest Voter Registration Education Project (SVREP) in Texas. The SVREP focused on securing resources and support to build voter education and registration campaigns in the Southwest. An affiliated organization, the Midwest Voter Registration Education Project, expanded these efforts into the Midwest region. Through the work of the SWVREP in Texas, the number of Mexican American registered voters in that state rose from 488,000 in 1976 to approximately 1 million by 1986.[11] Even with low turnout rates, this increase in the number of Mexican American voters, combined with changes in the political structure, enabled more Mexican Americans to seek office with a reasonable chance of being elected.

The SVREP continues to play a critical role in the Southwest and Midwest. It holds training and organizing sessions throughout the country to teach Latino community activists how to organize effective voter registration and get-out-the-vote campaigns. Its research arm, the William C. Velásquez Institute, gathers and analyzes information to improve political participation in Latino and other underrepresented communities. From its inception, SVREP has organized more than 2,200 voter registration campaigns in fourteen states and has trained over 100,000 volunteers.[12] As a result of these efforts and the work of other organizations, Latino voters have increased dramatically, from 2 million in 1974, when SVREP began, to 7.7 million in 2001. The SVREP continues to build on its previous efforts; in 2004 it set a goal of 10 million Latino registered voters and 7.5 million votes cast in the presidential election.[13]

❏ *Panethnic Latino Political Leaders Organizations*

The increase in Latino elected officials prompted the formation of other organizations that would represent the interests of these officials. In 1975, Congressman Edward Roybal formed the National Association of Latino Elected Officials (NALEO). This organization, composed of elected and appointed officials from both parties, has provided issue analysis, training, and advocacy at the local and national levels. NALEO grew from a small organization of Latino activists and elected officials into a prominent political institution that is well known for its research and analysis of issues related to the election of Latinos, as well as naturalization and citizenship issues.

In addition to this national organization of Latino elected officials, organizations have formed to serve the needs of Latinos at specific levels of government. In 1976, the National League of Cities established the Hispanic Elected Local Officials (HELO) constituency group to encourage communication among local elected officials. HELO also makes recommendations to the League of Cities on major public policy issues affecting Latino communities. Later, the National Association of Hispanic County Officials, a constituency caucus of the National Association of County Officials, was formed to represent the interests of Hispanic elected officials at the county level.

At the federal level, the Congressional Hispanic Caucus (CHC) was established in 1976. There were five original Latino members of

Congress—Herman Badillo (NY), Baltasar Corrada (PR), E. "Kika" de la
Garza (TX), Henry B. González (TX), and Edward Roybal (CA)—involved
in forming the caucus. Its purpose was to monitor legislative and other gov-
ernment activity that affects Hispanics. By 2004, there were twenty-five
Hispanics in Congress, including two Portugese Americans. The
Congressional Hispanic Caucus is comprised only of Democrats.
Republican Hispanics formed a separate caucus that includes five mem-
bers. Together, Latinos comprise 5.7 percent of all members of the House.
With the election of two Hispanics to the U.S. Senate in 2004, they now
represent 2 percent of the Senate.

❏ *Breakthroughs by Latinos in the 1980s*

In the wake of these legal efforts and the development of Latino leadership organizations, Latino politics in the 1980s expanded as candidates
were elected to a number of important public offices. At the statewide executive level, Toney Anaya was elected as New Mexico governor with the
backing of an estimated 85 percent of the Mexican vote in 1982.[14] He was
the second Hispanic elected as governor in that state, following Jerry
Apodaca, who was elected in 1974. Anaya was only the third Latino elected
to a state governor's office in the contemporary period. He served only one
term.[15]

At the municipal level, Federico Peña became the first Mexican
American mayor of Denver, Colorado, in 1983. Peña was a MALDEF
attorney in the 1970s. In 1978 he won a seat in the Colorado legislature,
and he rose to become the minority speaker of the Colorado House of representatives.[16] In 1983, Peña ran for mayor of Denver, a city where
Mexicans were not a majority population and had little access to the corri-
dors of power.[17] Even though Mexican Americans were 18 percent of the
population and only 12 percent of voters, they played an important role in
his election. The SWVREP had recently registered 6,000 new Latino voters, and they contributed to Peña's margin of victory. Peña was known not
as a strong Hispanic-identified candidate but as a politician who happened
to be Hispanic.[18] He built an electoral coalition that included downtown
developers, unions, liberals, blacks, and the Mexican American community
to win office. His politics could be characterized as moderate progrowth
and prodevelopment.

In 1982, Henry Cisneros became mayor of San Antonio, Texas, the
largest U.S. city with a Mexican-majority population. Cisneros, the
descendant of an elite family that had migrated to the United States during
the Mexican Revolution, was closely identified with the large Mexican
American community. Cisneros's ability to run as an at-large candidate
served him well when he decided to run for mayor of the city in 1981. He

won the election by forging a citywide electoral coalition of downtown business interests and the Chicano majority population. Cisneros was able to mobilize the diverse currents within the Chicano community while keeping the support of the city's Anglo elites. His skillful use of personal politics that transcended the barrio made him electable to citywide office. Peña and Cisneros both were able to achieve prominent elected political office by winning the backing of multiple class and racial forces at the same time.

❑ *Emergence of Cuban American Politics in South Florida*

While Mexican Americans and Puerto Ricans were using legal challenges to force open previously gerrymandered districts, Cuban Americans in South Florida used a combination of legal challenges and naturalization and registration drives among first-generation refugees to achieve a limited number of electoral offices by the early 1970s. The first Cuban elected to office was Manolo Reboso, who was elected to the Miami City Commission in 1973 after being first appointed to the position. The difficulties of penetrating the Democratic Party's nomination process, combined with the generally held view that the Kennedy Administration had let the Cuban community down during the Bay of Pigs invasion and Cuban missile crisis of the early 1960s, led the majority of Cuban Americans away from the Democratic Party and spurred the exiles to register as Republicans.[19]

However, others did not meet the growth of Cuban political influence with support. Instead of a cooperative atmosphere, a growing divide emerged: "the growth of Cuban voting power, together with a sudden new wave of a large number of refugees brought by the Mariel exodus, soon touched off a backlash among whites in Dade County."[20] A 1980 referendum attempted to nullify Dade County's support for bilingualism. The referendum passed easily. The vote polarized along ethnic lines, with 71 percent of non-Hispanic whites voting for it and 85 percent of Latinos voting against it. This tension between Hispanics and non-Hispanics would sharpen as the electoral strength of Cubans grew in the 1980s.

As the geographic concentration of Cubans grew into sprawling ethnic enclaves, whites fled, which increased the opportunities to elect Cubans into multiple offices. This further enhanced the power of the Cuban exile community. One form in which their growing influence was manifest was the establishment of the Cuban American National Foundation (CANF) in 1981. While other Latinos were focusing their efforts on achieving political power to address domestic issues and win political office, Cubans were strongly concerned with U.S. foreign policy. CANF raised and spent large amounts of money lobbying members of Congress to support legislation that kept up the pressure on Cuba.[21]

The growing political clout of the Cuban American community was evident after the redrawing of electoral districts and the creation of new single-member districts. In the early 1980s, following redistricting, Cuban Americans were elected to the legislature in Florida, and soon a Cuban American caucus was formed. At a national level, the Republican Party reached out to the Cuban community to build a base "to establish itself in the usually Democratic-controlled state."[22] The electoral strategy was to run Cuban candidates against Democrats and to promote Cubans into government posts. One result of these efforts were clearly evident in 1984; 80 percent of Cubans voted for Ronald Reagan for president, a far higher percentage than Puerto Ricans (18 percent) or Mexicans (30 percent).[23]

Outside the south Florida area, Cuban Americans are usually not the dominant Latino group in urban centers; in Chicago, Boston, and other cities they are less tied to the Republican Party and more interested in forging multiracial electoral coalitions.[24] For example, New Jersey congressman Robert Melendez, the son of Cuban immigrants, was born in New York City. He eventually moved to New Jersey, and in 1974 he was elected to his first position on the Board of Education of Union City, New Jersey. From 1986 to 1992 he served as the mayor of Union City; he was elected to the New Jersey State Assembly 1987–1991 and the New Jersey Senate 1991–1993. After this long career in local and state politics, in 1992 he was elected to the U.S. House of Representatives and become the first Hispanic from New Jersey to serve in Congress.[25]

■ Multiracial Coalition Politics, 1983–1993

As Latinos made important electoral gains in the early 1980s through legal challenges, changes in the Voting Rights Act, reapportionment, and voter registration growth, both parties began to court Latinas and Latinos as candidates for office. Multiracial coalition politics with a goal of achieving minority-group political incorporation were put to the test in the 1980s in some of the major metropolitan areas.

In Chicago, Latinos had a small presence in city politics prior to 1983. No Latinos had been elected to the city council, and only 2 percent of the city's employees were Latino, even though they were 19 percent of the city's population.[26] In 1983, African American congressman Harold Washington defeated two white candidates in the Democratic primary, including incumbent Mayor Jane Byrne and Richard M. Daley, son of the legendary machine mayor. Washington fashioned a liberal-progressive coalition that included almost all segments of the African American community plus liberal and progressive whites, Asians, and Latinos. While the established Latino community leaders initially supported the two white candidates, a group of Latino activists decided to back Washington because of his opposition to the Simpson-Mazzoli immigration bill and his fight against attempts to dilute the Voting Rights Act.[27] When Washington won the Democratic primary,[28] most Latino voters switched their support. Latinos voted 75 percent for Washington in the general election and helped provide the margin of victory against the white Republican Party candidate.[29] Latinos then served in the Washington administration and helped build a progressive multiracial administration both as insiders and as advocates for the Latino community through the newly formed Mayor's Advisory Commission on Latino Affairs.

In 1986, as a result of a legal challenge to the drawing of the city council districts, the courts ruled that the 1981 district map was discriminatory and required the city to develop an alternative plan. Four majority-Latino wards were drawn in the revised plan, in addition to several new majority–African American wards. The Latino wards were split evenly between the two major concentrations of Latinos in the city: two on the north side, where most Puerto Ricans resided, and two on the near south side, where the majority of Mexicans lived. In a special election held that same year, four Latinos were elected to the city council. Thus Latino representation increased from one member of the Chicago City Council to four.

The Latinos on the council represented different political allegiances, with two of the four closely aligned with Harold Washington: Jesus "Chuy" Garcia (who later became a state senator) and Luis Gutierrez (who later became the first Puerto Rican congressman from the Chicago area). These two viewed themselves as part of a progressive and reform agenda to transform Chicago politics. Both had arisen from grassroots community organizing to become local elected officials.[30] The other two were more closely identified with the Democratic machine. Also, in 1986, Miguel del Valle was elected state senator from District 5 in Chicago, which contained a slim Latino population majority but not a Latino registered-voter majority; thus he demonstrated the ability of Latino candidates to be elected in districts where they were not the majority of registered voters.[31]

Unfortunately, in 1987, a year after the election of the four Latinos to the council, Washington collapsed and died after successfully winning a second term in office. In the ensuing election, African Americans were divided between two black candidates. Richard M. Daley ran again and emerged victorious in 1989. This time, the majority of Latinos voted for Daley.[32] Daley's electoral victory in 1989 broke up the progressive "Black and Brown" coalition at the city level, as he built his own electoral coalition that included a large turnout of white voters who were not divided between white Democratic Party candidates, combined with a small percentage of black voters (the others being divided between multiple black candidates) and strong majorities from the Latino population. The Latino voters shifted from 70 percent support for Washington in the 1987 Democratic primary to 50 percent for the African American candidate in the special election. By the 1995 mayoral elections, more than 80 percent of Latinos voted for Mayor Daley.[33] Among those who supported the Daley electoral coalition in the late 1980s was Luis Gutierrez, who had come out of the Puerto Rican independence movement and sat on the city council. Gutierrez would later win support from Daley for a new congressional seat created by apportionment in 1992.[34]

In Philadelphia, Wilson Goode was elected mayor in 1983, having won a close Democratic primary against former mayor Frank Rizzo. Goode also built an African American–Latino–liberal alliance. The Latino population was only 4 percent of the city in 1980, with nearly three-quarters of these Puerto Rican. Given the predicted closeness of the election, Latino voters were courted. Puerto Rican voters voted for Goode more than two to one in the primary and 77 percent in the general election.[35] In 1987, when Goode ran for reelection, his percentage of the Latino vote was 70 percent in the primary. The rate was lower because state representative Ralph Acosta endorsed Goode's opponent, Ed Rendell, who would become Philadelphia's mayor in the 1990s.[36]

In Boston, a progressive African American candidate, Mel King, ran for the office of mayor in 1979 and 1983. Both times he was unsuccessful in winning the election; however, he was successful in building a multiracial coalition, including strong support from Latinos.[37] During the 1983 campaign, the combination of a Latino candidate for office and the Mel King campaign brought out large numbers of Latino voters, with a "Latinos for Mel King" committee drawing wider attention to their presence in the campaign.[38] In all three cities, multiracial coalitions headed by African American candidates were highlights of the campaigns.

■ Black and Latino Politics: An Unfinished Story

The success of the Mel King and Harold Washington multiracial electoral coalitions, combined with African Americans being taken for granted by the Democratic Party, prompted the Reverend Jesse Jackson to seek the party's nomination for president in 1984. Jackson called for the formation of a "rainbow coalition" of all races, particularly those historically disenfranchised by the political system—minorities, women, youth, and poor people. In many northern cities, African American and other voters participated in electoral politics for the first time. This included many Latinos who had previously viewed electoral politics as ineffective at best. The Jackson campaign was part electoral campaign and part social movement; the energy and enthusiasm it generated drew many into the campaign who were either alienated or part of society's historically disenfranchised elements: blacks, Latinos, Native Americans, Asian Americans, and the poor.

In 1984, Jackson, who had been largely unknown in the Latino community, except in Chicago, captured 33 percent of the Puerto Rican vote and 17 percent of the Mexican American vote in the Democratic primaries. Jackson's support for the Farm Labor Organizing Committee (FLOC) in its fight for better wages and working conditions won its endorsement. FLOC organizers campaigned for Jackson in Texas and helped him win delegates to the state convention in Hidalgo County, south Texas.[39] In New York City, where Jackson won every Latino-majority district, the organizing was carried out by grassroots activists with little help from elected Hispanic leaders, none of whom endorsed Jackson.[40] In New York and other parts of the country, grassroots "Latinos for Jackson" committees were formed, with varying degrees of success.

In 1988, when Jackson ran for the second time for president, he garnered 7 million votes nationwide in the Democratic primaries. A highlight of Jackson's second run was his winning the popular vote in New York City with the strong support of Puerto Ricans. Jackson won 53 percent to 40 percent for Michael Dukakis, his primary opponent. This time, all of the major Puerto Rican elected officials in New York supported Jackson. Jackson also garnered considerable support from the city's labor unions, notably Local 1199 of the Health and Hospital Workers, which had a large membership of Latinos.[41]

In contrast, while Jackson increased his vote total from 1984, he won only 21 percent of the Mexican American vote in the Texas primary.[42] While Jackson made significant inroads in the Latino community, his opponent, Dukakis, did better outside the Northeast. In Texas, Dukakis carried 55 percent of the Mexican American vote, which was pivotal for him to win this state's primary. By the time California held its primary in June, Dukakis already had secured the nomination and won the Mexican American vote by a two-to-one margin. In Los Angeles the Latinos for Jackson committee included many community activists. Some of them would go on to enter electoral politics themselves; for example, Gil Cedillo and Gloria Romero became state senators from the Los Angeles area. Throughout the 1988 presidential campaign Latinos played an important role in boosting Jackson's vote totals but also in securing the nomination for Dukakis. Latinos demonstrated that even without fielding their own candidate for president, they could be influential in determining who received the nomination in the Democratic Party.[43]

Following the Jesse Jackson campaigns for president in 1984 and

1988, other biracial and multiracial campaigns took place. In 1985, black and Latino political leaders in New York City could not agree on a candidate to challenge incumbent mayor Ed Koch. Herman Badillo announced that he would run and sought the endorsement of African Americans. However, the black leaders felt that Badillo's attempt to run for mayor in 1977 had divided their efforts to elect a black candidate. Rather than support Badillo, the black leaders endorsed an African American state assemblyman, blacks and Latinos divided their votes, and Koch easily won the race.[44]

Despite these problems, efforts at building rainbow coalitions in New York City continued four years later in the mayoral race of 1989. An African American, David Dinkins, the Manhattan borough president, was elected with the majority votes of African Americans and Latinos and a substantial minority (35 percent) of white voters. The Dinkins campaign again demonstrated the power of multiracial coalition building. Dinkins successfully united black leadership and won the support of many Latinos and white liberals. As in Chicago, the chance to elect the city's first African American mayor mobilized large turnouts in the black community. In the Democratic primary, Dinkins had bested incumbent mayor Koch, and in the general election he defeated Republican candidate Rudolph Giuliani. Dinkins also won the support of almost half the white liberals, a majority of Latinos, and a quarter of the white ethnic Democrats.[45]

Four years later, in 1993, Dinkins lost his rematch with Giuliani, a federal prosecutor, as white ethnics turned out in higher numbers to support him, while African American, Latino, and white liberals turned out in lower numbers for Dinkins. With African Americans not as numerous a voting group as they were in Chicago, and faced with strong interethnic tensions, Dinkins was unable to keep the multiracial coalition together. Some Latinos were disappointed that Mayor Dinkins had not done more to address some of their long-standing problems.[46]

Rainbow politics also spread to smaller communities. In Hartford, Connecticut, Puerto Ricans built a progressive coalition with white liberals and African Americans and won control of the city government in 1991. Having begun to participate in this city's electoral politics in the early 1970s, Puerto Ricans had emerged from having only one representative on the city council in the late 1970s to win three of the nine council seats in the 1991 election. These candidates captured the majority of votes in a city with less than 28 percent Latino population and where they were only the third largest racial group after whites and blacks. Puerto Ricans used identity politics to build in-group coherence but also used multiracial politics to have a citywide impact.[47]

The Hartford multiracial coalition, however, was unable to maintain political control, and a more conservative slate replaced it in 1993. The coalition had found it more difficult to work together to achieve legislation and policy agreement in office than to mobilize as candidates for office. As noted in an account of this period, "Only a few understood that although black and Puerto Rican interests were different, a mutually beneficial coalition was possible."[48]

At the end of the rainbow politics period, multiracial electoral coalitions were generally hard pressed to demonstrate their ability to maintain dominant local governing coalitions capable of holding on to power and advancing the interests of Latinos and the other underrepresented racial minority groups. However, efforts to build cooperative black-brown political coalitions continue, because in most large urban centers these two groups, along with Arab Americans, Asian Americans, and Native Americans, find themselves living and working side by side.

■ Latino Empowerment Efforts in Latino Communities

In addition to efforts of Latinos in large cities to build multiracial coalitions, and to build their own political base of support, the actions of Latinos in communities where Latinos were the majority or near majority population brought important breakthroughs in this period. In many towns and cities, Latinos had recently become the majority population or had been the majority population yet had no or limited representation. In California in the mid-1980s to early 1990s, a series of political organizing efforts illustrate the stirring of a new political animal, the Latino electorate.

A lawsuit filed in 1985, *Gomez* v. *City of Watsonville*, which challenged the unfairness of the at-large electoral system, was emblematic of numerous voting rights litigations that were filed during this period. After the defeat of city council candidate Maria Bautista, community activists met with representatives from the Mexican American Legal Defense and Education Fund (MALDEF). They discussed the possibility of a lawsuit against the city of Watsonville for a discriminatory at-large electoral system that prevented the election of Latinos to office due to the racialized voting patterns of whites in the city. Soon after, MALDEF attorney Joaquin Avila filed suit on behalf of three Chicano residents of Watsonville: Waldo Rodriguez, Patricia Leal, and Cruz Gomez. The suit charged that Watsonville's at-large system violated the Voting Rights Act of 1965 by its systematic denial of Latino representation.

In 1987, a U.S. district judge ruled against the plaintiffs. While acknowledging that racially polarized voting existed, he questioned the degree of political cohesion among Latinos, since 50 percent of the city's Latino population lived outside the proposed "Latino" districts. In July 1988, the U.S. Ninth Circuit Court of Appeals overturned the decision, finding historical and contemporary racial discrimination against Latinos in California. The appellate court ruled that Watsonville's at-large method of electing city officials violated the Voting Rights Act, as it diluted Latinos' voting strength. The appellate court also rejected the notion that Latinos in Watsonville were not a politically cohesive group. The court said that creating two majority-Latino districts, as proposed under the MALDEF plan, would create a politically cohesive voting group.[49]

As the city was deciding whether to appeal the decision, the Chicano community was organizing to demand that the court's decision be accepted. On January 10, 1989, Chicano community residents packed the city council meeting; representatives of the League of United Latino American Citizens (LULAC), the United Farm Workers of America (UFW), and social service organizations were present, along with cannery worker activists and the plaintiffs in the case. They presented petitions demanding that the city not appeal the decision. They told the city council that the Chicano community was tired of the entire history of discriminatory treatment by city government, including discrimination in city employment and an inferior level of services in the Chicano neighborhoods. Despite this united and vocal opposition, the city decided to appeal the decision to the U.S. Supreme Court.[50]

On March 20, 1989, the Supreme Court refused to hear the city's appeal, forcing the city to cancel the elections set for May and to schedule district elections. This set the stage for the first district elections in Watsonville since the alderman system had been dismantled in 1932. Watsonville had not had a Latino on the city council from the time it was incorporated in the 1800s until 1987, when Tony Campos, a wealthy businessman acceptable to the local political power structure, had been elected in citywide elections.

The electoral campaign for the first district elections was extremely intense. For the first time, Chicanos and Latinos realized they had a legitimate opportunity to win an election. In the seven district races, five Latinos and one Native American ran for various council seats. However, only one Latino, Oscar Rios, won a seat on the council, in the city's District 2, which was predominantly Latino. Following the election, some questioned whether the change to district elections had benefited the Latino community, since only one Latino was elected. However, this analysis neglects an important point. Latino voters had turned out in record numbers for the first time in Watsonville, doubling what the turnout had been in 1987 in the same precincts. The district campaign unleashed pent-up frustration with the local political system. To elect Rios, a grassroots campaign of volunteers was organized, including cannery workers, Chicano students from surrounding colleges and Watsonville High School, and community residents. The election took on the air of a community campaign. Based on these efforts, Rios was the only Latino to win his race. The communitywide effort went door to door, several times to every household, to solicit support.[51]

An important community campaign for political incorporation occurred almost at the same time as the Watsonville voting rights campaign. The city of Pomona, California, located in east Los Angeles County, began undergoing a major demographic shift in the late 1970s and went from majority white to majority black and Latino by the 1990s. Between 1965 and 1984, out of sixteen candidates from racial and ethnic minorities who sought election to the city council, only two Latino candidates were successful. In 1985, five Pomona residents filed a lawsuit claiming that the city's at-large system violated the Voting Rights Act. In 1986, the U.S. District Court dismissed the lawsuit, but in 1990, Pomona voters adopted a district election structure. By 1993, the city council became majority Latino with four members and with one black member.[52] Pomona was an important example of how minorities have joined together to achieve political incorporation.

In southeast Los Angeles County, a number of suburban cities had gone from being predominantly white working-class communities to being predominantly Mexican working-class communities by the 1980s. As growing numbers of Latino working families moved into affordable housing in Bell, Bell Gardens, Commerce, Cudahy, Huntington Park, Pico Rivera, Maywood, and South Gate, whites moved to outer suburbs farther south and east. Yet in these communities, despite the demographic changes, there was not a corresponding demographic change in the elected and appointed officials. Latino electoral representation was almost nonexistent.

In Bell Gardens, Latinos grew frustrated with the lack of representation and took decisive action. Bells Gardens' population of 43,000 was nearly 90 percent Latino. It was home to predominantly poor working-class renters. In 1990, the all-white city council passed a zoning ordinance that attempted to control population density by rezoning properties; this would have led to the demolition of hundreds of homes and apartment buildings and eliminated the use of "granny apartments," garages that had been turned into living quarters.[53]

The predominantly Mexican American residents got angry and decided to do something about this injustice. They went out, registered voters, and organized a recall election that threw out of office the mayor and three other white city council members in December 1991. The political establishment was stunned, as city leaders had cultivated the support of prominent Chicano politicians, including Congressman Marty Martinez. The residents had been successful by organizing a grassroots campaign that went door to door to build support to overturn the new zoning ordinance and recall the incumbents. At the next election, a majority of Latinos were elected to the city council.

The Bell Gardens story was viewed initially as a "revolt that would bring majority rule to all the Southland cities where local governments defy demographics."[54] Other efforts to elect Latino representation followed in other nearby cities. By 1994, most of the city councils in southeast Los Angeles County were becoming majority Latino. Unfortunately, in many of the poor and working-class communities, such as Bell Gardens, Maywood, and Cudahy, the achievement of Latino political dominance in local government came at a time where there were scarce economic resources. This severely limited the ability of the new crop of Latino elected officials to address problems of poverty, crime, and unemployment. Nevertheless, the Bell Gardens campaign opened a new era of Latino politics in the county, as grassroots leaders emerged who were more representative of the population in numerous Latino majority communities. Now Latinos also had multiple locations to gain experience in local politics, so these city councils provided an important training ground for future leaders.

With the growth of Latino leadership, the issue of representation takes on a different character: Latino candidates for office must distinguish themselves from other Latino candidates based on their record of community service, community ties, interest group support, and get-out-the-vote operations. As Latinos have been elected to office, the question arises, how representative is the bureaucracy that is responsible for carrying out public policy? Should the bureaucracy reflect the demographic characteristics of the population?

Political incorporation theorists Rufus Browning, Dale Marshall, and David Tabb view the composition of the workforce hired or appointed to city jobs as an important measure of minority groups' political incorporation.[55] As Latino elected officials have assumed the power, they have also changed the composition of civil service and key appointed city offices to reflect the demographics of the community and to improve communication with a largely Spanish-speaking population. In many of these Latino-majority cities, Latinos hold city manager, city attorney, police chief, and other key management positions. In other southern California cities, where Latinos were not the majority population, there were still few Latinos in key management positions by the start of the twenty-first century. When surveyed at that time, local Latino elected officials were less concerned with the ethnicity of the applicants for these key administrative positions and more concerned with their qualifications.[56] Nevertheless, having a representative bureaucracy remains an important measure of whether Latinos are politically incorporated, and it is apparent that when Latinos are in charge of political decision making, it is more likely that they will not only elect the representatives of their choice but hire them as well.

The majoritarian representation principle that is a hallmark of U.S. democracy is now evident in these majority-Latino communities. However, the economic resources to solve many of the systemic problems are often not available. Doing away with poverty is not the same as achieving political representation for Latinos. Ongoing stark racial and class stratification and discriminatory behavior also compel the development of community activism.

■ Politics by Other Means: Nontraditional Methods of Political Struggle

In addition to efforts to participate in electoral politics in many of the barrios and colonias, grassroots organizing efforts to challenge the status quo and fight for specific demands have served as means to achieve political influence. The history of such organizing dates back to when Mexicans were first denied access to the political process as Anglos became the dominant population in the Southwest. Later, as new immigrants arrived from Latin America in the twentieth century, they moved into ethnic enclaves and barrios, often without legal documentation. Many Latinos organize around their values and their beliefs about their rights, based on their sense of cultural belonging rather than on their formal status as citizens.[57] For many Latinos, their physical communities are locations of opposition to controlling structures and of the construction of a collective identity as a people. Day-to-day relationships among neighbors, families, and coworkers provide the basis for group mobilization efforts. While this book's focus on electoral political activities precludes a longer discussion of this important topic, it is important to note the role that Latinas from distinct ethnic communities have played in politics in various forms, as often these local campaigns transform individuals into community activists and candidates for office.

Often the key organizers in issues and struggles that affect the Latino community are women, who enter politics having been excluded from the male-dominated political arena in their own community and from the larger society: "Their activity tends to be collective. The issues raised were intimately connected to the community."[58] Women's organizing can take the form of organizing a community program to promote literacy, supporting coworkers in a workplace, or reclaiming cultural identity.[59] In Boston, Latinas built grassroots efforts that emphasized "the connection between everyday survival and political action; it also focuses on the connectedness between people at the local level as they struggle for social change."[60] While efforts by Latinas to organize in their community are not a new phenomenon, in the 1980s and 1990s these efforts blossomed throughout the nation and transnationally. For example, in Denver, Chicanas and other Latinas formed Hermanas en la Lucha to build alliances with indigenous women outside the United States. They targeted the struggle and women in Chiapas "in part because they saw their struggles for resistance as having important parallels with their own battles in the United States."[61]

In Los Angeles, one organization among many that formed during this period was the Mothers of East Los Angeles, established in 1984. A group of several hundred women came together to oppose the construction of a state prison in Boyle Heights. The group emerged from a Catholic parish on the east side of the city. The women marched, protested, and lobbied, leading to the defeat of the proposed construction site in 1992.[62] Later the group organized to oppose a municipal waste incinerator and an oil pipeline that were to be located in their community. These women provided an independent voice and organizing strength that were similar to efforts in other communities.

For many Latinas, the struggle for social change is simultaneously a struggle to create community. Often it takes the form of defense of their dignity on the job. In San Antonio, 1,100 workers who had labored for many years in a Levi-Strauss plant were laid off in 1990 when the company moved its U.S. plant to Latin America to stay competitive with other clothing manufacturers, even though the plant was profitable. The laid-off workers, predominantly Latinas, formed an organization known as La Fuerza Unida. These women then traveled throughout the country speaking against corporate greed. They launched a national boycott of Levi's labels. Their effort to improve the settlement package for laid-off workers has been an example to others victimized by corporate greed and globalization.[63]

In El Paso, displaced women workers formed La Mujer Obrera in 1981, after a long textile workers' strike against the Farah clothing company. La Mujer Obrera has survived more than twenty years as a grassroots community-based organization. Led by women of Mexican descent, the organization supports low-income women workers and their families.[64] In 1990, La Mujer members organized a hunger strike and chained themselves to their sewing machines to dramatize the poor working conditions and the flight of companies to Mexico and other low-wage locations. Later they pressured federal, state, and local government agencies to provide assistance to NAFTA-displaced workers.[65] One worker explained the need for an organization of women workers: "There was no place for women workers to meet and talk as women. . . . There was no representation of women's values and needs. There was a lack of respect for women as workers."[66]

Latinas have also acted as community watchdogs once Latino officials achieve elected office. If an elected official no longer stays in touch with or represents the interests of a community, Latina community networks and organizations are often the first ones to challenge his or her effectiveness. The presence of grassroots community organizations, as well as labor unions, in Latino communities supplies an important link to those histori-cally unrepresented by those in power.

■ Latinas: Political Activists and Leaders

Since the Southwest became part of the United States at the end of the Mexican-American War, Mexican American women have been active in politics including being delegates to the constitutional convention of vari-ous Southwestern states, and winning elected office.[67] In the 1930s, women helped build middle-class organizations such as the League of Latin American Citizens (LULAC), and were leaders in a number of labor organ-izations among cannery and farmworkers.[68] For example, in 1938 in San Antonio, pecan shellers went on a spontaneous strike after their pay was cut by 20 percent. A young dynamic labor radical, Emma Tenayucca, played a leading role in helping to organize the strike. After six weeks, and living on tortillas and frijoles, the workers won the strike and established a union.[69] In the 1960s, Chicanas sought a leadership role in the emerging Chicano movement and to articulate a distinct identity out of the long history of exploitation they suffered as women and Mexicans.[70] Puerto Rican women have played similar roles in building community organizations as activists and leaders in the 1960s and 1970s Puerto Rican movement. The experi-ences in these movements led many of them to form separate organizations focused on Chicana, Latina, or Hispanic women's issues.

■ The Rise of Latina Politicians

Latinas also began to seek political office in the 1960s and 1970s. Virginia Musquiz was active in the Crystal City struggle in the 1960s and ran for city council and for state representative. She also organized the high school walkouts in 1969 and the political campaign to take control of city government.[71]

In the 1970s, however, there were only a handful of Latinas elected to office. One of the pioneers of Latina legislators was Olga Mendez, a state senator from New York. She was elected in 1978 and was the first Puerto Rican woman elected to a state legislative body. She remained in this posi-tion until 2004, when, after changing her party affiliation from Democrat to Republican, she was defeated by New York City Council member Jose M. Serrano. Texas has had the largest delegation of Chicanas in elected office: Irma Rangel of Kingsville was elected in 1976 as state representative, and later Lina Guerrero of Austin was elected as state representative as well. Judy Zaffirini of Laredo was elected to the Texas State Senate in 1984 and held this position for decades. In 1987, according to the National Association of Latino Elected Officials (NALEO), there were 592 Chicana/Latina elected officials nationwide, but there were still no federal officeholders.

In 1989, this changed when Ilena Ros-Lehtinen (R-FL), a Cuban American, became the first Latina elected to Congress. Her election was followed in 1992 by the election of two additional Latinas, one from New York City and another from Los Angeles: Nydia Velasquez (D-NY) became the first Puerto Rican woman and Lucille Roybal-Allard (D-CA) became the first Chicana elected to the U.S. Congress. Subsequently, more Mexican American women legislators have been elected from southern California: Grace Napolitano, Hilda Solis, Loretta Sanchez, and Linda Sanchez. The election of five Latinas from one region of one state is not a coincidence, as there is a growing presence of Latina political leaders throughout the southern California area. Each of them has built strong electoral coalitions based on local political forces. The elections of these Latina congresswomen reflect their strong ties to their communities and their political sophistication. These women are important role models and leaders in their communities on issues of concern to the Latino community.

The election of a growing number of Latina elected officials at all levels of government was due to a combination of factors, including some redistricting after the 1990 U.S. Census that created new open seats, term limits in many states that forced longtime politicians out of office, mentoring and development of candidates by Latina networks and existing Latina officeholders, and changing attitudes of Latino and other voters. Latina elected officials emerged from a wide variety of experiences as community leaders, progressive activists, professionals, business owners, and intellectuals.

Latinas' potential to win races for highly competitive offices has been generally underestimated. In some communities where Latinos have a sizable population presence, Latinas hold some of the highest-ranking elected positions. El Paso County Judge Dolores Briones was a Democratic Party activist and worked in the health field before winning office as the chief administrative officer of the county government in 1998; she now presides over the county's governing body, the Commissioners Court.[72] She won reelection in 2003, the first person to do so in many years in El Paso County. She has received high marks for being a bridge builder between conservative and liberal perspectives on the county commission. Yet there have only been four Chicanas elected to Texas County judge in the history of the state.[73]

In 1992, Puerto Rican Nydia Velasquez won the Democratic Party nomination over New York congressman Stephen J. Solarz, who was at the time a nine-term incumbent. She won the general election to New York's

Twelfth District with over 75 percent of the vote, and in 1994 she was reelected with over 90 percent of the vote. Loretta Sanchez (D-CA), a Mexican American and daughter of immigrant parents, defeated eight-term incumbent Bob Dornan, a controversial maverick republican, in 1996 in Orange County, California. Orange County is a traditionally conservative area but has seen large growth in its Latino population, and many of these Latinos became Democratic Party voters. Sanchez won by a razor-thin margin and then had to endure charges that noncitizens had voted illegally to bring her victory. These charges were eventually dropped.

In 2000, Hilda Solis (D-CA) challenged nine-term incumbent Marty Martinez in the Democratic Party primary in the San Gabriel Valley area of Los Angeles County. To defeat a fellow Mexican American incumbent legislator in the primary was viewed by most as an extremely difficult task. However, Solis easily outdistanced the incumbent Martinez, 68 to 31 percent. This convincing victory was due to several factors, including the incumbent's positions against gun control and abortion, among other stands that alienated his base of support, and the strong labor, women, and community support received by Solis in the campaign.

In many states, women must overcome various institutional and gender barriers. In New Jersey, three Latinas currently sit in the state assembly, where county political party chairpersons (predominantly male) have strong institutional power to control who gets party nominations. Women of color in particular have a difficult time breaking into and succeeding at politics in this environment dominated by party and personal loyalties.[74]

There is not a clearly delineated path to electoral office for Latinas. Some enter through participation in grassroots community efforts and social networks in the community. Others use more traditional means, becoming party activists, political appointees, or aides to elected officials.

Latino gays and lesbians also began to run and win office in the 1990s. Prominent Latino gay and lesbian elected officials include Margarita Lopez, a New York City Council member who was the first lesbian Puerto Rican elected to office in 1998. Massachusetts state representative Jarrett Barrios was the first Latino gay state legislator elected to office in that state. He represented the Cambridge area, near Boston.

■ Backlash, Voting Strength, and Diversity in the 1990s

In the midst of growing Latino influence in society and politics, particularly in areas where there are large numbers of Latinos, an anti–Latino immigrant backlash emerged. In 1994, a combination of economic, political, and demographic factors combined to dramatically change the political landscape of Latinos in the United States, with broad implications for the future of U.S. politics. In California, a small group of anti-immigration activists in Orange County, fed up with the proliferation of Latino immigrants in the southern California region, put an initiative on the California ballot to cut off all services for anyone not having legal status, including medical services and public education. At the time, Governor Pete Wilson was in the midst of a reelection campaign and needed an issue to promote his candidacy and propel himself into a run for president in 1996. The ballot proposition passed overwhelmingly with 60 percent support, though it was opposed by 70 percent of Latino voters. The organized opposition by the Latino community signaled a new day for Latino politics and contemporary American politics.

At the state level, Proposition 187 had the effect of politically mobilizing widespread segments of the Latino community including mutual aid associations, social service organizations, elected officials, and owners of Spanish-language media. One month before the November election, more than 100,000 Latinos demonstrated in downtown Los Angeles against the bill.[75] The demonstration culminated a series of rallies organized by Latinos, labor unions, teachers, students, and medical practitioners in both rural communities and large urban centers. There were also school walkouts by middle school and high school students, who proudly waved Mexican and other Central American flags in heavily Latino school districts. The Catholic Church and the Spanish media in the state opposed the measure as well.

The election results demonstrated that a substantial racial divide existed in Californians' views of immigration and the rights of the undocumented. Whites—the strongest supporters of the proposition—were 81 percent of all voters. The racial polarization of voting was most evident in counties with a large Latino population or a very small Latino population.[76] African Americans and Asian Americans were more evenly divided, though a majority of both groups opposed the proposition. The ethnic breakdown of the voters is shown in Table 4.1.

If the political opposition to immigration and the mobilization of the

Table 4.1   Voter Support for Proposition 187

Ethnicity/Race of Voters	Percent of Voters by Group	Percent Who Voted for Proposition 187	Percent Who Voted Against Proposition 187
White	81	63	37
Black	5	47	53
Latino	8	23	77
Asian	4	47	53

Source: Los Angeles Times exit poll, November 10, 1994.

California Latino community was ignited in 1994, it caught fire in 1996. Anti-immigrant efforts went national in 1996 with the passage of the Personal Responsibility and Work Opportunity Act (Welfare Act) and the Illegal Immigration Reform and Immigrant Responsibility Act (IIRIRA). The welfare act removed many federal services for noncitizens, and the illegal immigration act reduced many of the due-process procedures that had been required to deport those apprehended without U.S. immigration documents.

The Latino response to these and other anti-immigrant efforts is still being felt on a nationwide basis. Before Proposition 187 passed in 1994, naturalization rates of Mexican and Central Americans was extremely low, as most Mexicans and Central Americans expected to return home when conditions improved or civil wars ceased. Following the passage of Proposition 187, many Latino immigrants sought the protection of U.S. citizenship through naturalization. Many formerly undocumented Latinos who had obtained amnesty under the Immigration and Reform Control Act (IRCA) of 1986 were now highly motivated to become naturalized citizens.[77] Between 1994 to 1997 citizenship applications to the Immigration and Naturalization Services grew from 540,000 to 1.4 million, and most were Latinos. Between 1990 and 1996, 876,000 Latinos naturalized, and their voting behavior has changed the nature of the Latino electorate.

Because of Proposition 187's presence on the ballot in 1994, first-generation immigrants in California were twice as likely to have voted as their counterparts in states that did not have a similar anti-immigrant measure on the ballot. Second-generation immigrants in California were 83 percent more likely to have voted as their peers elsewhere. By contrast, third-generation Latino "citizens in California were only 32 percent more likely to have voted than their generational peers in other states."[78] Analyses of voting from the 1996 national elections similarly indicate that naturalized Latino citizens were more likely to register and vote than native-born Latinos.[79]

Also, among newly naturalized Latinos in the post–Proposition 187 period, voting turnout was higher than that of other Latinos in California; the turnout rate was also higher in Texas and Florida, where there was no major anti-immigrant legislation at that time.[80] Another indication of the impact of new and energized Latino voters was in California's 1996 elections for president, Congress, and state house races. Latinos voted as a unified bloc and voted Democratic by a majority of 70 percent statewide, much higher than their previous rate of 60 percent.[81] In 2002 the National Association of Latino Elected Officials (NALEO) observed that 68 percent of Latinos in Los Angeles and 59 percent of Latinos in Houston had registered to vote since 1995.[82]

Another trend that has emerged in addition to new citizens and voters among Latinos is a new breed of Latino politician. The old guard Latino politicians won in districts overwhelmingly populated by Latinos, usually as the result of "paying their dues" and waiting for their turn to run after an entrenched Anglo politician retired, or after redistricting efforts in the 1970s and 1980s. A common denominator for successful entry-level Latino candidates in the 1990s was that "they were relatively non-threatening, which distinguished them from the old guard first elected in the 70s and 80s. . . . The 1990s Latino generation 'shared a crossover appeal.'. . . They generally presented themselves as highly educated good sons who selflessly returned from college to serve their community almost as if it were an extension of their families."[83]

Another important addition to Latino politics in the 1990s was a growing activism of new Latino immigrants and refugees in politics. As discussed in Chapter 3, Central Americans including Salvadoran, Honduran, Nicaraguan, and Guatemalans had begun to leave Central America and come to the United States in the 1960s and continued in the 1970s and 1980s as their countries' economic and political conditions deteriorated. During the 1980s and early 1990s, many who fled civil conflicts began to support activities in this country for the struggles being waged in their homelands for greater democracy and an end to military repression.

As civil conflicts came to an end in the 1990s, many Central Americans turned their efforts to obtaining legal status in this country and fighting for the rights of political refugees. While Cubans were readily able to obtain refugee status, many Central Americans who fled political conflict have been unable to receive political refugee status. Many remain in this country on temporary visas or are undocumented. A whole generation of Latinos from Central American countries is unable to become citizens and therefore cannot participate in the full range of political activities available to most Americans, such as voting. They are unable to qualify for most government services or for government jobs and continue to face an uncertain future.

In addition, getting a foothold in politics in the U.S. for Central and South Americans is made more difficult because, in most locations where they live, they are usually a minority of the Latino population. For example, in Los Angeles County, while there are nearly 1 million Central Americans, they are less than one-third of the Latino population due to the large number of Mexican immigrants. In south Florida, the Nicaraguan population is heavily concentrated in cities such as Sweetwater; however, Cubans who arrived earlier and have well-established political machines dominate the political leadership in this city.

There are instances where nonmajority Latinos have achieved electoral office. In Miami, Maurice Ferre, a Puerto Rican, was elected mayor from

1973 to 1985 by building an alliance of black and white liberals. However, after Cubans became the dominant electoral group in the 1980s, this seat went to a succession of Cubans, including Manuel Diaz, who was elected in November 2001. In Connecticut a Peruvian American, Felipe Reinoso (D), is the state representative from the city of Bridgeport, where there are large numbers of Puerto Ricans. Representative Reinoso was elected president of the Association of Peruvian Organizations of the United States and Canada. The Association of Peruvian Organizations works for the full participation of the 1 million citizens of Peruvian descent living in the United States, of whom 65,000 lived in Connecticut in 2000. Rep. Reinoso said, "Peruvian-Americans currently constitute the most rapidly growing segment of the Latino population. In Connecticut we contribute to the overall economy of the state as we pursue active roles in business, education and various other professions, as well as increasing involvement in civic and community endeavors."[84]

Other Latinos elected in an area where they are not a member of the dominant Latino ethnic community include Juan C. Zapata (R), Florida's first Colombian American state representative. He was elected in Miami-Dade County, where Cuban Americans are the largest Latino group and Colombians are a much smaller segment of the population. His Republican Party credentials, his ties to Cuban American elected officials, and his Latino heritage enabled him to win election. In Chicago's Near North side, Mexican American Cynthia Soto was elected to the state assembly from a predominantly Puerto Rican area. She had to overcome opposition not only from the Daly machine but also from some who thought the seat should be reserved for a Puerto Rican. However, her pro–working family agenda and her political ties with Congressman Luis Gutierrez and other prominent Puerto Rican elected leaders enabled her to win victory in 2001.

The emergence of new voices in Latino politics in the 1990s is an indication of the growing diversity within the Latino community. As Latinas, new immigrants, emerging ethnic constituencies, third-party officeholders, gays and lesbians, and others infuse new perspectives into Latino politics, and as the strength of Latino voters grows, together they have the ability to extend Latino political influence in the United States into areas not exclusively populated by Latinos.

■ Conclusion

Starting in the 1970s, Latinos moved from being political outsiders to filling a growing number of elected and appointed offices. During the "rainbow politics" period, 1983–93, the number of Latino elected officials in the nation increased by 48 percent, which compared favorably with the

53 percent growth in Latino population during the same period. More impressively, the number of Latinas in public office increased by 194 percent during that period and has continued to grow subsequently.[85]

Many of the new crop of Latino elected officials were part of biracial or multiracial coalitions in large urban areas. In the 1990s, Latinos also made gains in heavily Latino-majority towns, cities, and county districts as restrictive at-large electoral systems, gerrymandered districts, and low participation of Latino voters began to change. In 1994, an anti-immigrant measure on the California ballot helped spark new energy in large numbers of Latinos to become active in politics to defend the rights of Latino citizens and noncitizens. Also, new energy from Latino immigrant political voices created a distinct independent presence.

In short, Latino political incorporation in the 1970s to 1990s increased dramatically, particularly in locations with high concentrations of Latinos. In most large metropolitan areas with a concentration of Latinos, Latino politicians have been elected to office. This reflects a change from nonvisible representation to symbolic representation and in some places more substantive representation. Latinos are now integral players in many of the dominant political coalitions that run urban governments. They have matured politically and can compete and win office in many cities. The next chapter will explore the dynamics of the contemporary U.S. political system and Latino political behavior.

■ Notes

1. Mexican American Legal Defense and Education Fund. "About Us—Founding of MALDEF." www.maldef.org.
2. J. Gomez Quiñones (1990), p. 159.
3. R. Brischetto et al. (1994), p. 242.
4. Ibid., p. 243.
5. Ibid., p. 246.
6. J. Gonzalez (2000), p. 179.
7. S. Baver (1984), p. 54.
8. I. Lucas (1984), p. 111.
9. T. Córdova (1999), p. 42.
10. *Política Social* (2002), p. 1.
11. R. Brischetto (1988b).
12. Southwest Voter Registration and Education Project, "About SVREP."
13. Ibid.
14. R. Acuña (1988), p. 419.
15. J. Gomez Quiñones (1990), p. 170.
16. R. Griswold de Castillo and A. De León (1996), p. 157.
17. C. Munoz and C. Henry (1990), p. 183.
18. R. Acuña (1988), p. 420.
19. M. Gonzalez-Pando (1998), p. 61.

20. J. Gonzalez (2000), p. 180.
21. M. de Los Angeles Torres (1999), p. 117.
22. Ibid., p. 122.
23. Southwest Voter Registration and Education Project (1984).
24. M. de Los Angeles Torres (1999), p. 124.
25. U.S. Library of Congress (n.d.).
26. M. de Los Angeles Torres (1991), pp. 166–167.
27. Ibid., p. 171.
28. J. Betancur and D. Gills (2000), pp. 67–69.
29. T. Córdova (1999), p. 40.
30. Ibid., p. 47.
31. L. Fraga (1992), p. 118.
32. R. T. Starks and M. B. Preston (1990), p. 88.
33. D. Pinderhughes (1997), p. 131.
34. J. Gonzalez (2000), p. 184.
35. Ibid., p. 180.
36. R. Keiser (1990), p. 66.
37. T. Travis (1990), p. 119.
38. C. Hardy-Fanta (1993), pp. 107–108.
39. S. Collins (1986), p. 190.
40. Ibid., pp. 186–187.
41. A. Falcon (1992), p. 154.
42. R. Smith (1990a), pp. 225–226.
43. R. de la Garza (1992), pp. 172–73.
44. F. Bonilla and W. Stafford (2000), p. 49.
45. J. Mollenkopf (1997), p. 109.
46. Ibid., p. 110.
47. J. E. Cruz (1998), p. 211.
48. Ibid., pp. 178–87.
49. W. Flores (1992).
50. P. C. Takash (1990), pp. 342–344.
51. K. Geron (1999).
52. C. Gottleib (1993), p. B4.
53. M. Davis (1992).
54. Ibid.
55. R. Browning, D. Marshall, and D. Tabb (1984).
56. L. Moret (1998), p. 105.
57. W. V. Flores with R. Benmayor (1997), pp. 1–6.
58. R. Rosales (2000), p. 189.
59. W. V. Flores with R. Benmayor (1997), pp. 1–6.
60. C. Hardy-Fanta (1993), p. 103.
61. A. Sampaio (2002).
62. M. Pardo (1998).
63. M. C. Y. Louie (2001), pp. 207–208.
64. La Mujer Obrera (n.d.).
65. M. C. Y. Louie (2001), pp. 202–204.
66. Grassroots.org (2002).
67. C. M. Sierra and A. Sosa Riddell (1994).
68. V. L. Ruiz (1987).
69. Texas Civil Liberties Union (1938).
70. A. Sosa Riddell (1974).

71. R. Acuña (1988), p. 332.
72. D. Briones, interview (2001).
73. J. A. Gutierrez and R. E. Dean (2000).
74. B. Fitzgerald (2003).
75. R. Acuña (1996), p. 158.
76. C. Tolbert and R. Hero (1996).
77. H. Pachon, L. Sanchez, and D. Falcon (1999), pp. 170–172.
78. S. K. Ramakrishnan and T. J. Espenshade (2001).
79. A. Vargas (1999–2000), p. 7.
80. A. Pantoja, R. Ramirez, and G. M. Segura (2001).
81. G. Segura, D. Falcon, and H. Pachon (1997).
82. NALEO (2002).
83. D. Ayon (2000).
84. F. Reinoso (2001).
85. NALEO (1994).

5

Voters, Parties, and
Latino Political Development

This chapter explores the contemporary features of Latino politics and simultaneously the contours of racial politics in the United States. Contemporary Latino political behavior has been forged in an environment historically dictated by others. There are several factors to consider when examining Latino politics at national, state, and local levels. The structural and legal dynamics that shape Latino electoral fortunes are themselves affected by a multiplicity of factors. This chapter addresses the roles of demographic change, party affiliation, voting behavior, types of electoral districts, and candidate characteristics. We will also consider strategies used by Latinos to achieve political incorporation. To begin with, let's consider the contemporary U.S. political system within which Latino politics operates.

■ The U.S. Political System and Latino Politics

All politics takes place on a variety of levels; we participate as individual members of society and as members of communities of interest. A basic foundation to successful political participation combines group cohesion and individual motivation. While a group may long to have formal representation in government, ultimately this requires an individual willing to seek office, run for office, and win elective office. Likewise, while an individual may wish to hold an elective position, to win an elected seat takes more than personal will. It involves the efforts of a group, or groups, of persons who cooperate to elect a candidate to office. Our winner-take-all system, based on political entrepreneurship and interest group politics, dictates that an individual who seeks office needs group support to achieve it. If we assume that Latinos seek to further the interests of the Latino population, as do other demographic groups in a pluralistic society, then it can be expected that Latinos will seek to participate in the political system as voters, volunteers, activists, and candidates for office. In these efforts candidates and elected officials will seek to further their individual goals and possibly to benefit their group's position in society (although not all Latino candidates run as ethnic candidates or identify with or seek to assist directly the Latino community).

The ability of any group, whether identified by race, gender, ethnicity, age, or issue, to gain political influence is based on a number of factors, including political and economic resources, level of organization, and knowledge of how the system operates to maximize a group's gains. For Latinos and other minority groups, the political system has historically been more a barrier than a resource to be accessed in the quest to gain full participation. The system of racial exclusion and domination has long worked to keep African Americans, Latinos, Native Americans, and Asian Americans out of elective, appointive, and civil service positions. The civil rights movement of the 1950s and 1960s dramatically moved these issues to the front of America's social policy agenda. The goal of inclusion in government was twofold: to end discrimination in hiring, promotions, and election to office and to share in the benefits of government. This included increased minority employment, minority administrators, minority contracts for business with government, economic development in minority communities, housing, and decent public services in predominantly minority communities.[1]

Each underrepresented group has a particular history and justification for representation. Latinos have a unique claim in American politics: they are both the forerunners to the establishment of the American political system and some of the newest participants in the political system. Some of the early Spanish and Mexican settlers established forms of governance in the Southwest that preceded the establishment of the U.S. government. Since 1965, new immigrants from throughout Latin America have dramatically changed the ethnic composition of numerous cities and states and have brought different political experiences and a different perspective to U.S. politics. Yet the majority of Latinos are born and raised in the context of the U.S. system, where representation in government is an important measure of a group's political progress.

■ Growth of Latino Population

In the United States "there were 14.2 million foreign born who reported a Hispanic/Latino origin in Census 2000, representing 45.5 percent of the total foreign-born population (31.1 million) and 40.2 percent of the total Hispanic/Latino population (35.2 million)."[2] Results from the 2000

U.S. census indicate that Latinos have grown to become the largest racial minority group, with a population of more than 35 million, or 12.5 percent of the nation's total.[3] The Latino percentage of the population is expected to grow to 20 percent by 2020 and close to 30 percent by 2060, based on current growth rates. The Latino population is also extremely young. In the total U.S. population, 25.7 percent were under eighteen years of age in 2000, whereas among Latinos 35 percent were younger than eighteen. The median age for Latinos was nearly twenty-six, while the median age for the U.S. population as a whole was thirty-five. Latinos and Asians have the highest rates of population growth due to both higher birth rates than African Americans and whites and high immigration levels. As noted by immigration scholars, "Given the disparity in birth rates between minorities and non-Hispanic whites, white children are expected to comprise less than half of the total under age-18 population by as soon as 2030."[4] While the Latino population is predicted to continue to grow faster than other groups, much of this population is unable to fully participate in the political process because of low citizenship and voter registration rates.

The Latino population increased 58 percent from 1990 to 2000, while the total U.S. population increased 13 percent.[5] The Latino ethnic population varies by group. In the 2000 census, Mexicans were 58.5 percent of all Latinos, which was a decline from 60.4 percent in 1990. Puerto Ricans were 9.6 percent of all Latinos, which also represented a decline from 12.2 percent in 1990. Cubans declined from 4.7 percent in 1990 to 3.5 percent in 2000. The remaining 28.4 percent were of "other Latino" origins (up from 22.8 percent). Of the 10 million "other Latinos" in 2000, 1.7 million were Central Americans, 1.4 million were South Americans, and 765,000 were Dominicans.

Unfortunately, the second largest category after Mexican was made up of those Latinos who did not specify a country of origin or descent; they checked the Spanish/Hispanic/Latino box but did not provide any additional information or simply wrote in "Hispanic" or "Latino" or "Spanish." The number of Latinos who declared only this general description was 17.3 percent (6.1 million) of the total Latino population.[6] This created a situation where the overall population grew but specific national origin groups appeared to decline in number. Thus this census makes a precise analysis of the growth patterns of distinct nationalities of Latinos difficult.

The high percentage of Latinos that declared only the broad category of Spanish/Hispanic/Latino can partially be explained by the self-identification of citizens in New Mexico and southern Colorado as Spanish Americans. These members of the Latino population views themselves as descendants of the original Spanish settlers. Beyond this segment of the Latino population, there were many others who did not indicate a specific nationality. In New York, New Jersey, Los Angeles, and other locations, then, census figures suggested that the population of specific Latino groups had declined between 1990 and 2000, even though knowledgeable community leaders argued that their communities had grown significantly. Many Latino activists criticized the U.S. Census for listing only some Latino groups and not others. Colombians, Dominicans, Ecuadorians, and others who had to write in their national origin in the Hispanic question found their numbers seriously underreported. A growing number of Latino leaders and organizations believe that the Census Bureau should and can correct this problem.[7]

In addition to the growth of new Latino ethnic groups, it is important to understand the geographic dispersion of the Latino population. More than 27 million, or 76.8 percent, of all Latinos live in the seven states with the largest Latino populations (California, Texas, New York, Florida, Illinois, Arizona, and New Jersey). Latinos in California were 11 million, or 31.1 percent of the total Latino population in the United States. In Texas, the Latino population accounted for 6.7 million, or 18.9 percent of the total U.S. Latino population. Further, in New Mexico, Latinos were 42 percent of the state's population, the highest percentage of Hispanos in any state.

Another way to view the distribution of the Latino population and its political impact is to examine the numbers of Latinos in the ten largest U.S. cities (see Table 5.1). In eight of the ten largest cities, Latinos are at least 25 percent of the population. In San Antonio, they already hold majority status. In Los Angeles, they are close to majority status. The more than 7 million Latinos in the ten largest cities represent more than one-fifth of the total Latino population in the United States. This means that much of the Latino population is concentrated in a few large cities. Of course, we must factor in that 40 percent of the Latino population is foreign born and most of these have not obtained U.S. citizenship.[8]

In addition to the high concentration of Latinos in urban areas, they

Table 5.1   Latino Population in the Ten Largest Cities

City	Total Population	Latino Population	Percent of Total
New York	8,008,278	2,160,554	27.0
Los Angeles	3,694,820	1,719,073	46.5
Chicago	2,896,016	753,664	26.0
Houston	1,953,631	730,865	37.4
Philadelphia	1,517,550	128,928	8.5
Phoenix	1,321,045	449,972	34.1
San Diego	1,223,400	310,752	25.4
Dallas	1,188,580	422,587	35.6
San Antonio	1,144,646	671,394	58.7
Detroit	951,270	47,167	5.0

Source: U.S. Bureau of the Census (2000c).

are "the most significant and fastest-growing sector of the working class in the United States. Within a few years, Latinos will make up more than a quarter of the nation's total workforce, a proportion that is . . . larger than this group's proportion of the total population."[9] Equally important from an economic point of view is that Latino workers are located in the light manufacturing and service sections of the economy that hold strategic importance for U.S. capitalism. In Los Angeles County, a center of postindustrial America, it is estimated that 50 percent of manufacturing workers are Latinos, both legal and undocumented workers from Latin America.[10] The high percentage of working-class Latinos, the industries they work in, and their impact on the economy has made them an inviting, and under some circumstances a successful, target for the labor movement to organize.[11]

■ Latino Demographics and Political Behavior

The Latino population continues to grow, with heavy concentrations in large urban areas and with Latino workers located in sectors of the economy that are strategically important. Yet demographic growth does not equate to the attainment of political power. A critical ingredient in building Latino political power is to increase Latino political participation. Political participation involves acts of influencing the political system by individuals and groups. Traditionally this takes the forms of attempting to influence the policymaking process or participating in the electoral process. When one studies Latino political behavior, it is essential to understand different dimensions of the Latino population: first, the total population of Latinos; second, the Latino voting-age population (those over eighteen); third, the *citizen* voting-age population; fourth, the *registered* voting-age population; and fifth, the turnout of Latino voters.

It is critical to make these distinctions when analyzing Latino political participation because of a few considerations. First, disenfranchisement of Mexican Americans in the Southwest dating from the 1840s, and of other Latinos who came to the country, has limited their full political participation historically. Second, the immigration of Latinos from throughout the Americas means there are large numbers who are in the process of transitioning into U.S. society. Among Latinos who migrate to the United States, only Puerto Ricans are U.S. citizens, by virtue of Puerto Rico's status as a U.S. territory. All other Latinos, including legal and illegal immigrants and political refugees, such as Cubans, have had varying degrees of both opportunities and obstacles to become naturalized citizens, register to vote, and vote. For example, 72 percent of Cuban Americans are citizens, while only 58 percent of Mexican descent are citizens. Large numbers of Latinos who have roots in Central America and South America are recent immigrants, and only 46 percent are citizens.[12]

A high percentage of Latinos, unlike whites and blacks, and similar to Asian Pacific Islanders, are not citizens. The high incidence of noncitizenship is the single most important factor limiting the political power of Latinos. In 1998, there were 20.3 million Latinos who were eighteen years and over. Of this number, only 12.4 million Latinos were U.S. citizens of voting age. Of this total, only an estimated 4 million Latinos voted in the 1998 elections—that is, 32.8 percent, of Latino U.S. citizens.

In the November 2000 election, 57 percent of Latino adult citizens were registered to vote; this was the second lowest registration rate among major racial groups. Latinos also trailed in voting. In the 2000 elections, an estimated 5.9 million Latinos voted, which was 5 percent of the total vote. Sixty percent of Latinos are not eligible to vote. There are more than 12 million Latinos too young to vote because they are under eighteen. Another 9 million voting-age Latinos are not U.S. citizens, so they are not eligible to vote. In the 2000 election, 79 percent of registered Latinos reported voting, which was lower than the 86 percent of registered non-Latino whites who reported voting. If we consider registration and voting together, only 45 percent of Latino adult citizens reported voting in the November 2000 election.

The impact of the foreign-born Latino population is important to note. The results of Census 2000 show that the Latino population has dramatically grown since the 1990 census, from 22 million to 35.2 million. By 2002, the population was estimated at 37.4 million, of whom 15 million, or 40.2 percent, were foreign born.[13] Of the foreign-born population in 2002, 52 percent entered the country between 1990 and 2002, and only 7.3 percent of those who entered in this period have become U.S. citizens. Of the total foreign-born Latino population in 2002, 26 percent entered in the 1980s, and 29 percent of this group have become U.S. citizens. The highest percentage of foreign born who have become U.S. citizens is found among those who arrived before 1980. It appears that length of residency in this country is a key factor in Latinos' propensity for naturalization.

The growth in the Latino voting-eligible population is evident in the following trends. There has been a growth in naturalizations of Latino foreign-born adults. Among persons from Latin America, naturalizations totaled 1.7 million from 1996 to 2000. Another trend is the youthfulness of the Latino population. There are currently 2.8 million Latinos between the ages of twelve and seventeen who are native-born U.S. citizens. Many of these young people will be eligible to vote by November 2008. Increases among naturalized citizens and potential new young voters can dramatically increase the total number of Latino voters.

While all communities have some members who do not vote, Latinos generally have the highest rate of nonvoting. This is a particularly vexing problem for a community that is historically underrepresented and underserved. Using survey data of Latinos in 1988, one scholar found that registered nonvoters and nonregistered U.S. citizens had similar characteristics: they had lower levels of education and income and were younger. Furthermore, not all Latino groups have the same voting characteristics, "Mexican Americans, the largest of the Latino national-origin groups, are significantly less likely to vote than Cuban Americans and Puerto Ricans."[14] However, as discussed in Chapter 4, the growth of anti-immigrant efforts in the mid-1990s helped spur Mexicans and others in the Latino community to naturalize and begin to participate in voting.

Another potential obstacle to increasing Latino voting rates is poor access to registration. Voting requirements vary by state. Historically there were numerous obstacles to voter registration by Latinos, including poll taxes, white primaries, literacy tests, and language barriers. The extension of the Voting Right Act of 1965 (VRA) to language minorities in 1975 provided its basic protections to specific language minorities. Previously, in places like Uvalde County, Texas, registered Mexican American voters were not allowed to place their names on voting lists, election judges deliberately invalidated ballots they cast, and Mexican Americans were also not allowed to serve as deputy registrars.[15] Today, states have different requirements for voter registration; some states' rules are more stringent than others, such as that voters must register at least thirty days in advance of an election.

With such a high percentage of Latinos who are nonregistered U.S. citizens, they are not targeted by campaigns because they are not on lists of likely voters. They receive little, if any, attention or encouragement to vote. If they do consider registering to vote, the process to do so is not made simple and efficient; rather, potential voters must find a registration form, fill it out correctly, and submit it in enough time to be able to vote. While all potential voters face the same obstacles, they are particularly difficult for new citizens who are unfamiliar with the U.S. political system. If you factor in the high percentages of non-English-speaking Latinos, then it becomes understandable why many Latino U.S. citizens do not register to vote.

In addition to those who could potentially vote but do not do so, there is an enormous undocumented portion of the Latino population who are not able to participate in voting. How large is this portion? According to various estimates, there are more than 8 million undocumented persons living in the United States, of whom more than 4 million are of Mexican descent, with additional numbers of other Latinos.[16] This large segment of the Latino community cannot participate in the voting process, except in limited circumstances in elections for school boards, such as in New York City, or in nongovernmental organizations. Nongovernmental organizations can serve as a conveyor belt to move new immigrants from inactivity and isolation to social and political activism, as they do not usually have citizenship requirements. For example, in labor unions, civil rights groups, education, and church-based groups, thousands of Latino immigrants get their first experience of participating in organizations and voting for candidates for positions within the group or voting to ratify a union contract agreement. This is an important first step in civic engagement for a segment of the immigrant population. It enables them to learn the value of voting and participating in community affairs. It breaks through the stigma of being undocumented and the fear of taking part in American society. It acknowledges these immigrants' role and value as contributing members of barrios and community and labor organizations. For many Latino immigrants, these forms of civic participation were not always available in their homelands due to political repression.

■ Latino Voter Turnout

In addition to the size of the Latino general population, citizenship status, and voter registration rates, the critical factor of Latino voter turnout must be explored if we are to gain a full understanding of Latino political participation efforts. Motivating Latinos to go to the polls has been problematic for a number of reasons. Similar to most voters, their voting has declined since the 1960s. For Latinos, there are particular factors of high noncitizenship rates and percentage of the population under eighteen; however, even among those registered to vote, Latinos participate at rates lower than those of other racial and ethnic groups.

To overcome this legacy of Latino nonpolitical participation, Latino civil rights organizations, legal defense organizations, and policy groups have been working to increase registration and voter turnout. These efforts have produced dramatic results. The number of Latinos voting has gone up sharply since 1994. From 1994 to 1998, Latinos voters increased by more than half a million. In 1994, the number of Latino citizens of voting age was 10.4 million, and the number of voters was 3.5 million. In 1998, the number of Latino voters rose to 4 million. In spite of these rapid gains, Latinos have lower voter turnout rates than white and black voters. For example, in 1998 in congressional elections, 47.4 percent of whites voted, 41.9 percent of blacks voted, and 32.8 percent of Latinos voted.

In the 2000 elections, the number of Latino voters increased from previous national elections; however, how to precisely measure the number of Latinos who voted in 2000 has been a subject of debate. According to the Voter News Service (VNS), which conducted exit polls during the

November 2000 presidential election, whites were 80 percent of the voters, Latinos composed 7 percent, blacks were 10 percent, Asian and Pacific Islanders were 2 percent, and all others were 1 percent. These numbers are based on self-reports of voters and as such are only a crude estimate. Exit polls tend to overreport voting results but cannot capture absentee ballots. The William C. Velásquez Institute (WCVI) challenged the VNS estimates that Latinos cast 7 percent of the national vote for president, which in actual numbers would have meant roughly 7.35 million Latino votes cast. There would have had to be a turnout rate of nearly 92 percent for Latinos to achieve this number, so it was said not to be a realistic estimate.[17] In contrast, the U.S. Census reported that the total Latino vote was 5 percent of all votes cast in the 2000 elections. This was based on surveying a sample population; however, the sample was four times larger than that of the VNS exit polls.[18] The Current Population Survey (CPS) of the U.S. Census Bureau is the most accurate national source that can be used to estimate the Latino share of the turnout.

Even with many obstacles, the growth in Latino voting-age population is expected to translate into increased numbers of voters. The WCVI estimated that there were 5.7 million Latino voters in 2000.[19] The goal of the Southwest Voter Registration and Education Project (SVREP) was to mobilize nearly 2 million new Latino voters for the 2004 general elections, raising the national total to 10 million Latino registered voters and 7.5 million votes cast, which would have represented a 30 percent increase in Latino voters since the 2000 presidential election.[20] The WCVI estimates in 2004 that there were 7.6 million Latino voters, which was an increase of 1.6 million voters from the 2000 election. Latino voter registration also rose above the 10 million mark for the first time, and 75 percent of all registered Latinos turned out to vote in the election. Latino voters represented 6.6 percent of all votes cast.[21]

Social issues can become important motivators for Latino voter turnout. Several ballot initiatives in California directly affected Latinos in the 1990s and the early part of the twenty-first century, and voter registration and turnout among Latinos increased significantly in response. Proposition 187, an initiative put on the 1994 ballot by anti-immigrant groups, which would have barred public education and public services to undocumented immigrants, mobilized large numbers of Latinos, citizens and noncitizens alike, in opposition. Proposition 187 spurred noncitizen Latinos to naturalize in unprecedented numbers, a trend that dramatically increased Latino political power in America's most populous state. Although California voters approved Proposition 187 on election day, Latinos went to the polls in record numbers to oppose it: "While Latinos have historically turned out in much smaller numbers than other groups, 57 percent of registered Latinos voted in 1994, according to the Southwest

Voter Research Institute, only three percentage points less than the electorate as a whole."[22] Latinos voted overwhelmingly against the proposition, 77 percent statewide.[23]

The turnout of registered voters gave Latinos a newfound sense of political muscle. Subsequent voter initiatives that ended affirmative action programs for the state of California and ended the state's bilingual education programs, in 1996 and 1998 respectively, also helped increase Latino voter turnout. In 1996, according to an exit poll of voters, 76 percent of Latinos opposed the elimination of California's affirmative action policy; this was a higher percentage than among African Americans (74 percent).[24] In 1998, 63 percent of Latino voters opposed the elimination of bilingual education and saw it as an attack directed at Latino immigrants.[25] This initiative helped to spur grassroots efforts to defend bilingual education by many Latina parent activists.

A study of Latino voters in California indicated that the Latino share of California's overall vote increased from 8 percent in 1988 to 12 percent in 1996 and 13 percent in 1998.[26] In a study of the 2000 general election in California, it was estimated that the Latino voter share increased to 14.8 percent and Latino turnout increased from 65 to 70 percent. In addition, Latinos made big gains in voter registration, with an almost 17 percent increase in registered Latinos since 1996 in this state. This increase resulted in 331,000 new Latino registered voters; notably, there are still more than a million eligible Latinos who are citizens but are unregistered to vote (see Table 5.2).

The William C. Velásquez Institute also studied the 2000 Latino vote in Texas and found that Latinos cast over 1 million votes in the 2000 election. Latinos represented 15.6 percent of the total votes cast in Texas, a decrease in share from 1996's 17.5 percent, as large numbers of Texas voters came out to support fellow Texan George W. Bush's race for the presidency. Latinos saw large gains in voter registration, which was up by 27.4 percent since the 1996 election. This increase translated into 419,000 new Latino registered voters. The WCVI study indicated that almost 694,000 eligible Latinos remained unregistered to vote, either by choice or because of lack

Table 5.2   Analysis of California Latino Voters, 2000

Latino voting-age population (VAP)	6,639,030
Latino citizen voting-age population (CVAP)	3,346,071
Latino voter registration	2,300,000
Percent registered VAP	34.6
Percent registered CVAP	68.7
Latinos not registered to vote	1,046,071

Sources: U.S. Census Bureau (2002) and WCVI estimates.

of effort to contact them. This large group of unregistered voters is unavailable for active voter participation and presents an ongoing challenge for the Latino community, which will not realize its full voting strength as long as so many remain outside the electoral process (see Table 5.3).

Anti–Latino immigrant sentiments also produced an upsurge in naturalizations to U.S. citizenship and contributed significantly to the increase in Latinos' turnout and their share of the vote in the late 1990s.[27] A demographic profile of California and Texas Latino voters in the 2000 election indicated that 47.6 percent were naturalized and voted after 1996 in California and 30.7 percent in Texas. Also, there was growth in Latino foreign-born voters, an increase of 53.6 percent in California and of 30.4 percent in Texas in the 2000 elections.[28]

Outside of Texas and California, other Latinos have also reacted with strong turnout to issues of importance within their communities. A major controversy arose over the case of Elian Gonzalez, a seven-year-old Cuban child who was found floating on an inner tube off the Florida coast. The discovery of this young boy, whose mother had died attempting to flee Cuba with him and twelve others, set off an international incident in 2000. Miami Cubans argued that Elian should be permitted to stay in Miami with his great-uncle Lazaro Gonzalez, since his mother had died trying to reach the United States. Almost all local Cuban American political leaders, including Miami Mayor Joe Carollo and Miami-Dade County Executive Mayor Alex Penelas, were outspoken in opposing federal government intervention to remove the child from his relatives' home. Panelas, a Democrat, announced that county law enforcement officers would not cooperate with the federal government in efforts to reunite Elian with his father in Cuba and openly criticized the Clinton administration's handling of the affair.

For Cuban Americans, the federal government plan to return Elian to Cuba was tantamount to giving support to Fidel Castro's government. For months, thousands of Cuban Americans surrounded the home where Elian stayed in Miami's Little Havana neighborhood to prevent the child's removal. Eventually, however, the U.S. government did remove the child and returned him to Cuba to be reunited with his father. In the

Table 5.3 Analysis of Texas Latino Voters, 2000

Latino voting-age population (VAP)	3,746,069
Latino citizen voting-age population (CVAP)	2,644,725
Latino voter registration	1,950,000
Percent registered VAP	52.1
Percent registered CVAP	73.7
Latinos not registered to vote	694,725

Sources: U.S. Census Bureau (2002) and WCVI estimates.

days following the removal, there were sporadic protest demonstrations and work stoppages in Cuban-owned businesses, particularly in the Cuban American strongholds of Hialeah and Little Havana.[29] Still seething later that year, the Cuban American exile community fueled a strong voter turnout in south Florida for George W. Bush in the 2000 presidential elections. Even though Democratic presidential hopeful Al Gore had taken a position closely resembling that of the Cuban exile community, calling for family counseling and not government intervention, Cuban American leaders blamed the Clinton administration for Elian's removal and supported Bush overwhelmingly, with 75 percent of their votes in Miami-Dade County. While the Cuban exile community was already in favor of the Republican Party, the Elian Gonzalez case intensified this support.

Another continuing controversial issue that directly affects the Latino community is bilingual education. While locations such as Miami-Dade County, with strong local Latino leadership, expanded their bilingual programs in the 1990s, in other states bilingual education continued to be under attack. In Colorado in 2002, Proposition 31, a controversial anti–bilingual education measure, was placed on the ballot; it was financially backed by Ron Unz, the California businessman who had successfully backed anti–bilingual ballot measures in California in 1998, Arizona in 2000, and Massachusetts in 2002. However, in Colorado, the anti–bilingual education initiative was defeated for the first time in any state through the construction of a bipartisan coalition that convinced a cross-section of voters to retain the existing program. Latinos statewide participated in the defeat of Proposition 31, as part of a broad coalition entitled English Plus. Latino community and parent activists—including Nita Gonzalez, daughter of the founder of the Crusade for Justice, Rodolfo "Corky" Gonzalez— mobilized voters to defeat the measure.

■ Party Affiliation of Latinos

Historically, party affiliation has been a strong marker of the political behavior of social groups in the United States. According to a 1999 national survey of Latinos, party affiliation of Latino voters is tied closely to ethnic or nationality group. Among all Latinos, 40.9 percent identify with the Democrats and only 25.5 percent identify with the Republicans. Among likely voters, 41.8 percent identify with the Democrats and 31.1 percent identity with the Republicans.[30] When this information is examined by national origin, almost all Latino ethnic groups show strong support for the Democrats (see Table 5.4).

Other than Cuban Americans, all major Latino ethnic groups were

Table 5.4   Party Affiliation of Latino Voters by Ethnicity or Nationality Group (%), July 1999

Nationality	Democrat	Independent	Republican	Total	Democrat Advantage vs. Republican
Puerto Rican	60.8	19.3	19.9	10.5	41.5
Mexican	39.4	43.4	17.2	60.5	22.2
Cuban	32.1	29.8	38.1	5.2	6.0
Dominican	66.7	24.2	9.1	2.0	57.5
Salvadoran	42.9	35.7	21.4	6.0	21.5
Other South/ Central American	46.7	44.2	9.1	10.1	37.6
All Latinos	43.3	37.8	18.9	100	24.4

Source: Washington Post/Kaiser/Harvard Latino Survey (July 1999) as reported in Gimpel and Kaufman (2001).

solidly in the camp of the Democrats. The Democrats' party affiliation advantage is strikingly high among Puerto Ricans (41.5 percent) and Dominicans (57.5 percent); both of these groups are located primarily in the Northeast region of the United States, with Puerto Ricans also having substantial numbers in the Midwest. Among Mexican Americans, the largest Latino population group, party affiliation with Democrats was 22.3 percent greater than with Republicans. While there is a high "independent" segment of this voting population, previous research indicates that Mexican Americans consistently vote for Democratic Party candidates.

In the 2000 presidential election, the Latino vote was 62 percent for Al Gore and 35 percent for George W. Bush. In Bush's home state of Texas, where there is a substantial Mexican American population, Latinos voted 53.6 percent for Gore and only 42.9 percent for Bush. In the state of New York during the 2000 election, more than 80 percent of Latinos voted for Gore, and only 17.6 percent voted for Bush.[31] Even in Florida, home to a high concentration of conservative Republicans, where Bush's brother was the governor, Bush barely defeated Gore, 49.5 to 48.4 percent, among Latinos. The closeness of this vote was due to growing numbers of non-Cuban Latino voters who now live in the state, particularly in the Orlando area.[32]

In 2002, the Pew Hispanic Center poll found that among Latino young people who were registered voters, party preference is much weaker among those aged nineteen to twenty-nine: 34 percent identified themselves as Democrats, 21 percent identified as Republicans, and 26 percent indicated they were independents.[33] With more than one-third of the Latino population currently under eighteen years of age, this trend toward independence could change party affiliation and voting patterns in the coming years.

In 2004, the Pew Hispanic Center poll surveyed the three largest Latino groups and reported that 50 percent of Puerto Ricans and 47 percent of Mexican Americans said they were registered as Democrats, while 18 percent of Mexican Americans and 17 percent of Puerto Ricans self-identified as Republicans. Only 17 percent of Cuban Americans were registered as Democrats, while 52 percent self-identified as Republicans. Mexican Americans were the largest bloc of self-identified independent voters, at 22 percent. Cubans made up a much smaller number, at only 9 percent independents.[34] These survey numbers indicated a recent decline in the number of Puerto Ricans who self-identified as Democrats, but growth in numbers of Mexican Americans and Cubans who identified with the Democrats. The apparent change in self-reported party affiliation may indicate some shifts in long-term allegiances among Latinos or may reflect the difficulty of measuring the voter attitudes of registered Latinos.

Following the 2004 election, a controversy arose over the percentage of Latino voters who voted for President Bush. The National Election Poll was commissioned by a consortium of media corporations to provide election day exit polling. The data concluded that 44 percent of Latinos voted for Bush. In a separate national poll, the *Los Angeles Times* arrived at a similar number for Latino voters. The National Annenberg Election Survey concluded that Bush received 41 percent of Latino votes. NBC, after first agreeing that 44 percent of Latinos voted for Bush, announced that they were reducing their estimate to 40 percent.[35] The WCVI estimated that only 33 percent of Latinos voted for Bush in 2004, which shows that although the Latino vote total rose in 2004, less votes went to Bush compared to 2000.[36] This is an important debate because it involves not only the methods used to conduct exit polling of Latinos, but also is crucial in determining if Latinos have begun to shift their allegiance to the Republican Party.

While party affiliation is a traditional marker to predict voter preferences, issues appear to play a strong role among Latino voters. Polling data in recent years have consistently demonstrated that Latinos have very strong views on key issues that eclipse party affiliation. This is evident among Latino voters and in the views of Latino elected officials. One recent poll found that 95 percent of Latinos supported bilingual education. Another poll found that approximately 85 percent of Latinos favored proposals to provide legal status to undocumented immigrants.[37] Such issues of concern in the Latino community may not be taken up by either of the two major parties. For example, the topic of negative attitudes toward immigrants, a strong concern among Latinos, is not being discussed explicitly by either political party. Similarly, Latinos from both parties are willing to support a larger government to provide better educational opportunities even if it means higher taxes. The national parties, however, have not made education a top priority in their campaigns.

■ Latinos and the Contemporary Structure of U.S. Politics

In addition to the demographics, voter turnout, and party affiliation of Latinos, the political structure plays a role in shaping Latino electoral fortunes. The obstacles that have historically prevented the development of Latino empowerment was explored in depth in Chapters 3 and 4. However, if we are to understand the current level of Latinos' political progress, it is necessary to briefly review their group experiences. Since this country was founded, Latinos have faced various discriminatory barriers put up by the government. There were very few Latinos outside the Southwest region before 1848, when the United States annexed the territories of California, Arizona, Texas, New Mexico, and parts of Utah and Colorado following the end of the Mexican-American War of 1846–48. Mexican citizens residing in these territories were incorporated as U.S. citizens. Though they were nominally granted citizenship, their voting rights were extremely limited, except in areas where they were the numerical majority. In these locations they retained more citizenship rights, including the right to elect their own representatives. As more Anglos arrived in the former Mexican lands, however, Mexicans became the minority, and strict rules were laid down to limit the power of Mexican American voters, such as the poll tax, white primaries, and English-only ballots.

The Progressive Era of American politics, which lasted from the late 1800s to the early 1900s, radically changed local electoral systems, as most jurisdictions changed to at-large electoral systems during the first half of the twentieth century. This was particularly true of cities in the South and the West, which urbanized in the twentieth rather than the nineteenth century. By the mid-1970s, 74 percent of southern cities and 79 percent of western cities elected councils at large, compared to only 52 percent of eastern and 50 percent of midwestern cities.[38] In 1991, among U.S. cities with populations larger than 250,000, 28 percent used at-large elections, 10 percent used district-only elections, while 61 percent were a combination of district and citywide election systems. That is, 71 percent of cities elected councils by a district or mixed system.[39]

Such Progressive Era reforms, while designed to root out corruption, had a negative impact on Latinos. Since in most cities Latinos tend to be segregated into barrios, the elimination of district elections, while other barriers to voting were retained, made it extremely difficult to elect Latinos to office. The change to at-large elections in the Southwest would exacerbate the lack of Mexican Americans holding elected office, except in New Mexico (where Hispanos were the dominant group), from the 1880s to the 1950s. While other Latino ethnic groups were present in the country during this period, it was in the Southwest, where large numbers of Mexican

Americans were concentrated, that this change had the greatest impact. In many cities, Latinos found it extremely difficult to win in at-large elections. By the 1970s, Latinos were challenging the at-large electoral structure and the use of gerrymandered district boundaries for inhibiting the election of Latinos.

The passage of the Voting Rights Act (VRA) of 1965, with strong support from the Johnson administration, was a result of the civil rights movement to end discriminatory practices that prevented black people from voting and being elected to office, particularly in southern states, where segregation of the races and discrimination against blacks remained strong. Section 2 of the VRA prohibits minority vote dilution, which is the use of voting laws and practices that discriminate on the basis of race, color, or membership in a minority language group. All voting procedures are covered under the law, including voter registration, qualifications of candidates, voting practices, and types of electoral systems. Section 2 also prevents local governments from using any electoral procedure that would deny a fair chance to racial and language minorities to elect candidates of their choice.[40] In 1975 the VRA was amended to extend voting-rights protection to language minorities. These amendments mandated bilingual ballots and oral assistance to those who spoke Spanish, Chinese, Japanese, Korean, Native American languages, and Eskimo languages. In 1982 the VRA was also amended to clarify that proof of discriminatory *purpose* or *intent* was not required under a Section 2 claim of voting discrimination.[41]

One of the most critical structural elements governing the electoral process is the design of electoral districts. The design of electoral districts, whether it is based on nonpartisan or partisan positions, is a political act. Political parties and a wide variety of interest groups, including women, chambers of commerce, racial and ethnic groups, seek to draw political boundaries to increase their opportunity to elect someone who will represent their interests.

As noted, a major obstacle to the election of minorities to office is the use of at-large, winner-take-all seats, where candidates must run and win election in an entire school district, city, or county. In an at-large election system, there are no districts. A candidate can reside anywhere within the political jurisdiction, and all registered voters living within the political boundaries can vote for the candidate. Again, the at-large electoral system is part of the Progressive Era reforms of the late nineteenth and early twentieth century, designed to eliminate the ethnic urban political machines that controlled politics at the local level.

In the 1970s, Latinos and African American groups successfully challenged many at-large elections in locations where they had a history of being unable to elect someone of their ethnic or racial group to local office due to racially polarized voting. The goal was to create "district elections which would provide increased representation for minorities and facilitate their inclusion into urban governing coalitions, and lead to policy equity for underserved areas of the city."[42]

Today, however, a problem is evident with district elections: if a minority group is heavily concentrated in one district and if there is voting along racial lines in that city, then the voting strength of the minority community may increase in the district where it is concentrated but weaken throughout the rest of the city, because they are a small minority outside the one district where they are concentrated. District structures do tend to lead to deference to the wishes of council members on issues that concern their districts. Decentralization of power appears to increase council members' ability to deliver to their constituents and claim credit for doing so.[43]

Nevertheless, there are still many communities that do not use district elections or other electoral methods that would enhance minorities' opportunities to achieve representation on elected bodies. In California, 85 percent of the school boards, municipalities, and special districts use at-large election schemes, and these constitute a significant barrier to the political incorporation of Latinos in many places.[44]

Modern redistricting of political boundaries occurs after a census, which entails the counting of all Americans every ten years. Because the U.S. Constitution requires that representation in the House of Representatives be based on state population, congressional districts must be redrawn by state legislatures to reflect population shifts. Through redistricting, the political party with the greatest number of members in a statehouse tries to ensure that the maximum number of its party members can be elected to Congress. State legislatures are also responsible for redrawing any other district boundaries for state offices. Subunits of government within each state are responsible for redrawing their own political boundaries, such as at the county, city, and school district levels. The redistricting process often involves what is known as *gerrymandering*, the drawing of district boundaries to maximize the number of representatives from the political party in power in that state.

The process of redistricting also involves three types of claims of bias. State and federal courts have generally ruled out the claim of bias by either of the two main political parties based on redistricting schemes by state legislatures. In other words, there is no valid claim of bias if a district is "too Democratic" or "too Republican" in registration. This is understood to be the prerogative of the dominant political party in each state. Instead, the first basis for a claim is the "one person, one vote" principle from the Equal Protection Clause of the Fourteen Amendment to the Constitution. This principle basically states that each person's vote should count the same as every other vote; that is why all legislative districts must be drawn with roughly equal populations. In the year 2001, the target number was 646,952 people per congressional district. Too wide a variance from this target invites a lawsuit.

A second group of claims are those brought under the Voting Rights Act by racial minorities who claim that the political lines unfairly divide them among different electoral districts, thereby diluting their voting strength. In Los Angeles County, a Mexican American had not been elected to the county board of supervisors since the 1850s, so in 1984, the Mexican American Legal Defense and Education Fund (MALDEF) filed suit and challenged the division of Los Angeles County's large Latino community into different supervisory districts, saying it had effectively prevented Latinos from electing a Latino.[45] In 1990, a U.S. district judge ruled in *Garza* v. *County of Los Angeles* that the county supervisors had violated the Voting Rights Act by intentionally denying Latinos an equal opportunity to elect candidates of their choice to the board of supervisors.[46]

A third group of claims is the opposite of the second. These are called "Shaw claims," for the U.S. Supreme Court case that set the precedent. These claims generally argue that too much attention is paid to race in drawing district lines, violating the Fourteenth Amendment's Equal Protection Clause. The Supreme Court in the 1990s asked states to redraw district boundary lines if the district had been drawn for obvious racial purposes. Congressional districts in North Carolina and Georgia had to be redrawn so as to eliminate boundaries drawn explicitly to elect African Americans.

Often, then, redistricting starts at the state capitol and ends in a courtroom.[47] Notwithstanding the Supreme Court decrees that a state cannot overtly fashion districts to ensure minority representation in Congress, Latinos have historically fought to establish districts to ensure the best opportunity for minorities to be elected. New district boundaries began to be established following the adoption of the VRA. The drawing of district boundaries is shaped by voting-rights legislation, court interpretation, and state and local politics.

The form of district that provides the best opportunity for minorities to elect candidates of their choice is known as the *majority-minority district*. Here boundaries are drawn such that racial minority populations are concentrated into districts where they are the majority population. If it can be demonstrated that there is racialized voting, with white and minority voters each voting for their own candidates, with the effect of limiting the voting choices of racial minorities, then the formation of a majority-minority district can be justified. It enables the voters in this district to elect a candidate of their own choice (whether minority or not).

There are several congressional districts that are more than 60 percent Latino but that have a non-Latino representative. In most of these cases, a liberal white Congress member who was responsive to the needs of the Latino community had been in place before there was rapid Latino population growth in the area. The power of incumbency has enabled these congressional representatives to hold onto their seats despite changing demographics. For example, Howard Berman, a liberal white Democratic Congressman from the San Fernando Valley area of Los Angeles County, had a district that grew to become 65 percent Latino in the 1990s. So that he could retain his seat, Berman's district was redrawn following the 2000 census to decrease the Latino population to 41 percent. The redrawing of this district did two things for Congress member Berman: it made it more difficult for a Latino to challenge him in the Democratic primary, and it diluted the Latino population into two congressional districts. In Houston, Texas, a liberal white Democrat, Gene Green, defeated Houston City Council member Ben Reyes in 1992. Reyes was well known in the Latino community, yet in a district with 60 percent Latino population and low voter turnout, Congress member Green not only won the seat but retained it in the next five elections.[48]

The dilution of minority votes has historically made it more difficult for Latino candidates to be elected. However, in an area that contains a high concentration of Latinos, it also creates opportunities for crossover Latino candidates. In California, crossover candidate Loretta Sanchez defeated long-time incumbent Bob Dornan in conservative Orange County, known for having a combination of Latino and middle-of-the-road voters. Her electoral victory signaled the potential for Latino candidates with moderate politics to win races in non-Latino-dominated electoral districts.

In addition to district characteristics, candidates' ability to obtain endorsements and financial resources is crucial if they are to gain credibility. Such resources are usually acquired through working as a staff aide, party activist, or community or labor activist. Credibility is crucial: those who fund campaigns are most likely to donate to campaigns that have a reasonable chance of victory. Endorsements establish candidates' legitimacy and also draw in other resources. Entering into this political environment requires excellent connections and strong community-based ties. Name recognition is also a valuable commodity, whether due to familial ties or to demonstrated leadership in an area of expertise.

As electoral barriers to Latinos were removed, both male and females began to run for office in diverse locations and at different levels of government. The next section explores the fortunes of Latinos at different levels of government.

■ Latino Population Growth and Congress

The legislative branch of the federal government includes 100 senators and 435 members of the House of Representatives. Obtaining one of these

offices is not easy; such seats are costly, extremely partisan, and very pres-
tigious. Latinos historically have not been well represented in the legislative branch of the federal government. In the 1970s, there were only three
Latino congressmen (two from Texas and one from California) and only
one U.S. senator (New Mexico). In the subsequent decades, there were dramatic changes in the number and gender diversity of Latinos elected to the
House of Representatives. Latinos are now poised to make even greater
gains in the House and possibly the U.S. Senate in the next decade.

In the 1990s, the growth of Latinos dispersed their population beyond
the traditional centers of concentration into suburbs, rural areas, and all
regions of the country. In nearly one-third of the nation's 435 congressional
districts, Latinos are now a significant portion of the population. In 134 of
these districts (31 percent), the Latino share of the population now exceeds
the national share of the Latino population.[49]

In 2000, there were nineteen Latino legislators. Of the top fifteen congressional districts with the greatest share of Latinos, four had a more than 75
percent Latino population: two districts in Texas, one district in Los Angeles,
and one district in Florida (see Table 5.5). Another seven congressional dis-

Table 5.5   **Latino Congressional Members, Percentage of Latino Share of
Population, and Total Percentage of Votes Received in 2000 Elections**

Name of Representative and State Represented	Percentage of Latino Share of Population	Total Percent of Vote Received in 2000 Election
Ed Pastor, AZ	62.5	69
Xavier Becerra, CA	64.3	83
Hilda Solis, CA	59.4	Uncontested
Lucille Roybal-Allard, CA	86	85
Grace F. Napolitano, CA	72.4	71
Loretta L. Sanchez, CA	62.3	60
Joe Baca, CA	50.8	60
Illeana Ros-Lehtinen, FL	66.7	Uncontested
Lincoln Diaz-Balart, FL	77.5	Uncontested
Luis Gutierrrez, IL	70.1	89
Robert Menendez, NJ	47.2	79
Nydia Velasquez, NY	48.6	86
Jose E. Serrano, NY	62.9	Uncontested
Ruben Hinojosa, TX	78.9	89
Silvestre Reyes, TX	78	68
Charles A. Gonzalez, TX	67	88
Henry Bonilla, TX	66.3	59
Solomon P. Ortiz, TX	70.5	63
Ciro D. Rodriguez, TX	65	89
Average Latino population in district and percent of vote received	63.3	75.9 (excludes races where there was no opposition)

Source: NALEO Research Brief (2001).

tricts were between 65 and 75 percent Latino population, and four districts were greater than 62 percent Latino. In sixteen of the nineteen districts, the Latino population was greater than 50 percent. Two other districts, one in New Jersey and one in New York City, had slightly less than 50 percent Latino populations but overall had predominantly Democratic-registered voters, which ensured that a Latino had a strong opportunity to be elected.

Following the 2000 census, Latino and Hispanic members of Congress increased by five. As of the end of 2003, there were twenty-four Latina and Latino congressional members, twenty Democrats and four Republicans. There are now two caucuses that represent Hispanic interests. The Congressional Hispanic Caucus was formed in 1976 and historically had a liberal social agenda. It now includes twenty House members, all of whom are Democrats: nineteen of Hispanic descent and one of Portuguese descent. In 2003, House Republicans formed the Congressional Hispanic Conference, which is composed of four members of Hispanic descent and three of Portuguese descent. The new Congressional Hispanic Conference caucus was formed because of these members' outrage at the Congressional Hispanic Caucus's opposition to the appointment of Miguel Estrada to the federal bench in 2003.[50]

While Latinos have steadily increased their numbers in the House of Representatives, they are still only 5.7 percent of the total number of members, less than one-half of their percentage of the total population. After the 2000 census, there were twenty-four congressional districts with Latino populations greater than 50 percent. In order for a larger number of Latinos to enter the House of Representatives, they will need to win in electoral districts where Latinos are not the majority of the population but perhaps a significant minority.

Though Latino fortunes have improved in the House of Representatives, the situation is not as optimistic for Latinos when it comes to winning a U.S. Senate seat, which requires winning at a statewide level. Before the election of Latinos to the Senate in 2004, there had been only three Latino U.S. senators in the history of the country. The difficulty of putting together the economic resources, the political network, and a sophisticated campaign operation have until recently held back Latinos from winning only but a handful of statewide electoral victories.

It is no coincidence that the only U.S. senators of color elected consistently over the past forty years have come from the state of Hawaii. Asian Americans are the majority population in Hawaii, and they have consistently elected Asian Americans to both houses of Congress since Hawaii's statehood in 1959. There is one Native American U.S. senator, Democrat turned Republican Ben Nighthorse Campbell from Colorado. Barack Obama became the only African American senator when he was elected in 2004. Even in New Mexico, a state where Hispanos were historically and still are a significant portion of the state's population at 40 percent, no Hispanos have been elected to the U.S. Senate since the 1970s.

The next challenge for federal representation for Latinos, besides increasing the number of Latinos elected in the House, is to elect a Latina and additional Latinos to the U.S. Senate. However, given the difficulty of entering the Senate, it will take the right candidate, under optimal conditions, such as an open seat that becomes available, for more Latinos to win election to the upper house, as occurred in Florida and Colorado in 2004. The lack of Latino and significant African American presence (who together made up 24.8 percent of the total U.S. population in 2000) in the U.S. Senate, where confirmations for federal judgeships occurs, where foreign policy is shaped, and where potential candidates for president often emerge, indicates how far the United States must travel to have both houses of Congress reflect the country's diverse population.

■ State and Local Representation of Latinos

Other than the offices of president and vice president and seats in Congress, all elections in the United States involve contests for state or local offices. While Latinos have held elective office in this country since the early nineteenth century, before the 1960s they held such office only in a few areas of the Southwest. Beginning in the 1960s, Chicanos in the Southwest began to run and win in a wide variety of local and state representative elections. In the 1970s, Cubans and Puerto Ricans began to win elected office in the Northeast and Southeast. In the 1980s, other Latinos also began to win election in local offices in different regions of the country. In the 1990s, Latinos of different ethnicities ran for office in all regions. They held elected office in thirty-nine states in 2003. The breadth of office holding by Latinos in nearly 80 percent of the states is an indication of their growth and potential strength nationally.

At the state representative level, there are different social conditions and ethnic demographics among the states. Nationally in 2003, there were 160 Latino state representatives and 51 state senators for a total of 211. There had been only 114 Latino state legislators in 1985 and 163 in 1995. Not surprisingly, the southwestern states had the largest numbers and percentages of Hispanic state legislators. In terms of party affiliation, in 1985, 61 percent of all Hispanic legislators identified with the Democratic Party, while 32 percent identified as independents and 9 percent as Republicans. By 2000, 86 percent identified as Democrats and 14 percent were identified as Republicans—a dramatic decrease of independents and increases of those identified as Democrats and Republicans.[51] In general, Latinos have historically found it difficult to win election for state representatives except in majority-Latino districts. This is clearly evident in Texas, where the House of Representatives is composed of 150 members: in 2001 twenty-eight were Latino (including six Chicanas), and twenty-seven of the twenty-eight were elected from majority-Latino population districts. In New Mexico, Hispanic legislators numbered forty-five in total, or 40 percent of the legislature, which was an increase of 10 percent since 1985.

In California, the situation has begun to change: Latino state representatives are being elected in non-Latino-majority districts. Out of the eighty assembly districts in California, there were seventeen districts with a majority-Latino population and only fifteen districts with a voting-age Latino population greater than 50 percent in 2001. Of the seventeen districts with a majority-Latino population, there were only five with a majority of Latino registered voters. All of these districts were located in Los Angeles County, home to the greatest concentration of Latinos in the country. Of the nineteen Latino members of the state assembly in 2001, fifteen were Democrats and four were Republicans. Of the Latino Democrats, thirteen were elected from Latino majority districts, and the other two were elected from districts where Latinos had close to a majority population. None of the Latino Republicans, however, was elected from a majority-Latino district.

In 2003, there were sixty-one Latino state senators from seventeen states, which included fifty-two Democrats and nine Republicans. The largest state-senator contingents were New Mexico with fifteen Latino state senators, California with nine, and Texas with seven. There were also 160 Latino state house representatives in twenty-five different states, including 132 Democrats and 27 Republicans. The largest contingents of assembly members include thirty from New Mexico, thirty from Texas, eighteen from California, and thirteen from Florida. However, in 2004 the total number of Latino state house representatives was only 2.8 percent of the total number of 7,280 seats nationally. In contrast, African Americans held 8.2 percent of the total seats.[52] In only one state, New Mexico, does the percentage of Latino elected representatives exceed the state's percentage of Latino voting-age population; in all other states, the percentage of Latino state representatives is lower than the percentage of Latinos of voting age in the state. This is one way to measure whether Latinos have achieved equality throughout the country, and clearly they have not done so.

At the local level, Latino officeholders hold positions in numerous states, as was evident in Table 1.1. While Latinos hold many high-profile seats as mayors and county supervisors and on city councils and school boards in urban areas, a critical look at these numbers indicates that in many respects the process of electing Latinos to office is still at its infancy in many local areas. For example, in the area of public education, an issue Hispanics ranked as their highest priority in determining their choice for president in 2004,[53] there were a total of 2,557 Latinas and Latinos elected to school boards in 2001. Of this total, 1,147, or nearly 45 percent, were elected in one school district, the Chicago School District, where school sites elect their own parent councils. Since these positions change quite frequently, many scholars, including those compiling the National Directory of Latino Elected Officials, do not count them. If these numbers are not included, there were only two members not elected from the Chicago local school councils in the state of Illinois as of January 2001. Furthermore, by 2003 this number had increased to only seven members statewide.[54]

If we look at the numbers of Latino school board members in 2003, there were 1,694 scattered throughout the country, nearly 83 percent of them in three states: California (510), New Mexico (158), and Texas (736). There were 575 Latinas, or 34 percent, among these school board members (see Table 5.6). School board officeholders have surpassed city council members as the largest cohort of Latino elected officials. Yet consider that there are more than 14,500 school districts in the country and Latinos represent less than 1 percent of the total number of elected leaders for public schools. The small number of Latino school board members is a reflection of a larger crisis in education for Latinos. Latinos are dropping out of high school annually at a rate of 46 percent, Latino students nationally have lower test scores on average than other groups, and they also have low rates of admittance at many higher-education institutions. The lack of Latino representation on school boards and administrative positions becomes an important issue to be addressed. If Latinos are not included in local policymaking decisions, they will be relegated to outsider status with limited influence on policy outcomes.

■ Strategies for Winning Office in Diverse Districts

Latinos are elected from a diverse range of electoral districts, from predominantly Latino-populated districts to those where Latinos are only a small percentage of the population. While they are mostly elected from dis-

Table 5.6 Latino Elected Officials, Education/School Boards, 2003

	Male	Female	Total
Education/school board	1,119	575	1,694

Source: NALEO (2003a).
Note: Chicago local school council members are not included.

tricts where Latinos are a significant proportion of the population, Latinos have found creative ways to cross over and win in non-Latino-majority districts. Here we will explore the strategies employed by Latinos to achieve elected office.

The election of Latinos in non-Latino-majority districts is an indication of the potential for more crossover Latino candidates from both parties in urban, suburban, and rural areas. In more conservative suburban or rural districts, crossover politicians tend to use campaign themes and craft their campaign message to build a mainstream, noncontroversial platform that does not emphasize national origin or ethnic identity. In urban districts, where Latinos may or may not be the majority population, crossover candidates tend to include a multiracial platform and focus on interracial coalition building.

The existence of a majority-Latino district may lead us to assume wrongly that Latino candidates win elections there solely by appealing to Latino voters. In a study of Los Angeles politics, Latino city council candidates used deracialized campaign strategies in order to win office in districts that had a majority-Latino population but included other ethnicities. In order to build cross-racial support, which was crucial where the Latino electorate was less than 50 percent of the voters, Latino candidates used political styles, issues, and mobilization strategies that deemphasized race.[55]

Whether Latinos are using mobilization strategies that deemphasize race is an empirical question that must be further analyzed. Nevertheless, where Latinos are the majority population and Latinos have previously been elected to office, there is an *intraethnic* competitive character to electoral contests. Latinos now regularly compete against each other in majority-minority districts for elected positions, and the ability to form alliances with pockets of selected voters often makes the difference between winning and losing. Also, name recognition and strong family roots in the district are usually essential factors for winning elections.

In areas where Latinos are not the dominant population, employing a variety of approaches is crucial to elect Latinos. For more conservative Latino Republicans, the use of campaign messages that appeal to non-Latinos has been effective in suburban California districts where large numbers of middle- and upper-middle-class homeowners are concerned about preserving property values, improving schools, and keeping crime rates low. In urban locations, where Latinos are not the majority population, Latinos must reach across ethnic and racial fault lines and build coalitions. The coalitional forms include the use of biracial, multiracial, multiple issue, and labor-Latino alliances.

Each political environment contains its own set of circumstances. Former U.S. Speaker of the House of Representatives Tip O'Neill said,

"All politics is local." This is an accurate description of the dynamics under which Latinos seek elected office. Latino political candidates and office-holders are affected by the local political structure, including the strength of political parties, the influence of a dominant political machine, and the level of political organization in the Latino community. There are also structural rules, such as whether positions are partisan or nonpartisan, that influence the degree to which officeholders are tied to party politics.

In theory, nonpartisan races limit the power of machine politics, and during the Progressive Era in the early twentieth century, many local communities, particularly in the West and Southwest, moved to a system of non-partisan offices. However, the dominance of one of the two main political parties in most geographic areas means that while candidates may not run as a party candidate, they have traditionally been nominated by, or received the support of, a local party committee. Party identification, while not nearly as strong as during an earlier era, is still a powerful predictor of electoral success in many communities. It is only in strong reform electoral districts, where party affiliation is nonexistent or secondary to strong independent candidates, that partisanship is not a decisive factor in election to local office.

Historically, the use of machine politics in government, with strong control by a political apparatus, is usually tied to the dominant political party. In urban areas, the dominant political influence was usually the Democratic Party machine, which was formed in the nineteenth century in urban areas by Irish and other European immigrants. The large numbers of Latinos in the Democratic Party and the presence of Cuban Americans in the Republican Party make a monolithic party identification not completely useful in a discussion of Latino politics. Instead, "Latino machine politics" involves established political leaders, usually Latino but not exclusively, who have worked their way up the ladder of elected and appointed positions; these politicians seek to bring along the next generation of political leaders they have mentored and groomed for elected office. They also assist them with financial backing from influential supporters.

A good illustration of the power and problems of this approach is the endorsement of non-Latino aides by Latino elected officials who give up their seats to move up or must leave them due to term limits. In 1994, Mexican American assemblyman Richard Polanco of California had to give up his seat due to term limits and endorsed his Anglo chief of staff, Bill Mabie, to fill his position. For many years his district had been a focus of civil rights battles, which resulted in court-ordered reapportionments to create Latino-majority districts. Many members of the heavily Mexican majority district agreed with California state senator Art Torres, who said, "It's an issue of maintaining and electing Latino candidates, especially in a district where we have fought so hard for Latino representation."[56] Antonio

Villaraigosa easily won in the primary, defeating Mabie, and went on to win a seat in the California Assembly in the general election.

In 2000, six years later, the same seat became available when term limits forced Villaraigosa out. This time, Jackie Goldberg, a progressive white woman, was supported by most of the Latino political establishment over Latinos in the race. Goldberg easily won the contest. This election frustrated many in the Latino community, who still felt that a Latino should represent the district because it had a majority-Latino population. Other voices in the labor movement and Latino community argued that Goldberg's platform and historically strong support for education made her an excellent candidate for this district. Her victory indicated that to win in large, diverse electoral districts, ethnic ties are not necessarily the primary consideration.

■ Generational Trends in Latino Power

In most places, except in northern New Mexico and parts of south Texas, Latinos' winning of elected offices is relatively new, having begun only in the 1960s; however, even in some of these places where office-holding is relatively new, there is already a third generation of Latino politicians, which "may and often does include more than one biological generation."[57] The first generation of politicians was made up of veteran community leaders who paved the way and won office for the first time. Many of these leaders came of age in the 1950s and 1960s and shared common experiences, attitudes, and behavior. The second cohort followed in the first generation's footsteps; many of them were loyal aides who bided their time until the opportunity arose. Many in this group began to assume office in the 1980s. Due to term limits and retirements of many of these senior leaders, a third cohort of politicians has emerged. This group is young and fresh out of university following the completion of advanced degrees.

The new generation of Latino candidates is ambitious, usually well educated, and hungry to make an immediate difference. In San Antonio, Los Angeles, Miami, New York, Chicago, and other cities with large concentrations of Latinos in elected positions, one can find mature Latino politics involving a mix of seasoned veterans, loyal aides, political activists, sons and daughters of elected leaders, and "up and comers" who are new to electoral politics. These forces are competing for electoral office, usually with two or even more different camps with strong leaders who promote their own protégés, heir apparents, or allies to run for office.

In these centers of Latino power, where one party dominates and political differences are not always substantive, the campaign style of the candidate, the campaign message, and the campaign organization are crucial for victory. In locations where partisanship and party allegiance are still the dominant local characteristic, party-nominated slates of candidates and allegiance to a particular political leader are often the primary factors in electoral success, rather than individual candidate entrepreneurship.

An example of a strong party machine is Chicago, with a strong mayor and ward system of politics. Allegiance to Mayor Richard Daley usually determines whether you have party and local machine resources at your disposal to run for city, county, or state office. While Chicago is heavily Democratic, there are real differences among the Democratic Party factions, which have resulted in at least three camps of Latinos. Chicago also has the distinction of being the only major U.S. city to contain large numbers of the two main Latino ethnic groups, Mexicans and Puerto Ricans, with the former being the larger numerically but the latter having more voters historically.

Chicago politics are not for the faint of heart. The first group of Latino elected officials are those closely aligned with Daley; almost all of these officials are Mexican American. An example of a Daley political machine supporter is Danny Solis. Solis, a student militant in the 1970s at Northeastern University, helped form the United Neighborhood Organization in 1986 and challenged city hall on education and housing issues. With the election of Daley as mayor in 1989, Solis became a loyal supporter of Daley on development issues. In 1996, Daley appointed him as the Twenty-fifth Ward alderman. Solis is unapologetic about his position in the Daley machine; he says he can accomplish more for his community as a Daley ally: "I don't believe I have sold out my philosophy of what I would like to do for my community just because I am part of the Machine."[58]

The Mexican American elected officials aligned with Mayor Daley tend to view themselves as moderate to conservative Democrats. They stress issues of economic empowerment for Latinos, rather than political empowerment. They believe Latino immigrants do not need a handout from government and are not victims; rather, they are hardworking, and many are entrepreneurs.[59] The Daley camp consistently runs candidates against the other two camps in order to increase its influence and isolate the other two camps.

A second group—predominantly Puerto Rican—works with Daley on some issues in order to obtain city and county policy benefits but retains a level of independence on other issues, such as active support for the efforts to stop the U.S. Navy from bombing the island of Vieques in Puerto Rico. This group of officials is aligned with Puerto Rican American Congressman Luis Gutierrez. State senator Miguel Del Valle, Cook County commissioner Robert Maldonaldo, and Twenty-sixth Ward alderman Billy Ocasio are part of this independent coalition of Latino political leaders. They helped elect Cynthia Soto as state representative from the West Town area of Chicago in

2000. Together, they are a formidable independent voice in local politics. They also work with African American legislators at the state level as part of the black and Latino caucuses.

A third group of officials remains intensely loyal to the progressive ideals of Harold Washington, the African American mayor who first reached out to the Latino community as part of his multiracial coalition in the 1980s. This group has been weakened by losses to the Daley Latinos. In the early 2000s it was headed by Chicago alderman Ricardo Munoz; it is unabashedly liberal and clashes with Daley on most major issues, challenging the city's priority of support for big business at the expense of working people and minorities. This group's base of support is predominantly in the Mexican American communities of Pilsen and Little Village.

■ Electoral Districts and Latinos

In addition to the role of majority-minority districts, generational transitions, political party influence, and local political machines, there are a few other strategic considerations in the election of Latinos. One issue is the type of electoral district. An electoral district with distinct population demographics and characteristics may encourage a certain type of candidate to seek election. The percentage of Latino population, the percentage able to vote, and the class composition of the Latino population are also important factors to consider when analyzing the type of Latino candidate who may run for office.

There are four general types of local electoral districts, based on the demographics of the area.

1. *Predominantly Latino district.* The Latino population of these districts is greater than 60 percent. This is usually considered a safe district for a Latino candidate. Here Latinos are the dominant ethnic or racial group and generally do not need support from any other ethnic or racial groups to win office, unless there is more than one Latino candidate. However, in cities with a majority Latino population, there are usually other considerations. In El Paso, Texas, a city with a 75 percent Latino population, Ray Caballero won the 2001 mayoral race. He was only the third Mexican American to win this office in 120 years. While Caballero did not run as an ethnic candidate per se, he was clearly perceived as an ethnic candidate by the press and the local Mexican American community. As a prominent local attorney, he remained cautious about introducing the question of race and focused on building strong inroads into the affluent West Side of El Paso in addition to mobilizing the Mexican American community.[60]

In several cities in south Florida, California, New Mexico, and Texas, where Latinos are the overwhelming majority of the population, the focus is generally on economics rather than inclusion. Latinos in majority-Latino cities and towns are no longer fighting for minority integration but instead for more economic resources for development and housing in poor areas and constituencies.[61] Activists wage the struggle to obtain economic resources from those in city hall, many of whom are Latino, and from those who are influential in the business community.

In cities with a greater than 60 percent Latino population, there is usually strong Latino political influence because the majority of elected and appointed officials are Latino. Communities small and large with a high-percentage Latino population—El Paso and Laredo, Texas; Las Vegas and Sunland Park, New Mexico; Miami, Hialeah, and Sweetwater in Florida; Huntington Park, Calexico, and Maywood in California—have majority or total Latino control of the political institutions. In these majority-Latino communities, there is often intense competition between various factions, each usually tied to a particular local politician, and between differing approaches for how to address and solve problems.

2. *Mixed district.* Here the Latino population is 40–59 percent. Latinos may be the dominant ethnic group by population but are not necessarily the dominant group of registered voters. Latinos still need support from several other communities of interest if they are to win citywide elections. In some cases, they may be viewed as a threat to "take over" politically, upset the dominant coalition, and transform the traditional black-white paradigm. In San Antonio, where Mexican Americans are the dominant ethnic group with 58 percent of the population, Ed Garza's campaign for mayor was a mainstream campaign with little media or popular discussion of a "Mexican takeover" of the city. On the other hand, the mayoral race in Los Angeles in 2001 became racially polarized, with white liberals and Mexican Americans pitted against African American and conservative white voters. In both cases, Latinos were the dominant ethnic group; in San Antonio, however, white voters were comfortable voting for a Latino, while in Los Angeles, white voters were divided between a liberal white candidate and a liberal Latino candidate, and African American voters felt strong loyalty to the white liberal.

3. *Growing Latino influence.* In these electoral districts, the Latino population is between 25 and 40 percent. Here Latinos are perceived as a rising political force, but Latino registered voters tend to be considerably fewer. Latinos must rely on others to win, for usually they cannot win city-wide elections without strong support from one or more communities of interest—a segment of white voters, black voters, or Asian Pacific Islanders. Latinos who run as citywide candidates appeal to both their own ethnic base and at least one other ethnic community. An example of this situation is the Fernando Ferrer mayoral campaign in New York in 2001.

Ferrer built a coalition of black and brown supporters to mount a serious campaign against a white liberal candidate for the Democratic Party nomination. Blacks and Latinos made up the majority of the population but not the voters. In this scenario, a Latino candidate must devise a strategy that can sufficiently increase the Latino voters and/or appeal to a significant minority of white or black voters, depending on which group has the most number of voters.

In 2001, Latinos won elections for mayor in some cities where Latinos were not the majority population but where there was a well-qualified candidate. In Austin, Texas, accountant and council member Gus Garcia was overwhelmingly elected as mayor, with 60 percent of the vote in a city where Latinos were 30 percent of the population. Garcia had broad support among Latinos and almost all other constituencies. He had grown up in the border region that was heavily Mexican. He came to Austin in the 1960s and began his political career in 1967 by protesting the lack of Hispanics on the city's Human Relations Commission. He eventually joined the city council before running for mayor.[62] In Hartford, Connecticut, Eddie Perez, a longtime Puerto Rican community activist, won election as mayor. Puerto Ricans and African Americans were 40.5 percent and 37.9 percent of the population, respectively. They forged an alliance and elected Perez as Hartford's first Latino mayor. Perez had migrated from Puerto Rico in 1969, risen from poverty including dependence on welfare and involvement with gangs, and eventually went into church and community organizing. He ran for mayor to help address many of the long-standing problems he had been trying to solve as a community activist.

In Houston, another city where Latinos made up less than 40 percent of the population, Cuban-born Republican Orlando Sanchez challenged African American incumbent mayor Lee Brown in 2001. This race split along racial lines, as 90 percent of African Americans voted for Brown and 75 percent of Latinos voted for Sanchez. The high number of Latino voters was widely viewed as an indication that Latino voters, when given a choice to elect one of their own, even one who is in a different party, will cross lines to elect that person. Sanchez was a registered Republican in a city with a seemingly strong political machine of Mexican American Democrats in office (Sanchez would have been the only Latino Republican and the only Cuban American) and a high percentage of registered Latino Democrats. In a city with 37 percent Latinos and 25 percent African Americans, Sanchez counted on a voter base of conservative whites and the majority of the Hispanic community. He ended up with 49 percent of the vote to Brown's 51 percent. He won 75 percent of the Latino vote. Summing up, he concluded that the reason he lost was that white voters had not turned out in sufficient numbers; meanwhile, a strong turnout of African American voters, coupled with 25 percent of Latino voters along with labor and white liberals, resulted in the reelection of Brown.[61]

In each of these cities, while Latinos were not the majority population, they were a significant minority of the population and put forward strong, viable candidates with name recognition, citywide visibility, economic resources, and crossover appeal beyond their own national-origins. While only one of them was successful in 2001, it was demonstrated that Latinos can run credible and viable campaigns against well-funded opponents, if given the opportunity to demonstrate their electability.

4. *Predominantly non-Latino district*. Here Latinos are not perceived as a political threat to dominate local politics, for the Latino population is usually 25 percent or less. Latinos run as mainstream candidates and tend to downplay ethnic identification. A current example is Ron Gonzalez, the mayor of San Jose, California, who was elected in 1998. While Mexican Americans are a strong and visible ethnic group in the city, their percentage of the population was less than 30 percent at the time of the election, and their voter registration rates were considerably lower. Yet the combination of a visible community and an attractive crossover candidate with previous electoral and business experience was attractive to a cross-section of voters. Another example is Ray Martinez, mayor of Fort Collins, Colorado, a community with an 8.5 percent Latino population. Martinez was a retired police detective when he won his election in 1999. With his law-and-order credentials, he is a prototype of the Latino crossover elected official with strong appeal to a non-Latino-majority population.

This phenomenon of Latinos winning in locations where they are a small percentage of the population and are not yet perceived as a political threat to established forces represents a growing trend. In cities where the Latino population is 25 percent or less of the total population, its electoral influence is usually still limited to a few electoral districts where Latinos are the dominant population. For example, in San Diego, California, the Latino population was 25 percent of the total population in 2000, and Latino electoral influence was focused within the Eighth District, where there was a majority Latino population. Ralph Inzunza, an example of the new generation of Latino political leaders, represents this district. He was only thirty-two years old when elected and had been involved in politics from a young age.

It is important to look at the impact that Latinos have on city or county government, not just in districts that were created to enable a Latino to achieve elected office. While such redistricting may give Latinos a seat at the table of power, it may mask the limited power that Latinos are able to exercise overall. District elections structurally produce a situation where each council member has the most influence on issues related to her or his district.[64] This may create a situation of weak political incorporation, where Latinos are visible in leadership but are not a part of, or influential in, the dominant governing coalition that controls the politics of the broader community.

■ Types of Latino Candidates

In addition to the different demographics of electoral districts, there are different types of Latino candidates. The success of a candidate who emerges from a district and wins office is a function of many factors; one important factor is the type of candidate. Not all Latino candidates have the same characteristics. A candidate who arises from and runs in an electoral district that is predominantly Latino is more likely to strongly identify with his or her ethnic community. A candidate who did not primarily identify with and address the needs of a predominantly Latino district would have a more difficult time winning elected office in that district.

In an electoral district that is predominantly non-Latino, the Latino candidate may identify with his or her ethnic community; in terms of campaign issues, however, he or she is more likely to be a mainstream candidate who runs on universal issues, rather than issues that more explicitly address the needs of the Latino community. An example would be to run a campaign calling for quality education for all, versus support for bilingual education as a primary means to achieve quality education. In electoral districts where there is strong heterogeneity and multiple ethnic groups, and no one dominant ethnic or racial group, a Latino candidate will likely need to conduct a campaign that appeals both to her or his own ethnic community and to a mainstream, non-Latino, audience.

The following summary notes the general characteristics of the main types of Latino candidates:

1. *Strong ethnic identification.* Candidate is known as strongly identified with his or her ethnic community. May have little contact or experience outside that ethnic community.
2. *Combination candidate/officeholder.* Acts at times as an ethnic politician and at other times as a mainstream non-ethnic-specific politician. This candidate may have begun his or her political career as a strong ethnic officeholder and, over time and numerous political races, while retaining ties in the ethnic community, built ties beyond this community to other potential allies.
3. *Crossover candidate.* Candidate is primarily known as a mainstream politician, and ethnic identification is played down. This candidate has usually built a career outside of the ethnic community

in business, education, or politics. He or she may or may not have strong ties to the ethnic community.

This summary is meant to provide the reader with a general sense of the types of candidates who are emerging nationally. The existence of at least three types of candidates is an indication of the breadth of offices being sought by Latinos today. Previously, the prototypical Latino candidate was either a Latino community activist or a staff member of an elected official. Today, Latinos from all walks of life are running for office. More explicitly probusiness and fiscally conservative candidates are running for office in partisan and nonpartisan races, and in primaries of both major parties. It is also more common to find candidates who are lawyers, business owners, union activists, as well as more women running for office. The possible scenarios and the types of candidates they generate are worth further exploration.

When districts contain a sizable Latino population but the voting group is not greater than 50 percent, you are likely to find a Latino political candidate who has two campaigns, one that is a stealth ethnic-specific campaign, quietly mobilizing his or her ethnic voting population, and another that is thematically mainstream, inclusive, and not ethnic specific. An example was the 2001 Villaraigosa mayoral runoff in Los Angeles; he essentially ran two campaigns, a grassroots mobilization of the Latino community that he turned over to other Latino elected officials and community organizations, and a citywide campaign that emphasized his cross-ethnic appeal with universal issue themes.[65] The Orlando Sanchez campaigns for mayor in Houston in 2001 and 2003 were also conducted with a strong Spanish-language outreach to the Spanish-speaking community and another campaign that targeted conservative white voters.

When Latino candidates run in districts that are overwhelmingly non-Latino, Latino candidates are most likely to run campaigns deemphasizing their ethnic heritage and focusing on reaching out to other ethnic groups and interest groups for support. In this situation Latino candidates will seek to cross over and be acceptable to other communities of interest, which requires downplaying one's ethnic heritage and ethnic community support so as not to be perceived as a "Latino" candidate but as a candidate who happens to be Latino. The successful mayoral campaigns of Ron Gonzalez in San Jose, California, in 1998 and for reelection in 2002 serve as examples. This type of campaign is possible if the candidate's political career follows a noncontroversial development path, such as that of a business owner or a professional. If one has a history as a strong community or student activist, it is not easy to remold one's history to placate more conservative voters.

Historically, Latinos were elected from predominantly Latino districts. In Latino-majority districts, there is often intense competition among

Latinos for office. Here the relative strength of political machines is crucial in producing potential officeholders. In such districts, however, the relative strength of an individual officeholder may not be transferable to someone from his or her camp. However, running as the son or daughter of a former or current elected official can be extremely important for name recognition. Still, the nature of individualized politics in America makes a simple designation of an heir apparent not a good predictor of who is likely to win an office being vacated by a longtime incumbent. It is necessary to examine the relative strengths and weaknesses of individual candidates, community ties, campaign message, organization, and resources to analyze the merits of Latino candidates.

As Latinos seek to run and win in districts where Latinos are not the majority population, they must appeal to a cross-section of Latinos and non-Latinos, be they other people of color or white voters. Potential Latino candidates who are part of the pipeline of candidates that can cross over may have more appeal to run for offices that are more diverse than those whose appeal is focused on representation of the Latino community. Table 5.7 illustrates the relationship between the demographic characteristics of a district and the type of candidate who is likely to seek office.

Distinct electoral districts as defined by population demographics and the corresponding types of candidates they may produce are not applicable only to Latino candidates. Most Asian Americans officeholders, other than those from Hawaii, are elected in districts where they represent only a small percentage of the population. This tends to produce Asian American candidates who use crossover appeal to a wide variety of voters.[66]

The notion of crossover appeal is not new in political analysis. The ability of minority candidates to win elections in districts where they were not the numerical majority has been a vexing problem historically. Before the Voting Rights Act of 1965 was passed, there were very few instances of white voters electing nonwhites to office, particularly in the segregated South and Southwest. What then is the optimal strategy for electoral success for Latinos?

Table 5.7   Latino Candidate Types and Types of Electoral District

	Dominant Latino District, > 60% Latino Population	Near Dominant Latino/Mixed District, 40–59% Latino Population	Rising Latino District, 25–40% Latino Population	Small Latino District, < 25% Latino Population
Ethnic politician	X			
Combination politician		X	X	
Crossover politician				X

■ The Relevance of Racial Identity
   Politics in the New Millennium

The current trend of Latino elected officials (LEOS) being primarily ethnic representatives is not based solely on a strong sense of ethnic solidarity; rather, it arises from the structural arrangement in which they are elected from predominantly majority-Latino districts. In the near future this situation will most likely continue to be the predominant context in which Latinos will be elected to office. The concentration of Latinos in relatively compact electoral districts remains the primary means for Latinos to be elected to office. However, as the Latino population disperses throughout the United States, an increasing number of Latinos will seek office in areas where they are not the majority population.

As conditions change, what will be the optimal strategy by which Latinos can achieve electoral success? Will racial politics still be their primary strategy for election to office? According to David Metz and Katherine Tate, who studied black and white voters in a series of contests involving black and white candidates, the choice of an electoral strategy largely depends on contextual factors. Racially polarized voting is a byproduct of the ways race has been used in politics to win elections and achieve political goals.[67]

In a continuing demographic trend, Latinos are moving into areas where they had had little or no presence previously, and it is anticipated that the number of LEOs elected in these districts will grow in the future. As of 2004, Latinos had been elected in thirty-eight states. For example, in 2000, there were four Latino Republicans in the California State Assembly from districts with an average of 16 percent Latino registered voters. In these four assembly districts, Anglos were nearly 73 percent of the registered voters, and the Democratic registration margin was −7.4 percent. The decisive factor in these districts was not Latino voters; rather, non-Latino voters decided the outcomes by voting for Latinos.

In one of these districts, an affluent and ethnically diverse suburban area in eastern Los Angles County, Republican Robert Pacheco won elections for the Sixtieth Assembly seat in a district that had less than 40 percent Republican voters. Pacheco's victory is illustrative of the crossover appeal of nonthreatening Latinos in middle-class areas. These candidates have potential to gain the support of voters of different racial and ethnic groups by highlighting their extensive education and professional skills and by focusing on universal issues such as lower taxes, better schools, and crime reduction.

Compared to the districts where California Latino Republicans were elected, in the sixteen assembly districts where Latino Democrats were elected the average percentage of Latino registered voters was nearly 42 percent, while the Anglo percent of registered voters was 39 percent (see Table 5.8).

According to a study by Morgan Kousser (2001), the voters in California are not colorblind. The likelihood of a Latino being elected to the assembly in 2000 was most likely in districts where Latinos made up a majority of the registered Democrats. This occurred nearly 89 percent of the time. In districts in which Latinos were 30–50 percent Democratic Party registrants, Latinos were successful only 50 percent of the time. When the district's registration was less than 30 percent Latino Democratic, only 5 percent of Latinos were elected.[68] While this study focused only on one state, it is illustrative of the continuing significance of racialized voting patterns and the importance of maintaining electoral districts where Latinos are the majority of registered voters to provide the best opportunities to elect Latinos to office.

For Latinos to achieve electoral victories beyond majority-Latino districts, it is necessary to devise strategies that reflect local conditions. In some areas, spreading out the Latino population over a larger number of districts to increase conditions for a strong crossover candidate to win may be the best strategy. Even though Latinos are not a monolithic community that votes and thinks alike, having a solid minority of potential voters increases one's chances of winning an election, as there is a natural base of supporters to build a successful election coalition. In areas where Latinos are almost the majority or slightly more than the majority of the population, an appeal to non-Latinos combined with a distinct mobilization effort of the Latino community is critical for electoral victory. The biracial coalition strategy may work best under these conditions, because the Latino voting-age population will likely be small due to low voter turnout, a significant

Table 5.8   Ethnic and Partisan Differences in the California Assembly Districts in the 2000 Elections

Traits of Average District	Party and Ethnicity of Winning Candidates, November 2000	
	Latino Republican	Latino Democrat
Number of Districts	4.0	16.0
% Latino registered voters	16.1	41.8
% Black registered voters	5.1	9.9
% Asian registered voters	5.9	8.8
% Anglo registered voters	72.9	39.4
% Latinos of voting age population	25.2	55.7
Democratic registration margin (D-R)	−7.4	29.1

Source: J. Morgan Kousser (2001), p. 22

percentage of the population being too young to vote, and a large segment of the population being noncitizens. For example, in the 2001 Los Angeles mayoral election, Latinos composed 47 percent of the population, yet they constituted only 22 percent of the voters.[69]

Where there is not a majority of Latino voters, a Latino candidate needs to broaden his or her support by appealing to non-Latinos. After winning the largest number of votes in the Los Angeles mayoral election in 2001, Antonio Villaraigosa spent almost all of his efforts appealing to non-Latino voters in the runoff against the eventual winner, James Hahn. In this case, with Latinos constituting the largest ethnic group but not the majority of voters, he was unable to overcome a negative media campaign and the fear among many non-Latinos that Latinos were poised for a political takeover of Los Angeles.

In the successful 2001 campaign of Ed Garza for mayor of San Antonio, his electoral strategy was to actively campaign for white voters and virtually ignore Mexican American voters in the barrios. He counted on Mexican Americans turning out to vote for him even though he did not specifically campaign for them. He spent few resources encouraging Mexican American voters. This was a different strategy from the one that had been used by Henry Cisneros's successful mayoral campaign twenty years earlier.[70]

In areas where Latinos are a minority of the voting population, the focus on mainstream, universal issues rather than ethnic-specific issues has been used to achieve elected office. Latinos' adoption of an electoral platform that emphasizes nonracial issues that appeal to white voters is similar to how African American candidates, in districts where they were a small minority of the population, were able to get elected in several large cities and win the governor's house in Virginia in the late 1980s. Some scholars termed the experiences of such African American candidates *deracialization*.[71]

Minority candidates in districts where there are diverse population groups have used various methods to broaden their appeal. Some of these candidates have prioritized building ties with liberal white voters, as in Antonio Villaraigosa's campaign for Los Angeles mayor in 2001. Others have focused on building coalitions with African American voters against entrenched Anglo power holders, as exemplified by the Chicago mayoral campaigns of Harold Washington in 1983 and 1987. Still others formed candidate-centered campaigns where race was not a dominant part of the campaign message, such as the Federico Peña campaign for mayor of Denver in 1982, the Ron Gonzalez mayoral victory in San Jose in 1998, and the Ed Garza campaign for mayor of San Antonio in 2001.

The utility of building the traditional model of political incorporation, where a biracial coalition of liberal whites and racial minorities join together to empower minorities, may be appropriate only under certain circumstances, such as where there is a strong liberal tradition of electing minority candidates or supporting biracial coalitions.

In districts where Latinos are the dominant majority population (60–70 percent or more) LEOs will continue to run as ethnic candidates and fight for the interests of their ethnic communities and other disadvantaged constituents. In other locations, where they are a small percentage of the population, Latinos may be elected where they are not perceived as a threat to take over political control of the area. This is a reflection of the duality of Latino politics. Historically, Latinos have fought to be placed in Latino-majority districts in order to have the strongest opportunity to elect an ethnic candidate of their choosing. However, as naturalization and voting rates grow among Latinos, and as non-Latinos change their racial voting patterns, having supermajority-Latino districts may cease being a requirement to achieve elected office.

On the one hand, the electoral districts where they are the majority of the population remain the best locations for Latinos to achieve electoral representation. On the other hand, they are running and beginning to win in districts where they represent less than the majority of the population. Some Latinos do not want to be perceived as "ghetto politicians" who can run and win only in supermajority-Latino districts. They define themselves and their platforms as appealing to a broad cross-section of voters of different races and nationalities.

The bunching of Latino voters into supermajority districts may potentially limit the total number of seats that can be created where a Latino candidate has the opportunity to win an election. Dispersing Latino voters too widely can either increase the number of Latino elected officials or backfire and cause Latinos to lose more races. Will political entrepreneurs in the Latino community be able to win office in more non-Latino-majority districts? Will there be slow, incremental expansion of the number of LEOs because district lines that were drawn after the 2000 election tend to protect incumbents in most states?

Majority-minority districts, political parties, and candidate-centered and crossover politics have all played roles in creating conflict within the Latino community over how to expand Latino influence. In California, a debate erupted among Latino civil rights activists during the 2000 census redistricting efforts. MALDEF and the Mexican American Political Association (MAPA) charged that the state's redistricting efforts provided for an incumbent protection plan at the expense of Latinos' rights to elect representation of their choice. MALDEF accused Latino state legislators of sanctioning the redistricting plan—which had been put forward by the brother of liberal congressman Howard Berman—to protect their own seats rather than to increase Latino voting strength. Arguing that Latinos are still not equally represented, MALDEF and other civil rights organizations pressed to have additional majority-Latino population districts at the congressional level. MALDEF, MAPA, and League of United American Citizens (LULAC) chapters in the San Fernando Valley picketed the offices of Representative Berman (D-Mission Hills) over the proposed congressional map, which would divide up Latino voters in the valley into two congressional districts in 2001.[72]

Leading LEOs who had helped shape the redistricting plan countered that elections are not just about the racial identity of the candidate; they are about the candidate's stand on issues of critical importance to the Latino community. If a non-Latino candidate or incumbent is supportive of Latino concerns, then the Latino community should support her or him. Likewise, some LEOs believed it is wrong to limit themselves to seeking office in "safe" Latino districts.[73] Pointing out that Latinos were already being elected to office in non-Latino-majority districts, they argued that "electoral politics and issues are no longer just about race."[74] They believed that the redistricting plan would strengthen Latino districts and lock in the Democratic majority in the California state senate and congressional delegation for the next ten years. As two Latina state senators stated, "In the era of term limits, . . . we should not relegate ourselves to only a few court-imposed barrios."[75] Miguel Contreras, secretary treasurer of the Los Angeles Federation of Labor, added, "MALDEF doesn't walk precincts. They don't get out the vote. They do it all on numbers. . . . MALDEF has done good work in the past, but here they are out of date."[76]

Some LEOs have gone so far as to challenge Latinos' continued reliance on the courts to settle boundary disputes; instead, they argue Latinos should expand their influence by winning in districts where they may not be the majority population. This division is more than a local spat among old allies; it is a debate about the current stage of development in the Latino movement. According to one scholar-activist, it has to do with whether "the Latino vote is respected, without respect to whether or not Latinos vote for Latino candidates."[77]

While the growth in the number of LEOs will continue in cities, counties, and electoral districts nationally in the next decade, there is another battle that is being waged in the areas where Latinos are already established as the predominant social group. The struggle in predominantly Latino areas is no longer for descriptive representation; rather, it is for a higher level of *substantive* representation. In these Latino-majority districts, ethnic voters have been voting for ethnic candidates for many years; they vote for the candidates that most closely represent their views and are well known to them through community involvement as businesspeople or community activists.

In addition, differences between various political camps, usually within the same political party, exist in most cities and electoral districts. Elections thus become contests between the different organized interests seeking to maintain or to transform the existing political order. This process occurs in small towns and big cities, in all regions, and among and between ethnic Latino groups. For example, in Chicago, the pro-Daley (regular) Latino Democrats and the independent Latino Democrats have waged intense intraethnic campaigns for electoral power in Latino-majority districts for more than a decade. In New York City, there has been intense competition among Dominicans for city council seats. There are two major camps of Cuban Americans that vie for political office in Miami-Dade County.

This marks a healthy process of growth within Latino politics. Without a centralized leadership structure of well-established national leaders, most Latino leadership is localized and is tied to either business or community groups. While the National Association of Latino Elected and Appointed Officials is an umbrella organization of Latino elected officials, it does not attempt to provide leadership and direction to all LEOs. The Congressional Hispanic Caucus, another important leadership forum, also does not attempt to provide leadership to all LEOs. National civil rights organizations such as LULAC and the National Council of La Raza focus on their specific missions to address the needs of their community. There is no formal mechanism for this to occur, nor would it necessarily be advisable given the broad diversity of views that exist within the Latino community. This means that for the foreseeable future, Latino political power will be built primarily at the state and local levels by local and regional networks of Latino activists and within political parties. There will continue to be uneven development, with Latinos being elected in some states at all levels of government at higher rates than in other states, due to differing historical patterns of integration into local and state political systems.

■ Conclusion

The continuing growth of a diverse group of Latino elected officials will likely produce more Latino candidates who will seek to build panethnic Latino coalitions to seek electoral office. In other situations, there will be intense competition among Latino candidates from different national origins to win seats in majority-minority districts. The ability of candidates to construct broad coalitions, both intraethnic and interethnic, will be critical to electoral success. Candidate-centered politics, as opposed to a common group effort by Latinos to occupy an electoral seat held previously by an Anglo, became the predominant means to achieve office in the 1990s.

Today, ambitious Latino candidates are seeking to run for office in districts where Latinos are not the majority population; rather, they seek to run where Latinos are a sizable minority and can provide a base of support on which the candidate can build. Instead of focusing solely on turning out votes in the Latino area of an electoral district, they seek to expand their influence to non-Latino areas.

The debate in southern California between Latino civil rights organizations, elected officials, and organized labor is not unique to that area. The 2001 mayoral race in New York resulted in Republican Michael Bloomberg defeating Democratic candidate Mark Green in a city with a Democratic voter registration advantage of 5:1. Coming out of the primaries, Green led in the polls. He failed, however, to mend fences with Latino community and labor leaders and with African American leaders after a hard-fought primary in which charges of unfair tactics by his campaign were not resolved. Green received only lackluster support from Puerto Ricans, African Americans, and labor movements and lost the general election. One prominent Latino labor leader pointed out that labor unions must start putting the interests of workers over ethnic politics if they are to succeed in electing labor-friendly city officials.[78]

There are also fault lines within the Latino community, and with close allies, over strategic questions for the twenty-first century. How can the number of seats where Latinos have a credible opportunity to win office be increased? Should the creation and retention of majority-minority seats remain the primary objective of voting-rights litigation? Or is it more important to create new districts where Latinos are the largest ethnic group, but not necessarily the majority population, if Latinos are to extend their opportunities to win election? Notwithstanding the effort in the state of Texas to redraw district boundaries in 2003 after lines had already been established, most redistricting efforts concluded in 2000 or 2001, with district lines fixed for the next ten years. A key variable to observe in these early years of the twenty-first century is growth or change in population within districts and how this affects the electoral chances of Latinos. Also, how long will Latinos wait before challenging entrenched incumbents who now represent districts with majority or near-majority Latino populations?

This chapter has provided a broad overview of Latino politics and the involvement of Latinos in the electoral process. There is not space to fully explore other avenues of political participation in which Latinos are engaged; however, as electoral participation is an established means of political involvement, it provides a marker of the progress of Latino politics. The next three chapters will closely explore the process of Latino political empowerment nationally, and in four cities, from political disenfranchisement to political incorporation.

■ Notes

1. R. Browning, D. Marshall, and D. Tabb (1997), p. 10.
2. Migration Policy Institute (n.d.).
3. U.S. Bureau of the Census (2001b).
4. J. Gimpel and Kaufman (2001), p. 1.
5. U.S. Bureau of the Census (2001b).
6. B. Guzman (2001).
7. A. Falcon (2001).
8. R. R. Ramirez and G. de la Cruz (2002).
9. V. M. Valle and R. Torres (2000), p. 4.
10. Ibid., p. 5.
11. R. Milkman (2000).
12. Pew Hispanic Center and Kaiser Family Foundation (2002a).
13. R. R. Ramirez and G. de la Cruz (2002).
14. Louis DeSipio (1996), p. 117.
15. R. de la Garza and L. DeSipio (1997), p. 75.
16. E. Porter (2001); J. Passel (2002).
17. William C. Velásquez Institute (2000c).
18. S. Sailer (2001).
19. William C. Velásquez Institute (2004b).
20. Southwest Voter Registration and Education Project, "10-4 Campaign."
21. William C. Velasquez Institute (2004a).
22. G. Rodriguez (1996).
23. *Los Angeles Times* (1994).
24. *Los Angeles Times* (1996).
25. *Los Angeles Times* (1998).
26. Latinos Issues Forum (1998).
27. A. D. Pantoja and G. Segura (2000).
28. William C. Velásquez Institute (2000a, 2000b).
29. CNN.com (2000).
30. *Washington Post*, Henry J. Kaiser Family Foundation, and Harvard University (2000).
31. Voter News Service (2000).
32. J. Gimpel and K. Kaufman (2001), p. 7.
33. Pew Hispanic Center and Kaiser Family Foundation (2002a).
34. Pew Hispanic Center and Kaiser Family Foundation (2004).
35. William C. Velásquez Institute (2004b).
36. Ibid.
37. America Online and Time Warner Foundation (2002).
38. H. Sanders (1979).
39. A. Bridges and K. Underwood (2000), pp. 51–52, based on T. Renner and V. De Santis (1993).
40. Center for Voting and Democracy (n.d.a).
41. United States Department of Justice.
42. A. Bridges and K. Underwood (2000); B. Grofman and C. Davidson (1992).
43. A. Bridges and K. Underwood (2000); J. L. Polinard et al. (1994).
44. J. Avila (1997).
45. J. Regalado and G. Martinez (1991).
46. R. Acuña (1996), pp. 72–73.

47. J. Richman (2001).
48. M. Barone and G. Ujifusa (1999), p. 1,590.
49. NALEO (2001b).
50. Hickey (2003).
51. C. E. Menifield (2001b).
52. Center for Voting and Democracy (n.d.b).
53. Pew Hispanic Center and Kaiser Family Foundation (2004).
54. NALEO (2003), p. 70.
55. K. Underwood (1997b).
56. R. Lopez (1994).
57. R. de la Garza and D. Vaughan (1985).
58. C. Hernandez-Gomes (2001).
59. S. Mendoza, interview (2001).
60. D. Romo (2001), p. 2.
61. G. Rodriguez (2002a).
62. R. W. Gee (2001), p. 1.
63. J. Williams (2001); L. Rodriguez (2001).
64. J. L. Polinard et al. (1994).
65. M. Gold (2001).
66. J. Lai (2000), p. 219.
67. D. H. Metz and K. Tate (1995), p. 277.
68. J. M. Kousser (2001), p. 9.
69. *Los Angeles Times* (2001).
70. H. Flores (2002).
71. J. P. McCormick and C. E. Jones (1993).
72. M. Finnegan (2001).
73. M. Escutia and G. Romero (2001).
74. Ibid.
75. Ibid.
76. T. Edsall (2001).
77. A. Falcon (2002).
78. S. Greenhouse (2001).

6

Variations on Power: Miami, San Antonio, and Los Angeles

To study the extent of the progress of Latino politics at the local level, political incorporation theory is useful as it focuses on minority group mobilization, governing coalitions, incorporation into the institutions of power, and policy responsiveness to racial minority interests. Chapters 6, 7, and 8 will explore in more depth the process and extent of political incorporation by Latinos in large and small communities. While each local arena undergoes a unique political development, there are also patterns of electoral (dis)empowerment. In Table 5.8 the relationship between population size and the type of political actor likely to win electoral office was highlighted. In addition to demographic and individual-level characteristics, factors such as the extent of coalition building, financial resources, political support, and many others have an impact on electoral results. The three case studies in this chapter were selected to highlight Latino group experiences in different regions and in different local contexts in order to compare their pathways to political incorporation.

The first case study is Miami, Florida, a large metropolitan area. In only a few decades Cuban American immigrants have transformed this city and become the dominant politic force in the region. The second study is San Antonio, Texas, where Mexicans, who had led local politics until the 1840s, over time lost control to Anglo newcomers. For the next 130 years Mexican Americans were marginalized politically, even though they were the majority population. In 1981, a Chicano mayor was elected, and in 2001 a Chicano was again elected mayor. We will consider why it took so long to regain political control in a city originally dominated by Mexicans, why Chicanos were unable to retain the mayoral seat after the early 1980s, and how they were able to win the office again in 2001.

The third case study is Los Angeles, California, the location of the largest number of Latinos in the country, yet a city that did not elect a Latino mayor in the twentieth century. Latinos make up the largest ethnic or racial group in Los Angeles but have not been able to build a successful coalition to win the top seat. This case study explores the pathways to office for Latinos in Los Angeles and analyzes some of the reasons why Latino political incorporation has been slow in the nation's second-largest city.

■ Cuban American Politics in South Florida

In some cities in the 1980s, Latinos and African Americans worked together on issues of reapportionment and single-member districts and built multiracial electoral coalitions. In other places, however, strong working relationships were not forged. One location of sharp racial divisions is the south Florida area. The Voting Rights Act and subsequent amendments provided legal justification for fair representation of racial minorities in areas of concentration. While African Americans and Latinos nominally worked together in south Florida, reapportionment after the 1980 and 1990 censuses did not result in greater coalition efforts. Instead, white liberals and African Americans alike viewed the rapid growth of the largely conservative Cuban American community as a threat to their power and authority. The "natural allies" of Latinos in other cities were not their allies in Miami-Dade County. Why did this conflict occur? What pathways to political empowerment did Cuban Americans adopt to achieve electoral success?

As Cubans began to arrive in Miami in the early 1960s, African Americans were embroiled in a long battle for civil rights. After many years of struggle, in the 1970s and 1980s African Americans gained a limited number of elected and appointed positions in Miami-Dade County through the implementation of single-member districts in large cities and concentrations of voters in small communities. They won the majority of city council seats in Opa Locka and Florida City, as well as seats on the city of Miami Commission and the Miami-Dade County Commission. While African American electoral success grew, there were systemic economic problems that remained unresolved and boiled over into four riots in the 1980s, all precipitated by incidents with the police, that "crystallized a widespread anger among black Miamians over both the failure to keep pace economically and the lack of a political voice."[1]

In the 1980s, black Miamians struggled to advance economically in an environment where they were geographically divided into separate neighborhoods that were not connected to one another and politically isolated from potential allies. Historically, due to the race-conscious placement of some black settlements in unincorporated areas, blacks had played an almost insignificant role in the politics of municipalities, with most residing in unincorporated parts of Miami-Dade County where they lacked political clout.[2]

As African American fortunes stalled, Cuban American political fortunes grew dramatically in the 1980s. Much of the political change occurred because of changing demographics in Miami-Dade. A look at the demographics of the county reveals the rapid change from Anglo numerical majority to Latino majority in four decades (see Table 6.1).

The Cuban American population grew in numbers and economic strength; political incorporation came later. At first, prominent exile leaders such as Manolo Reboso and Alfredo Duran, who participated in the Bay of Pigs invasion in Cuba in 1961, escorted Anglo politicians to Little Havana, Hialeah, and Westchester to build ties with them and gain whatever small number of Cuban American votes were available at the time. This symbolic politics approach is typical of first-generation immigrant politics in the United States, where prominent members of the immigrant community serve as a link to society. In the early stages of their resettlement, Cubans refugees had not yet gone through the process of becoming citizens and registering. Anglo politicians would identify community leaders and "would reward them with political patronage, access, and influence."[3] Later, leaders from the Cuban American community developed their own political machines capable of delivering votes.

For their efforts in supporting Governor Askew and other Anglo politicians, both Reboso and Duran were appointed to local political office in Miami beginning in 1972. They were Democrats and heroes within the Cuban exile community because of their participation in the Bay of Pigs invasion in 1961. In 1972, Reboso was appointed to an open seat on the city of Miami Commission, the first Cuban exile to hold this position, and later won reelection in 1974 carrying seventy-one out of eighty-two precincts. In 1973, Duran was appointed to fill a vacancy on the Dade County school board and became the first Hispanic on this board. Even though he was a Democrat, and this was still a traditionally southern

Table 6.1   Miami-Dade County Population, 1960–2000

Year	Non-Hispanic White Number	Percent	Black Number	Percent	Hispanic Number	Percent	Total Number
1960	748,000	79.8	140,000	14.9	50,000	5.3	938,000
1970	788,000	61.6	190,000	14.9	299,000	23.5	1,275,000
1980	776,000	47.3	282,000	17.2	581,000	35.5	1,639,000
1990	614,000	31.2	398,000	20.3	953,000	48.5	1,965,000
2000	466,000	20.7	457,000	20.3	1,291,000	57.3	2,253,000

Sources: Thomas D. Boswell (1994); U.S. Census Bureau (2000b).

Democrat stronghold, he was ousted from office by the voters in the 1974 countywide election due to local Democrats' hostility towards Cuban American candidates.[4] Another Hispanic would not be appointed to the Dade County school board until 1980.

During the 1970s, the number of Cubans who became American citizens more than doubled: in 1970, 25 percent of the Cuban exiles had become citizens, and by 1980, the percentage had risen to 55.[5] Thus Cubans were now poised to expand their electoral influence. In 1978, Jorge Valdes was elected mayor of the city of Sweetwater, and Raul Martinez was elected mayor of Hialeah; both cities bordered Miami and had rapidly grown into Hispanic enclaves with strong Cuban American political influence. Around this time Cubans also began to be elected to office in the Little Havana section of Miami, where they had settled upon arrival in the early 1960s. The highest concentration of Cubans has remained in Little Havana, where they still make up 70–90 percent of the population. While blacks in Miami-Dade County are dispersed, a majority of Hispanics reside in various geographically connected municipalities. These settlement patterns and the large numbers of Cubans in cohesive, contiguous neighborhoods provided a natural base from which to build political power.

As demographic change was occurring, a trend developed of employing district elections at state and local levels. Given the high concentrations of Cubans in densely populated areas of the county, the adoption of district elections facilitated the election of more Hispanic city and county elected officials, and several of them went on to win higher local, state, and federal offices.

During the 1980s, the Cuban exile community began to discard their earlier reservations about participation in American politics. With the political enfranchisement of thousands of newly registered Cuban American voters and the reapportionment of new electoral districts with high concentrations of Hispanics, Cuban candidates had opportunities to quickly move into important elected positions. Based on the redrawing of district boundaries in 1982, Cubans captured three seats in the Florida State Senate and eight seats in the House from the south Florida areas where Cubans were heavily concentrated. Having had virtually no representation up to this point, they gained immediate visibility and political clout. This was a dramatic leap for an ethnic minority group that had had virtually no presence in the area before 1960. In 1988, the burgeoning numbers of Cuban American legislators prompted the formation of the Cuban American Caucus in the state legislature. This caucus continues to this date. It was formed consciously as a Cuban American, not Hispanic, caucus.[6]

Another important milestone for Cuban American politics occurred when Xavier Suarez, a Cuban exile, was elected mayor of the city of Miami in 1985. He defeated former mayor Maurice Ferré, a Puerto Rican

Democrat, and Raul Masvidal, a Republican and Cuban American National Foundation (CANF) board member. By 1986, Latinos totaled 53 percent of Miami's registered voters, held majority control of the city commission, and held almost all of the city's major administrative positions.[7] Since 1985, except for three years in the mid-1990s, the mayor's seat has been held by Cuban Americans. Suarez held the post from 1985 to 1993, lost it, and then won it back in 1997, only to have the election results overturned by the courts because of absentee ballot fraud. Joe Carollo was mayor from 1996 to 1997 and then regained the seat until 2001, when he was ousted after numerous conflicts with members of the city's management team and personal problems.

The 2001 mayor's race included four major candidates, of whom three were Cuban Americans and one was Puerto Rican. Carollo and Suarez split the largest share of Cuban votes in the initial round and did not make the runoff. The runoff pitted Maurice Ferré, the only non-Cuban in the race and a proven vote getter among liberal white and black voters, against Cuban American Manny Diaz, a local attorney with strong business ties who had represented the Miami-based family of Elian Gonzalez.[8] Diaz's victory, like the earlier electoral victories of Carollo and Suarez, was largely attributable to the Cuban American vote. He defeated former mayor Ferré by 55 percent to 45 percent. As Ferre's campaign manager Manny Alfonso put it, "If you're not Cuban in Miami, you don't have a chance."[9] Diaz won 71 percent of the Hispanic vote but only 12 percent of the black vote and 32 percent of the white vote. In the heavily Cuban neighborhoods of Little Havana and Miami West, Diaz averaged 70 percent of the vote.[10] However, Diaz was not strictly a high-identity Cuban mayor: "Diaz seems likely to be a mayor who is Cuban. He didn't make ethnicity an issue during the campaign . . . and has a good rapport with blacks and white non-Hispanics, unlike Carollo."[11]

In addition to engaging in city- and state-level politics, Cuban Americans were busy seeking regional and federal offices in south Florida. From the late 1980s to 2004, four prominent Cuban politicians were elected, solidifying the growing influence of Cuban Americans in the region. In 1989, in a special election to replace longtime congressman Claude Pepper, State Senator Ileana Ros-Lehtinen won by mobilizing 94 percent of the Cuban American vote. Ros-Lehtinen was the first Cuban American candidate for Congress who had a real chance to win. She enjoyed near unanimous support in the Cuban American community. Her opponent carried all the other blocs of voters—Jews, Anglos, and blacks—but they represented only 47 percent of the electorate.[12] In this election, the important factors in the victory were strong political mobilization and solid ethnic-group voting by Cubans. The significance of Ros-Lehtinen's victory went far beyond south Florida, because she became the first Latina and the first Cuban American ever to serve in Congress.

In 1992, following reapportionment, a second Cuban American, State Senator Lincoln Díaz-Balart, was elected to Congress in Miami-Dade County. Here a seat that had always been held by a Democrat was conceded to Cuban American Republicans.[13] In contrast to the polarized election of Ros-Lehtinen, Diaz-Balart had only weak opposition in the Republican primary and no Democratic opponent in the general election. Diaz-Balart comes from a powerful Cuban family that was involved in government politics in the island nation before the Cuban revolution.

Following the 2002 reapportionment, Mario Diaz-Balart, younger brother of Lincoln, became the third Cuban American member of Congress from the south Florida region. Mario Diaz-Balart was born in the United States and began his political career as an aide to Miami mayor Xavier Suarez in 1985. He later served in both houses of the Florida legislature. In 2000, Assemblyman Diaz-Balart headed the committee that drew the new congressional district lines within the state. He then won the seat in November 2002. Thus within twelve years, Cuban Americans won three congressional seats and established themselves as a solid conservative voting bloc in south Florida.

Another political milestone for Cubans and Hispanics began in 1990. Hialeah council member Alex Penelas won a seat on the Miami-Dade County Commission after defeating Jorge "George" Valdés, who in the early 1980s had been the first Cuban American to ever sit on this commission. Penelas, a Cuban American Democrat, was a young attorney fresh out of law school and only recently elected to the Hialeah City Council. At the time, all eight of the county commissioner seats were at-large seats; candidates had to reside in separate geographic districts but had to compete across the county. Penelas won on the strength of Democratic Party support among liberal black and white voters (he received 85 percent of Anglo votes); he did not win a majority of the Cuban vote. In fact he managed to attract only 38 percent of the Latino vote, while Valdés won 62 percent.[14]

The Miami-Dade County government underwent a dramatic structural change in 1992, when it was required to change from at-large to single-member district elections. An alliance of black and Latino leaders had mounted a successful federal court challenge that compelled this change. The courts also abolished the position of county mayor, which left a vacuum, as no commissioner represented the entire county.

County Commissioner Alex Penelas proposed to modify the commission's structure by establishing the position of executive mayor. The person holding this position would be directly accountable to the voters, as opposed to a county manager appointed by the commissioners. The executive mayor would be elected countywide and would provide checks and balances to the newly elected district commissioners. County voters approved the initiative in 1992, with the election to take place in 1996.[15]

This structural change laid the basis for a run for this office by Penelas. In the 1996 race, Penelas was pitted against African American Republican and fellow county commissioner Arthur Teele. Teele sought to win the Hispanic vote by appealing to his party identification. Penelas sought to win Democratic Party votes among black and white voters and have the Hispanic vote swing toward him along ethnic lines.

Penelas won the election. The significance of his electoral victory lay in the power of ethnic voting. Penelas is a Democrat, yet he received virtually the entire Cuban American vote, which normally votes heavily Republican, and virtually none of the African American vote. He won over 60 percent of the total vote, including 60 percent of the Hispanic vote, but only 3 percent of the black vote. Teele won 84 percent of the black vote but could only garner 2 percent of the Hispanic vote.[16] In the racially charged atmosphere of south Florida, party identification meant less for local electoral office than ethnic identification.[17]

This type of bullet voting is not unique to Cubans in south Florida; many ethnic and racial groups in other locales exhibit similar behavior when given the opportunity to vote for "one of their own." The party crossover voting patterns of Cubans is similar to the voting behavior of African Americans in Chicago in the 1980s, when Harold Washington ran for mayor and received more than 97 percent of the votes of fellow African Americans, with an astounding 85 percent voter turnout.[18] Asian Americans crossed traditional party lines and voted for Republican Matt Fong for U.S. senator in California in 1998. During the 2001 Los Angeles mayor's race runoff, Latino candidate Antonio Villaraigosa won between 80 and 90 percent in heavily Latino precincts.[19]

While the vast majority of Cuban Americans have been in the United States only for two generations, most of the first generation of Cuban community leaders trace their fate back to the homeland politics in which their families participated before the Cuban revolution. This is a powerful common denominator for the first generation of political refugees and for many of the American-born second generation of Cuban Americans.

The impact of ethnic voting was never more evident than in the Elian Gonzalez case. As an elected official of a diverse county government, Penelas had managed to govern from the center on most issues. However, during the critical months of the Elian Gonzalez saga in 2000, Penelas returned to his ethnic roots and stood shoulder to shoulder with other Cuban American community leaders and elected officials to oppose U.S. government intervention in the case. This made him a hero in the Cuban American community of south Florida, but many Democrats were angry with him and accused him of being a closet Republican, particularly after he did not intervene in the recount of the presidential race in 2000 in Miami-Dade County. Even though Al Gore won Miami-Dade County by

30,000 votes, Democratic critics felt Penelas should have supported the continuation of the county recount. The difficulty of being both a Democrat and a Cuban American in south Florida is evident in a comment by Penelas: "Let me tell you, it is not easy being a Cuban-American Democrat. It has been very, very difficult for me to remain a Democrat because of the incredible pressure I've gotten from the Cuban-American community that's predominantly Republican."[20]

In recent years, new political voices have emerged in south Florida, however they are still relatively weak. For example, Cuban American Democrat Annie Betancourt was elected to the State Assembly from the Kendall area of Miami-Dade County. The demographics of this district were more racially and politically diverse than in other heavily Cuban districts. Betancourt, who believes in dialogue and easing the embargo with Cuba, ran for the Twenty-fifth Congressional District seat added in 2002. The well-funded and influential Mario Diaz-Balart easily defeated her, however, in the general election.

Although Cuban Americans account for fewer than a third of Florida's Hispanics, all three of the congressional seats, all three of the State Senate seats, and nearly all of the eleven State House seats in majority Hispanic districts were held by Cuban Americans as of the early 2000s. There are both partisan and national-origin factors behind this. Cubans bloc-vote in high percentages, and 90 percent vote Republican. The Republican Party controls the state legislature, where district lines are drawn, and a study by Allan Lichtman found that 83 percent of Cubans in Miami-Dade and Broward counties were put into majority-Hispanic House districts, compared with only 55 percent of non-Cuban Hispanics. This concentrated the votes of Cuban Hispanics, whereas the votes of non-Cuban Hispanics were more diluted.[21]

While Cuban domination of Miami-Dade politics will continue into the foreseeable future, in neighboring Broward County a more diverse contingent of South Americans and Puerto Ricans as well as Cuban Americans is being elected to office. In Broward County, which is 18 percent Hispanic, compared to neighboring Miami-Dade's 60 percent Hispanic population, there are six Hispanics, from judges to city commissioners, who hold political office. Many Broward residents are recent arrivals from South America. There are thousands of Venezuelans, Peruvians, Argentines, and Colombians living in Broward, and many of them are more likely to be tuned into their home country via Internet than into local politics. Some are dual citizens and are still allowed to participate in their home country politics; others, such as Cubans and Nicaraguans, are barred from participating in home country politics. Many of Central and South America's wealthy purchase homes in south Florida as a hedge against political unrest in their home countries.[22]

Large numbers of Puerto Ricans have moved to Orlando and other parts of Florida to work in the service economy, and their Democratic-leaning voting patterns have created another node of Latino voters in the state. In the coming decade, the Latino vote in Florida will be more contested and fluid.

■ Mexican American Politics in San Antonio

The contemporary struggle for political empowerment for Mexican Americans is largely a post–World War II phenomena. However, to understand current politics, it is necessary to look back briefly at San Antonio's history and race relations. One hundred years before the establishment of the Republic of Texas in 1836 and the state of Texas in 1845, Tejanos exercised self-government through the *ayuntamiento*, a local form of government. The colonization of Spanish Texas began in 1716, and the province's first *ayuntamiento,* called San Fernando de Bexar, formed in 1731. This form of government continued into the Mexican rule of Texas, 1821–1836, and its influence persisted afterward.[23] White settlers and a few Tejanos declared their independence from Mexico in 1836. Subsequently, a war of independence and eventually a war of conquest was waged by the United States against the Mexican government to gain control of the land and resources in the Southwest.

In 1837, the Republic of Texas gave San Antonio a municipal charter, under which the city formed an eight-person board of aldermen. The first councilmen were all Spanish surnamed, and the mayor was Anglo. In the years following 1836, city councils were composed of a majority of Mexicans. Up to 1844 the Mexican electorate outnumbered the Anglo vote in San Antonio. In 1840 and 1842, Juan Seguin was elected as mayor; however, he was to be the last Mexican American mayor until Henry Cisneros in the 1980s. By 1845, European Americans had squeezed Mexican Americans out of their dominant position on the city council.[24] The Mexican elite's influence declined as the newcomers monopolized banks and commercial enterprises.[25]

In 1850, Mexican Bexareños composed 47 percent of the population; by 1880 their share had declined to 30 percent, and by 1900, the Mexican population was only 25 percent of Bexar County, where the city of San Antonio is located. From the 1880s until the 1940s, white political machines were able to maintain power through the use of patronage. World War II brought military bases to San Antonio, however, and with them came federal civil service jobs that the local political machine could not control. Mexican Americans remained marginalized from local politics.[26] As alternatives, Mexicans built strong community organizations; many of these groups were based in or had active chapters in San Antonio, including the League of United Latin American Citizens (LULAC), which formed in 1929. After World War II, middle-class Latinos in San Antonio, particularly businessmen, formed ethnic chambers of commerce. Other local Mexican veterans' organizations appeared, such as the Loyal American Democrats. Civic and political groups such as the West Side Voters League and the Alamo Democrats also formed in San Antonio.[27]

Meanwhile, the Good Government League (GGL) formed in 1954, the latest in a long series of Anglo local political machines. This group was based in the affluent north side of the city. One of the organization's strengths was nominating slates of candidates for city council. In the period 1955–1971, the GGL won seventy-seven of eighty-one seats. The council candidates "consisted primarily of Anglos (78 percent), although there were a few token Mexican Americans (one in 1955, two from 1957–1971, and three in 1971)."[28] The GGL controlled not only who got elected but, more important, the policy agenda. The Anglo businessmen who led the GGL controlled the city's economic development and enhanced their economic interests.

In 1969, the GGL began to falter as the Chicano community began to organize to challenge the at-large electoral structure of city elections and to run independent candidates from the barrio. The Committee for Barrio Betterment formed in 1969, composed of Mexican American Youth Organization (MAYO) activists and Barrios Unidos, a community organization. This group was not tied to the Democratic Party machine nor to the GGL, which had battled each other for electoral control for many years.[29] While not successful due to the at-large electoral system, the Committee for Barrio Betterment swept the Chicano precincts against all the GGL candidates.

From 1971 to 1975, Mexican American voters expressed their opposition to the ruling Anglo political elite by supporting Mexican American candidates who were not supported by the GGL, rather than Anglo and Mexican American GGL candidates. From 1971 to 1973 the GGL's Mexican American candidates received less than half as many votes in the predominantly Mexican American precincts as they did in predominantly Anglo precincts.[30] In 1971, there was high voter interest in the Chicano community sparked by a campaign for mayor by Peter Torres, who challenged the GGL candidate, John Gatti. Voter turnout climbed from 33 percent in 1969 to 53 percent in 1971, "a level of participation which has not been repeated since."[31] The 1971 election marked the beginning of the end for the GGL, as its grip on the nomination of city council members began to weaken. In 1973, several prominent GGLers broke ranks and backed other non-GGLers, and GGL-backed candidates won only four seats. Conflict among San Antonio's elites enabled new organizations and political voices to emerge.

One important independent voice that formed during this period was the Citizens Organized for Public Service (COPS), which came together in 1974 to demand greater equity in city services and for improvements in the barrios of the south and west sides. COPS was initiated by Eddie Cortes, who was trained by Saul Alinksy's Industrial Areas Foundation in Chicago. He believed that for an organization to last, it must be anchored by institutions with deep ties to the community: "They discarded the PTAs as too caught up in school board politics, and settled instead on the Catholic parish networks."[32] Although COPS did not formally endorse candidates for political office, the organization worked through the Catholic parishes to conduct voter registration drives and to improve the political influence of those who had been historically locked out. According to two scholars of Mexican American politics, "The concentration of Mexicans in the Westside, and the presence of a stable community encouraged the growth of COPS and made possible an effective voter registration program."[33] COPS became an influential independent voice that remains active in San Antonio politics today.

A beneficiary of the transition in political leadership who brought his own personal political skills was Henry Cisneros. Part of the Cisneros family had arrived in New Mexico long before the American Revolution, while Henry's grandfather had come from Mexico in the aftermath of the Mexican revolution. The Cisneros family was well known and active in both Mexican and American politics. Henry Cisneros was a professor of public administration who had received his education in Ivy League universities after growing up in west San Antonio. He returned to San Antonio in 1974 and began his political career as part of the GGL slate of city council candidates in 1975. His uncle, Ruben Munguia, an influential political operative in San Antonio politics, recommended him for the GGL slate, and the GGL, desperate to find new potential leaders, nominated him. Cisneros won his seat with much assistance from the influential GGL. He ran his own campaign and at age twenty-seven became the youngest councilman in the city's history; that year he was the only GGL candidate to win without a runoff. Cisneros won the election with 52 percent of the vote. He received more votes among Anglos than from Mexican Americans. For example, in heavily Spanish-surnamed precincts Cisneros received only 44 percent of the vote.[34]

Meanwhile, a recent annexation into the city had prompted a review by the U.S. Department of Justice based on the 1975 Voting Rights Amendment. The annexation, which added more white voters, diluted the majority status of the Mexican American population. The Justice Department indicated that unless the city changed its method of electing council members to provide equitable representation of language and racial minorities, the area would have to be deannexed.[35] The city council proposed, and voters agreed, to change the city charter to replace at-large elections with a council of ten persons elected from single-member districts and a mayor elected at large.

Cisneros joined in the successful campaign for passage of the referendum. The transition to single-member districts created potential for institutionalized independent voices from the diverse communities in San Antonio. The 1977 elections produced the first city council with a majority of racial minority members. Mexican Americans won five of the ten seats, and an additional seat was won by an African American candidate. This was a major shift, not only in the descriptive representation of the city council but in the transfer of power to a more diverse set of political leaders, less tied to the traditional power brokers of the GGL. While the new commission's public policy did not radically shift away from the progrowth policies of previous commissions, it signaled the end of the "business as usual" type of politics in the city.

The 1981 election for mayor and city council were a watershed for Mexican American politics. For the first time in the United States, a Mexican American was elected as mayor of a major city. Cisneros won a convincing victory, capturing 64 percent of the vote, with large majorities in the predominantly Mexican American precincts and an average of 43 percent of the vote in predominantly Anglo Districts 8 and 10. Cisneros relied heavily on energizing the Latino, African American, and labor votes; the San Antonio Teachers Council, for example, ran his phone bank operation. Cisneros was an effective ethnic candidate who relied on his westside base of support and won in eight of the ten city council districts. He was defeated only in Districts 8 and 10, which were majority white.

When Cisneros vacated his council seat to seek the office of mayor in 1981, a less well known but equally important political effort unfolded. A group of local Chicana activists established an informal group to discuss running a Chicana for the city council seat, and they nominated Maria Berriozábal to run. The Chicana activists backed Berriozábal during a difficult campaign, and she went on to win election as the first Mexican American woman to serve on the city council. Her victory was viewed as a victory for all Chicanas. Berriozábal's election grew out of a collective process, and she brought a new style of politics that included empowerment for the neighborhoods she represented. She was known for bringing people she represented to the council chambers to speak for themselves, which was her definition of providing leadership.[36] Berriozábal's victory signaled the emergence of a Chicana movement capable of electing its own candidates, and it was a demonstration of the electoral potential of Latinas nationwide. Similar efforts took place to elect Gloria Molina to the California State Assembly from Los Angeles in the early 1980s.

During Cisneros's time as mayor, he governed from the center with a progrowth economic development philosophy but did not alienate his Chicano and Mexican constituency as he addressed issues of jobs, education, and improving neighborhoods. Mayor Cisneros supported major development projects, including the Alamodome sports arena, and annexation and tax breaks for the Sea World and Fiesta Texas theme parks. His administration lasted until 1989, when he decided not to run again.

The personal politics of Cisneros did not translate into another Mexican American winning the mayor's seat. Former mayor Lila Cockrell, who was not Latina, succeeded him. The Cockrell victory signaled maintenance of the business development philosophy in the city. Cockrell left after two years, and Mexican American council member Berriozábal ran for mayor in 1991. Berriozábal lost in a runoff, and it would be another ten years before a Mexican American would wage a serious contest to win the mayor's seat. It took until 1995 for Mexican Americans to regain five seats on the city council, and until 1997 for the sixth seat to be captured. Then for the first time the descriptive representation on the council reflected the city's Mexican population.

In 2001, city council member Ed Garza won election at the age of thirty-two as San Antonio's second Mexican American mayor. He parlayed his experience as an architect who worked for a development firm to secure business community support. He was not viewed as a threat to the progrowth interests that heavily influence politics and economic decision making in the city. According to one observer, "San Antonio's electorate is very divided in racial and ethnic terms. Anglo districts vote for Anglos; Hispanics vote for Hispanics."[37] Even though Mexican Americans are the majority population, an Anglo can more easily win a mayoral election because Anglos are usually more likely to vote than Mexican Americans. Mexican American candidates must cross over and appeal to Anglos to win an election.[38]

In contrast to Cisneros, who had campaigned heavily in the Latino community, Garza campaigned less in the Mexican neighborhoods and more in the heavily Anglo northside communities, as he counted on winning the support of the Mexican American community. A study conducted by the William C. Velásquez Institute found that nearly 97 percent of Latino registered voters cast their vote for Garza, while only 52 percent of whites voted for him. Latinos represented 60 percent of Garza's total support.[39] Latinos represented 36.6 percent of the total votes cast, though the Latino population is nearly 59 percent of the city.

While Los Angeles voters chose to elect an Anglo Democrat for mayor in 2001, San Antonio voters, both Mexican American and white, supported a Mexican American candidate. It appears that even in a city with a long history of marginalizing Mexican Americans and deeply racialized voting patterns, a Mexican American candidate who can appeal to both Mexican and white voters can succeed in citywide elections. The electoral victories of Cisneros and Garza demonstrate the power of different types of crossover candidates.

■ Latino Political Incorporation in Los Angeles

In contrast to Cuban Americans' rapid rise to political incorporation in Miami-Dade County, the rise to power of Mexican Americans in Los Angeles has come through a long, slow process. Very different from a new refugee population arriving with both economic and political resources, the Mexican population in Los Angeles have had a visible presence since the 1700s. Mexicans actually provided the political leadership for the city until the mid-1800s. Unlike the Cuban refugees, who were provided with various government assistance programs upon arrival, Los Angeles' population of Mexicans was ignored by the federal and local government and was forced to live in segregated neighborhoods in the eastern portion of the city and in unincorporated East Los Angeles. A manipulation of boundaries between city and county residents divided the population in half and weakened the political strength of the Mexican American community. This artificial political division was part of a much larger political disenfranchisement of Mexicans in the eastside area and throughout the state. District boundaries for state assembly and senate seats divided barrios into safe seats for white incumbents, while the political establishment largely marginalized Mexican Americans.[40]

The contemporary political incorporation of Latinos in Los Angeles began after World War II, with eastside community activist Edward Roybal's election to the Los Angeles City Council in 1949. Roybal held that office until 1962, when he ran and won a seat in Congress from the East Los Angeles area. That same year the city council seats were reapportioned, and East Los Angeles was divided among seven council districts. As noted by one scholar, "As a result of this fragmentation, Latinos could not be a majority in any one of the city's fifteen districts, although they heavily populated seven of the council's fifteen districts."[41] Although Roybal sought to have another Latino appointed to fill his unexpired term, he had been the only racial minority on the city council, and African Americans successfully lobbied the council to appoint Gilbert Lindsey to this seat. Lindsey then became the city's first African American officeholder.[42]

From 1962 to 1985, no Mexican or other Latinos were elected to city council or citywide offices in Los Angeles. This period was politically volatile, and the lack of elected local leadership weakened the influence of Latinos in city politics. Latino political influence in Los Angeles grew, however, at the federal and state levels. In addition to Congressman

Roybal, two Mexican Americans, Richard Alatorre (elected to the State Assembly in 1972) and Art Torres (elected to the State Assembly in 1974), were the other Latino elected officials from the Los Angeles area in the pre-1980s period. Not only did these elected officials have to represent the interests of their constituents at the state and federal levels, but they also became the de facto political leaders of California's whole Mexican American community because they were the only Latinos elected to the state and federal office at the time. By all accounts, the local political incorporation of Latinos during this period was low.

The gerrymandering of Los Angeles area political districts to limit the political participation of Mexican Americans, combined with their historically low voting rates, made it extremely difficult to elect a Mexican American to the city council. In the vacuum of leadership, outsider groups such as the La Raza Unida Party (LRUP) challenged the dominance of the two-party system and sought to establish their own electoral base in the early 1970s in the Los Angeles area. The LRUP ran a candidate for a state assembly seat in East Los Angeles, and although it was unsuccessful, it demonstrated that at least a segment of the Mexican American community was willing to consider third-party candidates. In 1974, the City Terrace chapter of the LRUP unsuccessfully led a campaign to incorporate East Los Angeles as a city. Unincorporated East Los Angeles included over 100,000 residents, more than 90 percent of them Mexican. Real estate and business interests that opposed the incorporation effort defeated this effort, and the Mexican American community remained politically weak.[43]

Meanwhile in the city of Los Angeles during the 1970s and 1980s, a biracial coalition was being forged between white liberals and African Americans. African American Tom Bradley was elected to city council in 1963, lost a racially charged mayoral race in 1969, and won the mayor's seat in 1973. He held this office for twenty years, retiring in 1993. While working-class Latinos were strong supporters of Bradley, the Latino community was at best a junior partner in this coalition and received only limited policy rewards and a few notable appointments to positions in the Bradley administration. Latinos were largely viewed as uninterested in politics. They had very low voter turnouts in city elections, and their voice and votes did not play a major role in Los Angeles politics until the 1980s.

Furthermore, as noted, a large percentage of the Latino population lived in unincorporated East Los Angeles, which bordered the eastern portion of the city. These residents of the county of Los Angeles were unable to vote in city elections. During the period between the 1960s and 1980s, Latinos were heavily concentrated in two council districts, the Ninth and Fourteenth. Gilbert Lindsay held the ninth council seat until he died in office in 1990. He had held this seat for twenty-seven years, and when it became vacant, another African American, Rita Walters, was appointed to fill it.

The Fourteenth Council District was held by two Anglo politicians from 1943 to 1985. This district included the heavily Latino East Los Angeles and the largely white Eagle Rock neighborhood. While numerically it had a smaller number of residents, it turned out a higher number of voters, thus perpetuating Anglo rule on the eastside. Art Snyder held the seat from 1967 to 1985, when he resigned after a strong challenge by community activist Steve Rodriguez in the 1983 council race and after surviving a recall effort in 1984. While East L.A. was in turmoil from the late 1960s into the 1970s, with the walkouts of tens of thousands of Latino high school and junior high school students in 1968, the Chicano Moratorium against the Vietnam War in 1970, and numerous other struggles, Latinos were forced to operate in a political system where each city council seat represented 200,000 people. Without strong financing, it was not possible to challenge incumbents who could afford to mount door-to-door campaigns and mail out campaign literature. Also, many residents were not yet citizens, and many of those who were citizens could not vote. So Snyder remained in office in the fourteenth council seat for eighteen years, which only added to the frustration and powerlessness of Los Angeles Latinos.

Meanwhile, African Americans in the city were more successful than Latinos in winning political representation, city jobs, and appointed positions.[44] While African Americans were able to win three of the fifteen city council seats, Latinos had no representatives on the council from 1962 to 1985. In 1985, however, Mexican American state assemblyman Richard Alatorre gave up his seat to seek the city council position vacated by Snyder. He was elected in the overwhelmingly Latino Fourteenth District, twenty-three years after Roybal had left the council. In 1986, as a result of a federal lawsuit contesting the 1982 reapportionment of district lines, an additional Latino district was created, resulting in the election of Gloria Molina to the city council in 1987.

The emergence of Molina and Alatorre in the 1980s reflected not the simple addition of brown faces to the black and white biracial coalition but the importance of the use of legal challenges and political recruitment networks by Latinos. Alatorre had emerged as a legislative aide to a non-Latino assembly member in the 1960s, and by 1972 he had won a seat in the assembly in an increasingly Latino district. In 1982, he was placed in charge of the assembly committee responsible for reapportionment. Most of the Latinos holding significant elected positions in the early 1980s gathered in a meeting and decided whom to support for various positions that would become available following reapportionment.

Two legislative aides sought support of the group for the state assembly seat that was vacated by Alatorre's move to the city council in 1982. Richard Polanco, an aide to Alatorre, and Gloria Molina, then an aide to assembly member Art Torres, competed against each other in the Democratic primary, and Molina won the primary and the general elections. At this point Molina became the first of a number of Mexican American women to run and win office in Los Angeles. In 1986, Molina again challenged the Chicano political establishment by not supporting its candidate for the seat vacated by Alatorre, who had won election to the Los Angeles City Council. In 1987, Molina decided to run for another seat, the vacated District 1 council position. She bested the Alatorre-supported candidate handily and was now well positioned to achieve an even more significant electoral post.

Molina was the daughter of a farmworker who had worked in the Carter administration in the 1970s; she built a grassroots base of young and working-class Chicanas into a strong electoral machine. As an outsider, Molina challenged the Anglo-black political establishment and the old-boy network of Chicano officials.[45] In the 1980s and early 1990s, the Alatorre and Molina camps put up rival candidates for almost every local election in the Los Angeles area. The recruitment networks provided money, resources, expertise, and campaign workers. Only a rival network could effectively compete with this level of campaign organization.[46]

In addition to the lawsuit charging malapportionment of city council districts, another lawsuit filed by the Department of Justice and the Mexican American Legal Defense and Education Fund (MALDEF) challenged Los Angeles County's 1981 reapportionment plan, which combined heavily Latino districts with white-dominant communities to dilute the Latino vote. The five members of the Los Angeles Board of Supervisors served a population of 8.5 million people and controlled a budget of over $13 billion in 1990. There had not been a Mexican elected to this board for 115 years. In June 1990, a U.S. district court ruled in *Garza* v. *County of Los Angeles* that the supervisors had violated the federal Voting Rights Act. New district lines were drawn to create a district that was 71 percent Latino population. In a 1991 election, Los Angeles City Council member Molina, after a hard-fought campaign against three other Latinos, including her former boss Torres, was elected to the board of supervisors.[47]

When Molina left the city council to run for the board of supervisors, a seat opened up on the council. Again with an Alatorre-backed opponent, Mike Hernandez won the endorsement of Supervisor Molina and was elected to office in 1991. The growing influence of Molina acted as a counterbalance to the more entrenched Alatorre forces. In addition to redistricting at the local government level, reapportionment for congressional districts occurred following the 1990 census. In the newly redrawn Thirtieth Congressional District, the conflict between the Molina and Alatorre forces continued as longtime representative Edward Roybal resigned and both sides put up candidates. The Molina-backed candidate, assembly member

Xavier Becerra, went on to win the contest. In the nearby newly created Twenty-fifth Congressional District, Roybal's daughter, Lucille Roybal-Allard, won easily and became the first Mexican American congress-woman.

The 1990 reapportionment brought a dramatic increase in the number of Latinos elected to office in the Los Angeles area. The redistricting of the Seventh District created the conditions to elect a third Latino to the city council. As Latino numbers continued to grow, other groups felt a corresponding decline in their political influence. In 1994, another Latino, Richard Alarcón, was elected to the city council from the northeast San Fernando Valley. Alarcón held this position for four years before he left to run for a state senator position in 1998. His razor-close election to this state senate seat showed the growing influence of Latinos in the San Fernando Valley section of the city and county of Los Angeles. For the first time, a Latino held a seat traditionally held by an Anglo. Perhaps more significant was that Alarcón won his election by defeating a prominent, and well-funded, former assembly member, Richard Katz. Alarcón's ability to turn out new Latin voters demonstrated how Latinos could be mobilized. Spurred by his get-out-the-vote effort, Latino participation doubled, rising from 6 percent of the primary voters in the district in 1994 to 12 percent in 1998.[48] Alarcón's victory was in part prompted by the rapid growth in the Latino population in the San Fernando Valley, which had reached 27 percent of the total valley population; in some parts of the northeast valley, Latinos are now the overwhelming majority.

After Alarcón vacated his city council seat, twenty-six-year-old Alex Padilla won a hard-fought campaign in 1999, defeating the candidate backed by the Los Angeles labor movement and Alarcón. Padilla, the son of Mexican immigrants, had returned from college on the East Coast and gotten involved in local politics. The Padilla race was preceded by the 1996 election of Tony Cardenas to the Twentieth Assembly District seat in the same part of the San Fernando Valley. Padilla worked for Cardenas and was in turn supported by him for his race. These two Valley Latinos have developed a stance of independence from the eastside political machines. They are not tied to the Molina forces nor to any other eastside forces. This represents a growth in Latino political power in another section of the city and county of Los Angeles and enhances the overall presence of Latinos in political power in the region.

Two later electoral campaigns provide further evidence of a diversity of views and a jockeying for position among Latinos, reflecting the growing sophistication, intergenerational conflicts, and political influence of Latinos in Los Angeles: the 2001 race for mayor and the 2003 race for the Fourteenth District. The 2001 race for mayor of Los Angeles demonstrated that the Latino community is not monolithic, as it initially backed different

Latino candidates, Antonio Villaraigosa and Xavier Becerra, who competed in the general primary. Villaraigosa obtained the largest vote total in the nonpartisan primary but did not receive 50 percent of the vote, so he was forced into a runoff with the next highest vote getter, City Attorney James Hahn.

While most Latinos backed Villaraigosa's candidacy, then assembly member Tony Cardenas and council member Padilla did not support him in either the general contest or the runoff with Hahn. Instead, they backed Hahn, an Anglo. Hahn was also endorsed by Richard Polanco, the former state senator who had lost to Gloria Molina in the 1982 state assembly contest that launched her electoral career. Polanco and the two San Fernando Valley officeholders were the most prominent Latinos to support the opponent of Villaraigosa.

In the runoff, Villaraigosa did very well among Latinos, garnering 82 percent of the vote, but he was unsuccessful in securing the majority of white and black votes and lost to Hahn. While Latinos were nearly 50 percent of the population in Los Angeles in 2000, they were only 22 percent of the voters (see Table 6.2).

The final vote total showed that moderate and conservative voters, African Americans, and San Fernando Valley voters were more inclined to support the liberal white Democrat, Hahn, who was viewed as tough on crime. Hahn won a decisive 80 percent of the black vote. This was due to several reasons. First, he had longtime family ties to the African American community, something that Villaraigosa did not have. His father was the longtime county supervisor for the area and had helped mentor a number of senior African American leaders there. African American politicians decided en masse, except for one prominent leader, to back Hahn in exchange for Hahn's continued support of African American police chief Bernard Parks. In the aftermath of the L.A. riots of 1992, police-community relations had been poor; Parks rose to become police chief in 1997 and had strong back-

Table 6.2   Exit Poll Results for Los Angeles Mayor in 2001 (percentage)

	% of All Voters	Hahn	Villaraigosa
Total	100	54	46
White voters	52	59	41
Black voters	17	80	20
Latino voters	22	18	82
Asian voters	6	65	35
Liberals	49	41	59
Moderates	29	62	38
Conservatives	22	73	27

Source: Los Angeles Times (2001).

ing in the African American community.[49] Another reason for Villaraigosa's defeat, according to some observers, was Hahn's use of negative campaign materials that trafficked in racial stereotypes, including a last-minute campaign ad that criticized Villaraigosa for supporting amnesty for a drug dealer and linked his image with the use of crack cocaine.

However, overriding any other factor at play in the mayor's race were the raw numbers in Los Angeles politics. Latinos made up 46.5 percent of the population but were not an equivalent percentage of the voters. The Latino electoral participation has been rising rapidly, from 8 percent in the 1993 mayoral election to 22 percent in 2001, but it remains far below a level commensurate with the Latino population. Again, part of the reason is that Latinos are a young population, with a sizable number still too young to vote. The other factor is a high proportion of noncitizens, including undocumented persons who reside in the city.

Beyond victory or defeat in this particular election, a significant potential ally for some Latino politicians emerged. Villaraigosa was a former union organizer, and he won the backing of the Los Angeles labor movement, which is growing and energized. The Los Angeles County Federation of Labor is a strong, well-organized political machine, under the leadership of Miguel Contreras, a former United Farm Workers activist. The L.A. County Federation voted to back Villaraigosa and put hundreds of its members into the streets to help elect him, even after several union locals with large numbers of African Americans had decided to back Hahn. The L.A. County Federation has more than 800,000 members in 350 local unions. It is perhaps the most influential labor council in America and has helped elect local, state, and federal officials who support labor's agenda.

The building of a labor-Latino alliance in Los Angeles represents a convergence of shared agendas by two rapidly growing segments of the population. Organized labor, opposite to its trend in many places, has been growing in Los Angeles County. More important, the county federation has brought together various unions from the public and private sectors, predominantly those representing immigrants, to work to elect labor-friendly candidates, many of whom were Latino. The Latino population is also heavily immigrant, working class, and increasingly unionized. Many are becoming citizens and registering to vote. In the city of Los Angeles in 2001, union leader Contreras estimated that 175,000 union members were registered to vote and that 31 percent of them were Latino.[50] While these numbers are not large enough to swing a citywide election by themselves, in combination with other allies they can have a decisive impact on a city council, state assembly or senate, or congressional race. The changing demographics, the increase in Latino voters, and the strategic alliance between Latinos and the burgeoning labor movement will most likely play a significant role in upcoming elections in the Los Angeles area, helping to shape positions on such critical issues as affordable housing, living wages, and economic development in the neighborhoods.

Since 2001, four Latinos have been newly elected to the city council, including Eric Garcetti, District 13, and Ed Reyes, District 1, in 2001, and Tony Cardenas, District 6, and Antonio Villaraigosa, District 14, in 2003. By 2003, then, with Padilla, five of the fifteen Los Angeles City Council members, or one-third of the council, were Latinos. While Latinos now have significant influence on a council in which they had no members as recently as 1984, there is not unanimity among them. These differences reflect the reality that these officeholders have risen to office in different parts of the city, with different constituencies. The diversity indicates that the dominant political machines of the 1980s and early 1990s no longer exist in the same fashion nor do they control the political fates of Latino politicians. While Gloria Molina, the senior locally elected official, is still a powerful figure, there are others who have important influence as well, including the San Fernando Valley politicians, the Latino congressional members, and new political leaders, many of whom are women. With the establishment of term limits in California politics, the jockeying for positions, particularly in the heavily Latino Los Angeles County, is constant and relentless, and at times it overshadows the important problems that need to be addressed in the community.

The ongoing conflicts that erupted within the Latino community in 2001 were again evident in the 2003 race for the Fourteenth City Council District seat. The race pitted Los Angeles City Council member Nick Pacheco against Antonio Villaraigosa. Pacheco had won his seat in 1999 in a crowded field seeking to replace Richard Alatorre, who had decided not to run for reelection after holding office for fourteen years. Eastsider Pacheco, having failed to win the support of Gloria Molina and State Senator Richard Polanco in that first run for office, had built alliances instead with Los Angeles Mayor Richard Riordan and Congressman Xavier Becerra. When Becerra ran for mayor in 2001, Pacheco backed him. When Pacheco came up for reelection in 2003, he had Becerra's and ex-mayor Riordan's support. However, in a two-person race, Villaraigosa, who also had strong ties to the district, more political endorsements, and an effective get-out-the-vote operation, won 56 percent of the vote and defeated Pacheco.

■ Conclusion

These three case studies highlight the complexity of Latino political incorporation. In three large Sunbelt cities with different political histories, economies, and political cultures, Latinos have achieved varying levels of incorporation. Latinos in Miami have gained full incorporation in just a few decades of concerted political activity. In San Antonio, Mexican Americans had what would be called in labor relations "a break in service." Before 1848, they led the city out of the transition from Mexican province to independent republic to statehood, and then they were unceremoniously excused and did not appear again as serious political actors until the 1960s when, in less than a decade of concerted effort, they retook the mayor's seat. Twenty years later, they took the majority of the city council; however, it would take until 2001 for the Chicano majority to obtain in the electoral arena what had been theirs in the 1840s: the majority leadership of the council and the mayor's seat. In San Antonio, Chicanos have only recently become fully incorporated. In Los Angeles, Latinos have yet to achieve full political incorporation. They have finally won one-third of the council seats in a city where they are the dominant ethnic group but not yet the majority of the population. Structural barriers, low voter turnout, racial polarized voting, and internal conflicts have weakened their power base in a polyglot world city, slowing progress toward political incorporation. Latinos in Los Angeles have achieved more than weak incorporation but have not yet gained strong incorporation. This could take the form of the election of a Latino for mayor and/or the election of several more Latino city council members. However, given the demographics of the city and chronic low voter turnout rates, Latinos will need to build alliances with other racial and ethnic groups to advance toward full incorporation.

These three case studies provide a window into the difficulties of translating population numbers into electoral victories. In each location, Latinos have grappled with the problem of voter registration and turnout. In Miami, Cuban Americans were able to overcome this hurdle more quickly. In San Antonio, consistent voter registration efforts coupled with higher voter turnout rates of Mexican Americans enhanced Mexican American candidates' opportunities to win office. In Los Angeles, the city with the largest Latino population in the nation, the reality is that only a relatively small percentage is able and willing to vote. As Latino voting rates increase, so will the chances for stronger Latino representation.

Together these studies highlight the diversity of political situations confronting Latinos in politics in large urban centers. Other large cities with significant Latino populations, such as New York, Chicago, Houston, and San Jose, also show that the structural barriers, the political obstacles, and the pathways to elected office and political incorporation are complex and multifaceted. Taken as a whole, these case studies provide a glimpse of the diversity of methods being employed by Latinos to obtain political power in large urban communities. In the next chapter, we will explore how Latinos in an agricultural community wrested power from entrenched agricultural and business interests and transformed the city of Salinas into a model of successful Latino political incorporation.

■ Notes

1. G. J. Grenier and M. Castro (1998), p. 37.
2. C. Warren and D. Moreno (2003), p. 287.
3. M. Gonzalez-Pando (1998), p. 60.
4. Ibid.
5. Ibid., p. 61.
6. D. Moreno and C. Warren (1992), p. 135.
7. R. Mohl (1989), p. 149.
8. C. Warren and D. Moreno (2003).
9. K. Ross, J. Weaver, and O. Corral (2001).
10. Ibid.
11. T. Bridges (2001).
12. D. Moreno (1996).
13. D. Moreno and C. Warren (1992), p. 179.
14. G. J. Grenier et al. (1994), p. 183.
15. D. Moreno, K. Hill, and L. Cue (n.d.).
16. G. J. Grenier and M. Castro (2001).
17. D. Moreno, K. Hill, and L. Cue (n.d.).
18. A. R. Hirsch (2001).
19. Tomas Rivera Policy Institute (2001).
20. A. C. Smith (2003).
21. S. V. Date (2002).
22. J. Kripalani (2003).
23. The Handbook of Texas Online.
24. J. A. Booth and D. R. Johnson (1983), p. 6.
25. R. Acuña (1988), p. 29.
26. C. Muñoz, Jr., and C. Henry (1990).
27. "Tejano Politics" (n.d.).
28. J. A. Booth and D. R. Johnson (1983), p. 23.
29. R. Rosales (2000), pp. 118–119.
30. R. Brischetto, C. L. Correll, and R. M. Stevens (1983).
31. Ibid., p. 85.
32. J. D. Sekul (1983).
33. C. Navarro and R. Acuña (1990), p. 213.
34. K. Diehl and J. Jarboe (1985).
35. R. Brischetto, C. L. Correll, and R. M. Stevens (1983), p. 88.
36. R. Rosales (2000), pp. 163–167.
37. H. Saunders, quoted in B. Zars (2001).
38. B. Zars (2001).
39. J. Trejo (2001).
40. R. Acuña (1988), p. 318.
41. J. Regalado (1988).
42. R. Sonenshein (1993), pp. 43–44.
43. R. Acuña (1988), p. 368.
44. R. Sonenshein (1997), pp. 52–53.

45. R. Griswold del Castillo and A. De León (1996), p. 156.

46. F. Guerra (1991), pp. 130–131.

47. R. Acuña (1996), pp. 72–74.

48. R. Dallek (1998).

49. After winning the mayor's race, Hahn decided not to support Bernard Parks to continue as Los Angeles police chief; in 2002 he was replaced with a former New York City police chief. In 2003 Parks ran for and won a seat on the Los Angeles City Council.

50. G. Skelton (2001).

7

A Surge of Representation in the Salinas Valley

T he city of Salinas, California, is a model of how a well-organized predominantly Mexican-origin community can achieve a fairly high level
of political incorporation within a short period of time. From 1980 to 2001,
Latinos went from zero representation in local political offices to winning a
number of significant electoral empowerment victories, including the
majority on local school boards and the Salinas City Council, the first
Mexican American Monterey County supervisor in the twentieth century,
and the first state assembly member from the Salinas-Watsonville-Hollister
area. They were also successful in both establishing district elections for
local judges and electing a progressive Chicano judge to the Superior
Court. The rapid transformation to visible Latino representation at the local
level occurred after many years of hard work by a dedicated group of
Chicano community activists and offers lessons for how to build Latino
political power at the local level.

This chapter is a case study of these group efforts; in particular, it
focuses on the potential to expand policy benefits through substantive political representation. Unlike large urban communities, where a viable biracial
or multiracial coalition was viewed as a necessary requirement for minority
political incorporation in the 1960s and 1970s, Salinas's Latinos have
achieved strong electoral representation largely through their own political
efforts. After gaining political control, Latino political leaders have
addressed issues of growth, housing, and quality of life, helping reallocate
policy benefits to the Mexican American community in ways that had not
been possible under all-white local administrations. How this occurred, and
why, is important for the study of racial coalition politics.

Salinas is also important because in most large urban contexts ethnic
and racial groups are constantly jockeying for greater political influence
with white voters and among themselves, but in the majority of Southwest
locations where Mexican Americans reside, the main demographic groups

161

in close proximity to one another are Anglos and Latinos. It is in these suburban and rural communities that Mexican Americans have an excellent opportunity to advance politically as their numbers increase. In most cases they do not have to compete with another racial minority group, such as African Americans, for political influence and electoral positions. In many of these communities, they are the majority population, and as more Mexican Americans undergo naturalization, register to vote, and become politically active, the possibility of increasing the ranks of Latino elected officials will grow exponentially. For example, in Los Angeles, California's largest city, five of the fifteen council members as of 2004 were Latino. Even if Latinos were to win another two or three seats over the next few years, this would not substantially change the overall numbers and clout of Latinos nationally. However, if Latinos can get elected in other suburban and regional center cities such as Salinas, the total number of Latino elected officials will grow dramatically. Not only is the Salinas case study significant for its local transformative value, but it offers important lessons for similarly situated communities in the Southwest and in other regions where Latino population growth has surged dramatically but where there is virtually no political representation, such as small cities in the South, Northeast, and Midwest. The Latino populations of many of these communities are mostly first-generation immigrants, yet with grassroots organization, electable leaders, and sufficient economic resources to run effective campaigns, the Salinas experience could be repeated.

Urban governments provide most government functions, especially those that directly affect the lives of residents. Basic local services such as police, fire, and social services are as necessary as those provided by the federal government. In addition, it is at the local level that the type and quality of housing, jobs, and education are contested. It is therefore important to study how policy benefits were distributed before and after Mexican Americans ascended to political leadership of Salinas, a regional agricultural center. As Latinos become a major presence in many parts of the nation, their process of political incorporation is instructive of how politics operates in cities with large Latino communities. It provides insights into the racial dynamics that have begun to unfold in the new millennium.

Salinas is the county seat of Monterey, California. This city had an estimated population of more than 129,900 people in 1996 and more than 151,000 people by 2000 (see Table 7.1).[1] It is located one hour's drive south of San Jose and thirty minutes inland from the coastal city of Monterey. Salinas was born out of *rancho* lands awarded to settlers by the Mexican government. A town was established in 1856, and the city was incorporated in 1874. Salinas is the food processing and shipping center of the Salinas Valley, which is internationally known for its mass production of vegetables and fruits. In fact, it is known as "the salad bowl of the world."

Table 7.1   Latino Population of Salinas

Year	General Population	Latino Population	% of Total Population
1890	2,339	n/a	
1900	3,304	n/a	
1930	10,263	n/a	
1940	11,586	n/a	
1950	13,917	n/a	
1960	28,957	2,586[a]	9.8
1970	58,896	4,760[b]	8.0
1980	80,479	30,577	38.0
1990	108,777	54,428	50.6
2000	151,060	96,880	61.1

Source: U.S. Bureau of the Census, various years.
Notes: a. No specific information on Spanish-surname or Latino population is available; however, the total foreign-born population was 2,838. Of this number, 252 were of Asian origin. The majority of the remaining 2,586 were of Latino or Portuguese origin.
b. This number represents the number of foreign born or of mixed parentage from Mexico. Another table lists a similar number of Spanish-language or Spanish-surname residents. This number is significantly higher—21 percent. However, since Salinas has a relatively high percentage of both Portuguese- and Spanish-surnamed Filipinos, I have used the smaller number of foreign born from Mexico.

A famous native of Salinas, John Steinbeck, used the city as the setting for his novels *Tortilla Flats,*[2] *Of Mice and Men,*[3] and *East of Eden.*[4] These fictionalized accounts of life in this community reflect the agricultural roots of the region. The agricultural character of Salinas drew migrants from the East, including Oklahomans during the Great Depression, and immigrants from Mexico. The waves of migrant labor since the 1930s has created a growing Latino community constituting more than 61 percent in 2000 (see Table 7.1).

■ A Brief History of Salinas

The roots of Latino political incorporation efforts can be traced back to the decades of discrimination and inequality faced by migrant farmworkers who labored in the Salinas Valley fields to produce fruits and vegetables for consumers but received poor compensation and little opportunity for advancement. The landowning elites who founded the city of Salinas in the nineteenth century tightly controlled the political and educational systems.

Efforts to improve the conditions of Chicanos began in the agricultural fields and in the educational arena. In the late 1960s, young Chicanos demonstrated in the streets of Salinas to demand the right to celebrate their history and culture. The inspiration for the young Chicanos was *campesinos* (farmworkers) who had been stirred into action by the organizing of the United Farm Workers of America (UFW). The UFW had a profound impact on the city of Salinas.

In 1970, the UFW was drawn to the city after the Teamsters Union unilaterally signed contracts with most of the lettuce growers in the area.[5] Having just completed the successful organization of grape workers in the San Joaquin Valley in 1965–1970, the UFW moved most of its leaders to Salinas to oversee what was to become one of the largest agricultural strikes in California's history and a nationwide lettuce boycott.

In 1970, when the UFW began to organize in the Salinas and Pajaro valleys, people of Mexican descent were in the process of establishing permanent roots in and around Salinas. Previously, the population of Mexicans had been small, made up mostly of migrant farmworkers. In 1950, only a small percentage of the population of Salinas was Mexican. These numbers did not begin to change until the ending of the Bracero Program in 1964, which enabled many Mexican workers to bring their families and settle in the area. Many workers lived outside the city limits in the East Alisal area.

The history of Salinas, similar to that of many cities in the Southwest, is closely linked to Mexico. After Mexico seceded from Spain in 1822, two ranchos in the Salinas Valley were granted to Mexican settlers: Sausal and Nacional. The ranchos were sold to white settlers following the Gold Rush of 1849. These early settlers formed the town of Salinas in the 1850s, which soon became the county seat of Monterey County, after a vote where Salinas' 150 new residents swung the election.[6] Many of the early ranchers wanted to make sure the county seat was moved out of the city of Monterey, which they viewed as "too Mexican" and too far off the north-south travel route. The city was incorporated in 1874.

From being only a small way station between Los Angeles and San Francisco, Salinas grew to 25,000 by 1960.[7] This population growth was fueled by the introduction of lettuce in the early 1900s and later artichokes and broccoli, which were the main agricultural crops and the dominant focus of the local economy. The development of a variety of crops and the start of the Great Depression in the 1930s drew large numbers of poor migrants, including a large number from the Dust Bowl of Oklahoma.

Mexican migrant workers also came to Salinas. In 1936, a lettuce strike organized by the Fruit and Vegetable Union erupted into a conflict between the new migrants and the townspeople, who were backed by the shed owners. A combination of local guards, vigilantes, and state and local law-enforcement forces attacked four thousand workers and sympathizers.[8] Workers were left beaten and bloody from this confrontation. The new settlers were not deterred, however, and more people continued to arrive. A huddle of shacks became Alisal, an unincorporated part of Monterey County. In 1960, the Salinas population was 28,000, and the Alisal area contained an additional 18,000 people, with a sizable percentage from

Mexico. Salinas and Alisal had a combined population of 46,000, making it the largest agricultural center in the region. Under the city of Salinas's general plan, the Alisal area was annexed into Salinas in 1963. This area was physically an integral part of Salinas, with almost as many people as north and south Salinas combined.

Beginning in the 1930s, the Mexican population grew rapidly, especially with the advent of the Bracero Program during World War II, when a shortage of farm laborers led the U.S. government to create a seasonal worker agreement with the Mexican government to bring temporary workers to pick vitally needed crops.[9] Following World War II, however, there were still very few Mexicans who lived in Salinas on a year-round basis.

Historically, a triumvirate of Anglo and Japanese agricultural interests, downtown banking and financial interests, and real estate developers controlled economic development in Salinas. During World War II, local Japanese farmers, along with all other West Coast Japanese Americans, were rounded up and placed in internment camps. The incarceration of Japanese farmers enabled other growers to purchase some of their land and limited the influence of Japanese farmers following the war. In the 1950s and 1960s, Salinas grew from solely an agricultural community into a manufacturing and retail center for the region. A Firestone tire and rubber plant opened, along with other major plants owned by Peter Paul Cadbury, Nestlé, Shilling, and J. M. Smucker companies. Thousands of Chicanos and Mexicans who had been drawn to the area for agricultural work were now being employed in the manufacturing and food-processing industries.

■ The Impact of the United Farm Workers on Monterey County Politics

The economic story of the early 1970s was the struggle in the fields to unionize farmworkers. As mentioned previously, in 1970 the UFW made it a top priority to organize thousands of lettuce and other agricultural workers in the Salinas and Pajaro valleys. For several years these farmworkers had been calling for the UFW to come and support them.[10] Lettuce growers in the Salinas and Santa Maria valleys, anticipating that they would be the next target of a UFW organizing campaign, had secretly signed contracts with the Teamsters to represent their field-workers, without even consulting with the mainly Mexican workers.[11] After intense negotiations between the two unions, a peace agreement was reached whereby any Teamster contracts would switch to the UFW.

When the 170 lettuce growers refused to switch unions, a general strike was called, and all lettuce was boycotted. More then 7,000 men, women, and children walked off their jobs in the lettuce and strawberry fields.[12] In one of the most dramatic episodes of the UFW organizing drive, Cesar Chavez refused to abide by a court order to stop the boycott against Bud Antle, the largest lettuce grower, who became the target of the UFW (even though it had signed a separate union contract with the Teamsters a decade earlier). A local judge ordered Chavez arrested in the Monterey County Courthouse in Salinas. Chavez went on a hunger strike. An around-the-clock vigil began, with thousands of farmworkers surrounding the courthouse. Finally, on Christmas Eve, some twenty days later, the judge relented and freed Chavez.[13] This incident received national publicity when Robert Kennedy's widow, Ethel Kennedy, traveled to Salinas to support Chavez, and it helped to galvanize more public support for the farmworkers' campaign in the Salinas area.

For most of the 1970s, Salinas was polarized as the powerful agricultural interests sought to prevent farmworkers from choosing the union to represent them. The Chicano and Mexican community was largely in support of the UFW, as many of these families included members who were farmworkers. However, politically the Chicano community was not organized, and in some respects there were contradictions in the community's response to the UFW. As noted earlier, the Teamsters Union had cut a deal with Bud Antle in 1961 and had unionized more than 1,000 workers, almost exclusively Mexican migrants who were sent back and forth between Salinas and Yuma, Arizona, during the dual harvesting seasons to prevent them from being organized by the Agricultural Workers Organizing Committee, a forerunner to the UFW.[14] Many of these workers were sympathetic to the UFW, yet they received better wages and benefits than nonunionized farmworkers.[15] The UFW was unable to secure strong union contracts within the lettuce industry, and the Teamsters Union let most of its contract lie dormant and did not enforce its provisions. The low level of unionization in the fields weakened organized labor's presence and kept the Mexican community without political power. The growers' power to control the fields meant that they continued to control the politics of the Salinas Valley as well. Without the strong presence of an active union like the UFW, farmworkers and their families had little hope of gaining a political voice in their employment terms and in their communities.

In addition to the power of the growers, the political inexperience of the Chicano community limited Chicano economic progress in the 1970s, and the lack of unionization meant that farmworker families were paid poorly. There was only a very small Chicano middle class, as few families were able to move from the working class into middle-class professions and small businesses. The economic difficulties of the Latino community were reflected in its early attempts to gain political incorporation.

■ Initial Efforts Toward Political Incorporation

Historically, a large number of Mexicans lived outside the city limits in the Alisal area. In 1963, the Alisal area was annexed to the city of Salinas; this action by the city helped prompt a movement for political inclusion for the Chicano community. An early political activist, Sally Gutierrez, was the first Latina to run for local office in 1970. While her campaign was unsuccessful, Gutierrez's attempt was an important first step in the Latino community's efforts to win political representation.[16] In addition to traditional electoral participation efforts, the UFW campaign to organize farmworkers exposed a broader lack of political power for all Latinos in the Salinas area. Many local residents began their involvement in local political issues by supporting the UFW and the lettuce boycott.

The Monterey County chapter of the League of United Latin American Citizens (LULAC) was founded in 1973. Also in the mid-1970s, Willie Velasquez, the founder of the Southwest Voter Registration Project, visited Salinas and discussed the need to build a local organization to do voter registration and education. From 1976 to 1978, a local community activist, Jesse Sanchez, developed a Salinas-based Southwest Voter Registration Project. By 1980, these efforts converged to begin running local Chicanos for office. Sanchez was elected to the Alisal Union School Elementary School Board in 1981. In 1982, Bill Melendez ran for Monterey County school superintendent and placed second. The effort to get Melendez elected showed the potential power Latinos had in the county, if they were organized and mobilized.[17]

While Latinos were beginning to be elected to school boards, the city council and mayor's seat remained firmly in the hands of Anglos. From 1970 to 1985, Latinos tried unsuccessfully four times to get elected to the city council. Each time, there was polarized voting, with Chicanos voting in large numbers for the Chicano candidate but white voters overwhelmingly rejecting Chicano candidates. As long as Latinos were a minority population, they would face an uphill battle to elect one of their own in citywide elections.

Finally, in 1985, a Cuban American businessman, Ralph Portuondo, became the first Latino elected under the at-large electoral system. Portuondo, a real estate developer, had the support of the white political establishment, a combination of agricultural interests and developers, that had governed Salinas for decades. Community activist Jesse Sanchez ran unsuccessfully in the same race. Sanchez received 70 percent of the vote in Chicano precincts but only 9 percent of the vote in white precincts.[18] The Sanchez defeat in 1985, coupled with the filing of a lawsuit in Watsonville (twenty miles away in Santa Cruz County) the same year to challenge that city's electoral system, had a big impact on Salinas's community activists.

Their strategy now shifted toward exploring legal options to challenge the citywide electoral system.

In early 1987, when a federal district court judge ruled that Watsonville's at-large electoral system did not discriminate, the reaction of local Salinas Chicano activists was to point out differences between Watsonville and Salinas: "In Salinas, it's very clear that you would have a majority of Hispanics in some districts, if the city was broken down into districts."[19] Three elements are needed to prove that at-large election systems are discriminatory. Sanchez pointed out that in Salinas "voting is polarized, Hispanics are geographically compact, and Hispanics are politically cohesive. . . . I think we can show that there is a legacy of discrimination and that a Hispanic from East Salinas could win if the city were broken into districts."[20]

On June 2, 1987, mayoral and council elections were held, and although no Chicano candidates ran from the East Salinas area, a grassroots organization, the Alisal Betterment Committee (ABC), endorsed three white candidates, including Al Styles, a resident of East Salinas. East Salinas contributed 21 percent of the total votes, including over 1,000 votes delivered through the efforts of ABC.[21] The actions of ABC grew out of a larger vision of local Chicano community activists, who decided not to run their own candidate but to endorse other candidates and continue to build their own grassroots organization. Later that year, an official of the Department of Justice came to Salinas to investigate local politics and determine whether there was discriminatory voting.[22]

In 1988, hiring practices in Salinas came under fire, as local Latino community leaders, including the LULAC, criticized the city for failing to hire and promote minorities and women. A member of the City's Affirmative Action Commission, Juan Oliverez, charged, "Even though we are making some strides, there's still not any hiring at management levels. . . . I'm not convinced there is a real commitment to Chicanos." Local LULAC chapter president Bill Melendez said, "Unless feet are held to the fire, they won't hire Latinos and minorities." Demands were raised to hire more bilingual public contact people, including recreation staff, police, fire, library, and building inspectors.[23]

■ Citywide Effort Wins District Elections

In late August 1988, following the path taken by community activists in Watsonville, Joaquin Avila, the attorney in the Watsonville case, filed a class action suit to end Salinas' at-large election system on behalf of three Chicano activists: Fernando Armenta, Simon Salinas, and Marta Nava (who had been the first Chicana to win office in Salinas when she was elected trustee of the Alisal Union School Elementary School Board following Sanchez's election). Avila filed a lawsuit charging that the city of Salinas's at-large electoral system diluted Latino voting strength and prevented Chicanos from being elected. As Sanchez noted later, "We could prove that voting was polarized. We could prove that when a Chicano was placed on the ballot, there was a higher Chicano voter turnout. If the elections were held by districts, a Chicano could win."[24]

Fearing the high cost of a court trial and the real possibility of defeat, city officials agreed to settle the matter through a local election.[25] According to Salinas city manager Roy J. Herte, "We watched what was happening in Watsonville. . . . We had no insurance policy to cover the costs of a suit, and no estimate of what it would cost, and we knew that once the precedent had been set over there, our chances of winning would have been remote."[26] The political establishment counted on being able to defeat the citywide measure, just as it had defeated eastside Chicano candidates previously.

Elections were scheduled for December 6, 1988. The election proved difficult for several reasons. First, proponents of district elections had to win an at-large election. This would require a heavy turnout in Chicano precincts (as Chicanos were not yet officially the majority population) and a substantial sympathy vote by Anglos. Second, there was very little time to prepare, as the elections were scheduled four months after the lawsuit was filed. Third, proponents of district elections had to urge voters to pass not one but three measures: measure 1 would establish district elections with six council seats; measure 2 would expand the size of the city council from five to seven members, and measure 3 would amend the process by which vacancies on the city council were filled.[27]

Local grassroots organizations used a combination of voter education and get-out-the-vote efforts. They were up against a Salinas City Council that gave "tepid support" and hoped the three measures would fail.[28] Using experience gained in previous elections, the Chicano community had developed an effective vote-generating operation. Volunteers went door to door throughout East Salinas, explaining the measures on the ballot. Supporters of district elections organized rides to the polling places on election day. While Chicano community sentiment ran high in favor of the three measures, the Anglo community overwhelmingly opposed district elections. When the votes were counted, district elections had won by only 107 votes, 3,507 to 3,400.[29]

The majority of the margin of victory came from the high Chicano voter turnout, accounting for 35 percent of all votes cast. Voting was polarized along racial lines, as Chicano activists had consistently charged. Chicano precincts voted 85 percent in favor of the three measures, while white precincts voted 75 percent against it. Nevertheless, the small white vote in favor of district elections, combined with votes of Filipinos, who made up 5 percent of total voters and also favored the measure, were sufficient to tip the scales. After the votes were tallied, Sanchez commented, "The vote makes it clear that Chicanos are now a force in this community. What's really impressive is that we won this in only six months. . . . Now, we're finally going to have a Chicano on the city council."[30]

As the votes were counted, affirming the establishment of district elections in the city, a fierce battle erupted within the Chicano community. Two Chicano candidates emerged to seek the same seat on the council. Simon Salinas, a thirty-three-year-old schoolteacher in East Salinas and a plaintiff in the initial lawsuit against the city, faced two other opponents: Chicano attorney Juan Uranga and a non-Latina, Deloris Higgins, who owned a small business in East Salinas. Uranga was supported by the Central Coast Democratic Club and elected city officials. He also had worked for fourteen years as an attorney for the California Rural Legal Assistance and advocated for the rights of farmworkers. The differences between Salinas and Uranga reflected less their political differences than differences about who and how the community would select its elected leaders. Veteran community activists, many of who had worked since the early 1970s for the opportunity to elect a Chicano representative to the city council through the Alisal Betterment Committee, expected to discuss who would be the best candidate and then unite to work for that person's election. When Uranga decided to run without their endorsement and rely on the local Democratic leadership, some Chicano activists were angered. According to then attorney and now municipal court Judge José Velásquez, "We were shocked to find the Democratic leadership attempting to impose their hand-picked leader on our community."[31]

Simon Salinas said he was concerned with local issues—"my priority is not going to be pleasing Democratic higher-ups in Sacramento"—and that Uranga had too much "outside" support from as the Central Coast Democratic Club and other political leaders. Uranga, who used his fourteen-year experience with the California Rural Legal Assistance as evidence of his concern for East Salinas residents, was shocked by the tenor of the campaign: "Using negative campaigning as a strategy at this level of politics really surprises me."[32]

The competition between two viable Chicano community candidates sparked increased voter registration and participation. Lydia Villareal, Uranga's campaign manager, predicted a heavy voter turnout in District 2. "It's because of district elections," she said. "Everything flows from that. . . . The interest is much more immediate."[33] Signs from one camp or the other were visible in every store window on East Alisal Street. By election day, the differences between the two candidates' camps reached such an intense level that authorities had to be called in to keep the peace in eastside precinct polls. There was chanting, insults were exchanged, and there was even pushing in line as Chicano residents anxiously waited to vote for the candidate of their choice.[34] In the words of Monterey County voter registrar Ross Underwood, "Poll officers were forced into the role of yard-duty teacher. It was almost a carnival-like atmosphere."[35]

When the votes were tallied, 2,375 persons, or 43 percent of the 5,519 registered voters living in the city's newly created heavily Latino District 2, had showed up to vote. This was the highest voter turnout percentage in the city. In 1987, before district elections were approved, 966 voters, only 23 percent of the area's 4,132 registered voters, had cast votes for mayoral and council candidates. In that election, there had been three white council candidates and one Latino candidate.[36]

In the District 2 election in 1989, the clear victor in a hard-fought race was Simon Salinas, who captured 62.4 percent of the ballots cast. The election of the first Latino to the Salinas City Council, under the district election system, occurred just as Latinos were becoming the majority population. The 1990 census revealed what Chicano activists had been saying for some time: Latinos had become the majority population in the city (see Table 7.1). Their numbers had risen dramatically between 1980 and 1990. This demographic change, along with the change in the political structure, proved to be the winning combination for the election of Latinos. To change the electoral structure in a racially polarized environment such as Salinas, there must be sufficient numbers of Latinos present, and they must vote in large numbers.

In addition to a change in the structure, other ingredients are necessary to achieve Latino incorporation. The disenfranchised group must be organized, viable candidates developed, and issues clearly articulated. In Salinas, these conditions were met. Latinos had built grassroots community organization, and they had run electoral campaigns for school boards, superintendent of schools, city council, and other races. They had a community presence in these campaigns. There were identifiable community candidates with the potential to be elected, if the rules were changed to enable Chicanos to select a candidate who would represent their interests on the council. They had a captivating issue—the documented history of racialized voting. The citywide vote to change the electoral rules was historic, as it enabled wider participation by Salinas residents and greater opportunities to be elected through neighborhood campaigns.

The election of a community resident from East Salinas was a reflection of the strong ties and support that local community organization had constructed. The white businesswoman in the race, though an eastside resident, was no match for the mandate from the community for local Chicano representation. The contest between two well-qualified and well-known candidates indicated that already there were divisions within the Chicano community between various camps, not necessarily around major policy differences but rather regarding from whom they received initial support. Since neither Salinas nor Uranga had held elective office previously, this election came down to who was best able to register and organize new and existing voters.

■ Latinos Achieve Political Control, 1989–2001

Since 1989, Latinos have been elected on a regular basis to the Salinas City Council. The second section of this chapter discusses the progress of Latino political incorporation and examines whether the inequalities in benefit distribution to the Latino community that prompted the movement for political representation are affected by different political rule. While, as some scholars note, "equality is a complex and uncertain guide to public policy,"[37] the dominant paradigm in government since the Great Depression is to address societal inequalities with social programs. Yet most broad social programs have been the jurisdiction of the federal government. At the local level, there are numerous constraints that limit cities.[38] This section of the chapter will study the results of seven years of gradual Latino incorporation in Salinas, during which Latinos gained a majority presence on the city council.

We will review the first two years, 1989–1991, then briefly examine the years 1991–1993, when two additional Latino representatives were elected. Next, we will examine the period 1993–1997, when four out of seven city council members elected were Latinos. Finally, we will assess the 1998–2002 period, when the first Chicana mayor was elected. The latter period transformed Salinas into the largest California city with a majority-Latino city council.

Salinas represents an excellent case to examine this book's basic question: does electing Latinos to political office make a difference for the Latino community that elects them? The issue of equality underlying this study is complex. Are there group entitlements that flow from organizing a group's power to achieve electoral success? Are there observable differences in how social policy and policy benefits are distributed before and after Latinos take power? In addition, this chapter includes an analysis of the role of government bureaucrats to affect the setting of policy and the distribution of resources.

❏ The First Two Years, 1989–1991

An inequality of services and benefits for the Chicano community, such as a lack of low-cost housing, a lack of parks and recreational activities for youth, and little hiring of minorities in city government, prompted the drive for Chicanos' political empowerment. These issues began to receive more concerted attention from the city council after Simon Salinas took office. One of the first actions of the new city council was to form a citizen task force with broad representation from various segments in the city, with the responsibility to recommend an affordable housing program and funding to meet the General Plan's goal of making 10 percent of all new units affordable to lower-income households. There were 13,200 households, or 40 percent of all city households, estimated to be lower income in 1990. For a family of four, "lower income" was defined as an annual income of less than $23,000. During 1980–1990, virtually all of the city's single-room occupancy housing and group farmworker housing was lost to building closures or abandonment.[39] The groundbreaking work of the task force was to bear fruit with several housing projects in later years.

Also, the new council hired the city's first Latino city manager, David Mora, who brought experience and an ability to work with different forces to provide a fresh perspective to the city's administration. Mora came from the city of Oxnard, another community with a high percentage of Latinos. One of his accomplishments as Salinas city manager was the hiring of Latino, Asian, and black people to head six of the city's departments. In 1992 Mora noted, "When I was hired as city manager two years ago, I said I would go out and find the best qualified candidates and I also said that these would include more minorities. . . . I have always been convinced that there are qualified minority candidates out there. I hired the best people available."[40]

The hiring of an experienced Latino city manager and other people of color in management positions, in addition to the election of Latinos, may account for a change in policy benefits for the Latino community. The Robert Lineberry argument that it is primarily changes in government bureaucracy that affect the delivery of services, rather than elections of new public officials, is a serious challenge to the argument that it is primarily the political actor's relationship to the community that determines to what degree benefits are returned to the community.[41] If full-time bureaucrats distribute policy benefits in a colorblind fashion, rather than politicians who serve only on a part-time basis, does electoral empowerment matter? This question will be addressed after the changes in Salinas's government have been explored.

By 1991, a growing gang problem, which had been swept under the rug by previous councils, was addressed by the new city council. The council called a community meeting to hear testimony and gather insights on what to do about the problem. The head of LULAC, Juan Oliverez, spoke to the city council and called for action by the city to address the problem: "One thing's for sure, after the June election, there's going to be more Chicanos up there," which was a reference to the need for a more diverse council.[42]

LULAC, the Alisal Betterment Committee, and other community organizations continued to monitor city government and to fight for issues of concern in the Mexican American community. The election of Simon Salinas to the council of a rapidly growing Latino community, along with the involvement of experienced organizations and leaders, were signs that Salinas' Chicano community was well positioned to further advance Latino political empowerment.

❏ *Growing Empowerment, 1991–1993*

In 1991, during the next round of elections, a Chicano and a Chicana were added to the Salinas City Council. Fernando Armenta, a Monterey County Medical social worker, ran unopposed in the city's District 1, with a Chicano/Mexican population of 85 percent. The fact that he ran unopposed led some outside the Chicano community to ask pointedly whether there was an "east Salinas political machine and one of its leaders a godfather."[43] This perspective, common among many white voters, did not take into account that Chicano activists had worked together for many years in a careful construction of political campaigns, voter registration drives, and political organization. As Armenta's campaign manager, Jesse Sanchez, commented, there are practical reasons for getting community leaders together: "If you include all of those who are active in the decision-making process, they will support the person who comes out of that process. Everyone had a hand in selecting the person—by everyone, I mean those who are politically active, who walk precincts, who are volunteers. . . . Because they are a part of the process, they will defend their decision and that's a source of strength."[44]

Armenta was well qualified to be the next Chicano councilperson. He had worked for more than a decade on various campaigns, supporting Simon Salinas's campaign in 1989. He was born and raised in Salinas and had graduated from area schools, including Hartnell Community College. He had returned to the community after obtaining a master's degree in social work in San Jose. The fact that no one ran against him indicated that he commanded broad support from various groups in the community.

Anna Caballero, meanwhile, won in District 6, with a Latino population of only 25 percent. Her election had not been nearly as certain as Armenta's. Caballero, a well-known local attorney, had worked for several years for California Rural Legal Assistance before entering private practice in 1982. She was appointed to the city's planning commission from 1985 to 1989, becoming the first Chicana in any of Salinas's governing bodies. In

1989 she had worked to elect her husband, Juan Uranga, to city council, against Simon Salinas. The 1989 campaign had caused a split among Chicano activists. By 1991, Caballero had moved to another district, the wealthier and more diverse District 6. District 6 had a 10 percent Filipino population in addition to its 25 percent Latino population. Caballero ran a racially inclusive campaign, focusing on issues local residents had in common rather than accentuating the historical exclusion of Latinos from city politics. Caballero said, "This is the beginning of a bridging for Salinas. This is a diverse community. It was an opportunity for Salinas and even though we didn't say that, I think a lot of voters understood it. I think it appealed to many voters, casting a vote for a harmonious town."[45]

Caballero had traveled a distinctly different path to electoral office than that of the other two Chicano council members. Her campaign message was not the Salinas campaign message that a racist power structure controlled local politics and excluded Chicanos. Unlike Armenta and many other community activists, she did not grow up in Salinas; rather, she had come to Salinas to work in the CRLA in the late 1970s. She had witnessed firsthand the mistreatment of farmworkers and worked to defend their rights on the job and in the community. She became involved in politics less for reasons of Chicano empowerment than to bring communities together. Her campaign message was one of racial and class harmony.

For the next two years, these three Chicanos agreed that they would work together on issues of common concern such as affordable housing, the youth and gang problem, and the underrepresentation of Latinos in local government. While at first there were hard feelings and a lack of trust left over from the 1989 election, some of these differences were ameliorated over time in the context of a city council that was still predominantly white, with three white councilmembers elected through the district election system and a white mayor elected citywide.

❏ *A Chicano Majority on the City Council*

In 1993, Chicanos became the majority on the Salinas City Council, making Salinas the largest city in California with a majority-Latino city council. The biracial electoral coalition that generally leads to the strongest political incorporation was less evident in Salinas than in the cities studied by Rufus Browning, Dale Marshall, and David Tabb,[46] but the results were more substantial. In Salinas, in contrast to the Browning, Marshall, and Tabb model, Chicano activists achieved a council majority by organizing within their neighborhoods and electoral districts to elect progressive Chicanos to office with virtually no support from white voters—except in District 6, where Caballero ran and white voters were the predominant voters. The Latino council majority would not have been possible without Caballero's election in a non-Latino-majority district. Her election proved that Latinas could win office in non-Latino-majority sections of the city and broke down some stereotypes that Latinos could win only in Latino-majority districts and that non-Latinos would not vote for Latinos. This became important later in the decade, when Caballero ran for mayor.

In early 1989, there were no Latinos on the city council; the change in representation within just four years was unprecedented. This change in leadership, which had occurred only after a change in the electoral structure, indicated the symbiotic relationship between structure and agency. Once the structural impediment to change was removed, there was a tangible reason to organize: to win electoral seats. Winning a council majority for Chicanos was achieved not by incumbents winning reelection but rather by the election of two new members. Gloria Reyes won in a close race in District 4, defeating an appointed incumbent, Deloris Higgins. Roberto Ocampo won in District 2, the seat vacated by incumbent Simon Salinas, who decided to seek election to the board of supervisors. The city council now included Caballero, Armenta, Reyes, and Ocampo. Fernando Armenta commented, "I think it will broaden the sensitivity to the Latino community . . . and the sensitivity to all minorities and all walks of life."[47]

Over the next eight years, Latinos retained their council majority. From 1993 to 1997, only Reyes left the council, and Juan Oliverez, a longtime community activist and professor of ethnic studies at a local college, replaced her in District 4. Mayor Allan Styles continued in the position he had won in 1991, until he stepped down to run for a state assembly seat in 1998.

■ Latinos and County Offices

In addition to Latino community efforts to win in several district elections in the city, their sights were expanded to other electoral contests, including a campaign to redistrict boundaries for county supervisor seats. Since 1991, Chicano activists had pressured for a redrawing of supervisory boundaries to reflect demographic changes. They were successful in delaying three of five district elections. Chicano community pressure—especially from the La Raza Redistricting Committee, composed of Simon Salinas, Local 890 Teamster Union president Frank Gallegos, and other area activists—was exerted through a united front in numerous hearings and meetings to "review about three dozen maps, a lawsuit, a federal study of various plans, and a ballot measure."[48] The board of supervisors finally caved in, recognizing that they could not hold back the demographic and political changes taking place in the county. A new Monterey County district map for supervisors was drawn up in 1993, and elections were set for later that year.

Chicano community activists, as they had done since the early 1980s, met to discuss who should run for supervisor in District 1, the seat that would afford Chicanos the best opportunity to win election, with a Latino population of 68 percent (see Table 7.2). After the majority of local activists decided to support Jesse Sanchez, the principal organizer and architect of the Chicano empowerment, Salinas decided to run for the same seat. Once again, as in 1989, there was disunity in the Chicano community over whom to support to secure the first seat for a Latino, this time on the board of supervisors. Many longtime activists felt that Salinas had allowed individual advancement to overshadow the community unity needed to achieve Latino political empowerment. Nevertheless, the campaign began, with both sides hurling charges and countercharges.

By the time of the June elections, when the city of Salinas was electing Gloria Reyes and Roberto Ocampo to the city council, the two other Chicano candidates, Salinas and Sanchez, were battling for support and endorsements. Salinas garnered the support of organized labor (including the Central Labor Council, Communication Workers of America Local 9490, and the Building and Construction Trades Council of Monterey and Santa Cruz Counties), the Monterey County Prosecutors Association, North Monterey county growers, and several Chicano community leaders. Sanchez, who was an outspoken voice for farmworkers' rights, carried the support of most of the Chicano activists who formed the core of the Alisal Betterment Association and who believed it was Sanchez's turn to seek higher office.

Following the June primary, a runoff was set for August 3, 1993. After initially planning to run, Sanchez decided to withdraw from the race, citing the divisive nature of the campaign in the Chicano community. Salinas went on to win, thereby becoming the first Mexican American to hold a

Table 7.2   Monterey County Supervisor Districts

District	Total Population	% Latino	% Black	% Native American	% Asian/ Pacific	% White
1	67,095	68	2	1	3	26
2	71,634	22	6	0	8	63
3	72,165	62	4	0.4	1	32.6
4	72,540	12	8	1	0.2	78.8
5	72,125	7	10	1	5	77
Total	335,560	34	6	1	3	59

Source: Salinas Californian (August 21, 1992), p. 1.

board of supervisors seat in the twentieth century. Chicano activists who had sought to change the face of not only city government but county government as well were cognizant of the progress that had been made; however, they wondered, at what cost? How significant was the division that had developed between Salinas and Sanchez? Did this represent the end of the Chicano community's efforts to work together for Latino empowerment, or was it a reflection of the diversity of candidates and views within the Chicano political community?

Chicano activists were not content with electing one of their own to the board of supervisors. Another arena that did not reflect the changing demographics in the county was the judicial system. A key issue was to change the boundaries for municipal court judges, since while 33 percent of the county was Latino at the time, all nine municipal court judges were white. As community activist Jesse Sanchez commented, "Any institution, at least in our form of government, must reflect the community in which it functions. . . . Only when that happens do people truly feel it represents them."[49] The issue arose because Monterey County consolidated two municipal court and seven justice court districts into a single municipal court. Judges in the resulting court were elected on an at-large basis and served the entire community.

A lawsuit was filed in 1991 that claimed that Monterey County had violated the federal Voting Rights Act. The plaintiffs argued that the system robbed minorities of their voting strength and that none had been elected for decades. Their legal argument, however, was that Monterey County had failed to seek the approval of the U.S. Justice Department before consolidating the districts. Under the Voting Rights Act, Monterey County is one of four California counties required to clear any voting practice changes. It had become subject to federal oversight after under 50 percent of its voters took part in the 1968 presidential election (Yuba, Merced, and Kings counties were also subject to this ruling).

In October 1993, the board of supervisors agreed to split the 1994 judicial elections among seven districts. Civil rights attorney Joaquin Avila, who had been instrumental in challenging Salinas's citywide electoral system and redrawing the Monterey County Board of Supervisors district lines to reflect changing demographics in the county, viewed the board's decision to establish district elections of municipal court judges "the first victory in a statewide battle to reshape judicial elections."[50]

The issue of district elections for judges remained controversial. In 1994, there were no people of color on the municipal court bench. In 1995, Lydia Villarreal was appointed to the municipal court bench by then governor Pete Wilson. She was an attorney for eight years with the California Rural Legal Services in the 1980s; she then worked for the Monterey County District Attorney's Office from 1989 until her appointment. But

Judge Villarreal was forced to run for office almost immediately after her appointment, as part of the settlement of a suit alleging that the county had discriminated against Hispanic voters by consolidating a multiplicity of municipal and other local courts into a countywide court of limited jurisdiction.[51]

In 1995, in a court-ordered special election in a Latino-majority single-judge district, longtime Chicano community activist attorney José Angel Velásquez defeated Villarreal in a tight race. Velásquez was the first Latino to be elected to the county's municipal court (in 2000, he became a superior court judge following the unification of all county courts). He has remained on the bench and continues to advocate for farmworkers, the poor, and youth. Villarreal was later appointed to another seat on the bench in Monterey County in 2001 by then Governor Grey Davis.

■ City Jobs and Affirmative Action

The argument put forward by Marshall, Browning, and Tabb that following the ascent to power of minorities, the spoils of power, including the power to hire and appoint for city jobs, pass into the hands of those in power,[52] is substantiated in the city of Salinas. Salinas has had a long and controversial history of not hiring and appointing people of color and women. In 1980, after pressure by Chicano activists, the mayor and city council adopted the city's first formal affirmative action plan (AAP). The AAP included the following guidelines: "1) flexible and narrowly-tailored hiring/promotion goals designed to remedy prior discriminatory employment practices that had caused it to underutilize women and minority group members; and 2) EEO [Equal Employment Opportunity] policies designed to achieve a work environment free of discrimination on the basis of disability, race, national origin, sex, or age."[53]

Even though there was an AAP in place, Chicano activists filed several civil rights and employment discrimination complaints regarding the lack of hiring of minorities, particularly in positions not traditionally held by minorities, such as professionals, key management staff, and department heads. In one instance reflecting the vestiges of institutional discrimination, the city paid out $453,000 in 1993 to four firefighters to settle a civil rights lawsuit. The firefighters were of different races and genders, but the common charge was that discriminatory behavior and sexual harassment were not being dealt with by the city's fire department.

When Dave Mora was hired as city manager in 1990, he became the first person of color in this critical position. Mora vowed to hire more minorities in city government. By 1992, Mora had made good on his promise by hiring Latinos, Asians, and blacks to head six departments. He also hired Latinos for the positions of fire marshal and police captain.[54] Table 7.3 illustrates the change in demographics of city employment between 1975 and 1996.

It is apparent from the figures in Table 7.3 that Latinos, Asians, and women have benefited from the change in city hiring policies, whereas white males have seen their percentage share of the total workforce decrease dramatically. In 1994, the city's workforce was composed of 39.8 percent women and minority employees. This reflects a 13 percent increase of women and minorities hired and/or promoted since 1980.[55]

What types of jobs, however, have Latinos and women obtained? In 1994, the city of Salinas undertook a revision of its affirmative action plan. Based on local civilian labor force statistics in the 1990 U.S. census, the city had an overall goal of 45.4 percent representation of women and minorities. The 1994 report noted, "Despite its EEO progress in the last 13 years, the City's evidence shows that prior discrimination continues to have an adverse impact upon the selection of women and minorities for employment and promotion."[56]

In the broad categories of office/clerical, paraprofessional, service/maintenance, and skilled craft, there was minority representation of 43–59 percent. However, these numbers are deceiving when it comes to Latino representation, the majority population in the city. In the skilled craft and technician categories, Latinos were 25 and 26 percent respectively; thus some activists pointed out that Latinos were still underrepresented in the higher-paying skilled positions in the city. Also, Latinos held only three positions, or 15 percent, of the top-level administrator positions, albeit two of these were the key positions of city manager and assistant city manager.

Table 7.3   Salinas Workforce Comparison

	1976		1984		1996		Percentage + or − 1976–1996
	Number	Percent	Number	Percent	Number	Percent	
Latino	72	13.32	93	18.00	177	30.5	+17.18
African American	13	2.40	14	2.5	17	3.00	+0.60
Asian	27	4.99	47	8.50	20	3.45	+4.01
White	425	78.62	368	69.00	327	56.40	−22.22
Indian	3	0.55	5	1.00	6	1.00	+0.45
Total	540	100.00	528	100.00	580	100.00	
Male	432	80.00	412	78.00	411	59.00	−21
Female	108	20.00	115	22.00	169	41.00	+21

Source: Personnel director, City of Salinas (1996).

Thus Latino political power in the city bureaucracy had brought advances in total overall hiring; however, their political power was concentrated at the top, in the city manager and assistant city manager positions.

The hiring of those historically underrepresented for city jobs will continue to be controversial, particularly since the passage of California's anti–affirmative action law in 1996 that banned implementing hiring goals based on race, sex, or other categories. An affirmative action officer had attempted to aggressively challenge the hiring practices and institutional discrimination but faced a wall of indifference by other city officials; this person's departure in the mid-1990s did not bode well for quick solutions. Further, Salinas is governed by a civil service system that protects job security, so it is extremely difficult to remove high-ranking administrators from office, except for major malfeasance.

These institutional factors are difficult to change; however, in the years since the inclusion of Latinos, both elected and appointed, in city government, the dynamics of Salinas's city government *have* changed. More bilingual and bicultural staff have been hired, particularly in positions where there is direct public contact. Previously, Spanish-speaking members of the community had a difficult time communicating when they needed city services. In addition, there was diversity training for all city employees in 1994. The city's affirmative action commission had told the city council that the city's growing multiculturalism makes it important for city employees to understand different cultures and ethnicities. Commission members pointed out that the more city employees know about the public and each other, the more effective they can be. Chairwoman Helen Sicalbo said, "Salinas is what all of California's going to be by the end of the century, our diversity is going to impact our services. . . . It makes good business sense."[57]

Besides hiring goals and diversity training, there was more scrutiny to make sure that the process of hiring and promotions is fair. The city's affirmative action commission (now equal employment opportunity commission) has been proactive in overseeing the hiring process to make sure that there is no bias in the selection process. Yet institutional changes in nonelected positions can be slower than the process of electoral change. Salinas had an almost all-white administration in the 1980s. By the mid-1990s, there had been dramatic changes; but change has not come quickly enough for many in the Latino community, who believe that the face of government is only the start of real changes that must occur. Nevertheless, in the year 2000, according to the city's Equal Employment Opportunity Plan, the workforce "is now composed of 59.8% women and minority employees. This reflects a 24.8% increase in women and minorities hired and/or promoted since . . . 1984 when the City workforce was only 35% women and minorities."[58]

■ Economic Development Efforts and Latinos

The case of Salinas indicates that though there has been political progress, local economic development for the Latino community has not traveled a parallel track. Should a local government have a role in economic development? Does the election of a particular segment of a city—in this case Latinos—mean that this segment will benefit in terms of economic development?

Political power and economic power are not the same. The thesis of this chapter is that grassroots politicians will be able to return more benefits to their constituents than will politicians, who are primarily concerned with their own political and economic interests. In Salinas, by all accounts, the Chicanos elected in the first wave of Latino electoral empowerment were liberal to progressive in their politics; all of them ran grassroots campaigns and had strong ties to their community. They were not from the business community and did not run expensive, limited-voter-contact campaigns. An assessment of the actions of the new political leaders in Salinas is important to determine whether in fact grassroots politicians have provided benefits to the Mexican American community that it would not have received under an administration that did not have Latino representation.

In the context of an economy that is based primarily on agriculture, with large numbers of mostly Latino seasonal farm labor and tourist industry workers, what role does local government play in relation to the local economy? Specifically, was there a change in local economic development policy following the changes in local government after Latinos ascended to power? An examination of land usage, housing, and redevelopment indicates that in the 1990s the city council was active in shaping a direction for the city's economic development that directly benefited the Latino community.

The Salinas Redevelopment Agency (SRA) is directed by the Salinas City Council, which acts as the agency's board. The agency and council set goals that clearly reflect a concern for the needs of Salinas's Latino community. In 1996 these goals included working with the Hispanic Chamber of Commerce and the Alisal Merchants Association, using a central city tax increment and other interfund transfers, to develop an economic development plan for the East Salinas area and to develop farmworker housing in Salinas in cooperation with agricultural and other private interests.[59]

An analysis of the work of the SRA indicates that redevelopment has been used, as in many other cities, to improve a blighted downtown area, with funding for an updated intermodal transportation center and the construction of a tourist and educational museum dedicated to John Steinbeck. In addition, the SRA established funding for annexation and development of a retail shopping area in the Boronda section, which lies outside of the city's boundaries. However, in contrast to the usual focus on downtown development, the Salinas SRA helped eliminate blight in the heavily Mexican community of East Salinas, using public and private investment to improve the exterior façade of the area and supporting local community development without tearing down badly needed existing housing. What began in 1970 as a small redevelopment project on one block of Sunset Avenue in East Salinas was expanded in the 1990s into a broader program of community revitalization. This expanded role for East Salinas's redevelopment was directed by the Latino-majority city council. The SRA was also involved with implementing a farmworker housing assistance program, using $1 million set aside by the city council in 1993.

Redevelopment, in the hands of a liberal to progressive Chicano-majority city government, has redirected tax increment funds to improve predominantly Latino East Salinas, as well as to more traditional redevelopment projects. This kind of redevelopment was not undertaken by administrations of the 1970s and 1980s. This is a significant and observable change from the programs of previous probusiness city councils, whose development was carried out haphazardly, with no attempt to improve the economic well-being of the Latino community.

While the use of city resources to benefit the Latino community was evident during the Latino-majority era, the systemic problem of low wages endemic to the agricultural, tourist, and retail industries was not challenged. Instead, elected officials sought other means to improve the lives of the working poor. One means to address this problem was to build more affordable housing.

■ Building Affordable Housing in a Hot Housing Market

In 1993, following the election of a Latino council majority, $2 million out of the $5.4 million in housing funds obtained was directed toward farmworker and large family housing. The goal was to build more housing for low-income farmworker families. The city council consciously directed the housing funds toward those in greatest need. As one member said, "Who are the people with the greatest need? I think we should be giving to that greatest need."[60] Where in the 1980s the priority of the probusiness council was the building of expensive new subdivisions, the new council focused on building housing for low-income farmworker families. The result has been the approval of more affordable-housing money and the building of more units than at any other time. The building of more affordable housing units that accommodate large low-income families is directly related to the change in the composition of the city council, as new Chicano members made this issue a high priority and made sure that resources were directed toward those in need.

However, the demand for affordable housing in the city still exceeds the supply. Even with strenuous efforts, there is not nearly enough housing for farmworkers and other low-wage workers who have been drawn to the region. As Frank Brunings, Monterey County housing coordinator, said, "There is an incredible need for low-income housing based on the kind of industries growing in Monterey County. If you take a look at the kind of industries we have, they are all predicated on low-wage workers."[61] To illustrate the lack of affordable housing in this city, in 1998 the Monterey Housing Authority, which uses federal funds to provide low-income housing, had a 7,000-name waiting list. Also, the Monterey County nonprofit housing developer, the Community Housing Improvement Improvement Systems and Planning Association (CHISPA), which began in 1980, had built 460 units in Salinas by 2001 and received more than 12,000 applications for residency in these units. By 2004, CHISPA had constructed 1,600 affordable housing units in Monterey County, Watsonville, and Santa Cruz, many of them in rural, heavily farmworker communities. The need for affordable housing is illustrated by the fact that Salinas is one of the least affordable housing markets in the nation. According to the Monterey County Association of Realtors, local residents earn a median income of $55,600 a year, meaning that they can afford only 49 percent of a medium-priced home of $460,000.[62]

The directing of city funds to address the affordable-housing needs of large families, farmworker families, and the elderly involved new programs. These programs reflected increased city government awareness of the urgency of meeting Salinas's affordable-housing problem. The change in policy direction toward greater efforts at constructing more affordable housing began in 1990, with the establishment of a citizen housing task force that was spearheaded by Chicano community activists.

■ **Voter Registration and**
  Grassroots Participation, 1998–2002

Starting in 1998, a number of important changes have had long-term significance for local Latino and regional politics in Salinas. In 1998, Anna Caballero ran for mayor of Salinas and was victorious. Caballero was the first Latina elected mayor in the city's history. Her image as a consensus builder with good relations with the different segments of the city enabled her to win this office easily. She was conscious of her role as a woman in the campaign; as she said, "It's been a challenge for women to put themselves in leadership positions, and it's been a challenge for me."[63]

With the demise of ABC in 1993, there was no central grassroots organization to unite community activists to work out who would run for various electoral offices. The emergence of several potential qualified candidates, with limited loyalties to one another, and the lack of a strong local political machine to keep candidates and officeholders in check have led to a more fluid process, with new challengers emerging to compete against veteran politicians as seats open up. The new dynamics were evident in the campaign of Latina Sandra Pizarro for an open state assembly seat against the highest-ranking local Latino official, County Supervisor Simon Salinas. Pizarro, the daughter of a local restaurant owner, had lived outside the area for many years and built a political career in Sacramento. She returned to run for this seat with the backing of the Latino caucus of the California state legislature. Simon Salinas's strong ties to a local base of support brought defeat to Pizarro in the Democratic Party primary, but her candidacy indicated that people outside the local area now viewed the city of Salinas's politics as important enough to attempt to influence its outcome.

This competitive trend within Latino politics had begun with the race for the first district election for Salinas City Council in 1989, when two Latinos, Uranga and Salinas, competed for the same seat, and continued in 1993, with the competition for the Monterey County supervisor seat between two Latino community activists, Sanchez and Salinas. Today individuals deciding to run for office do so of their own volition, without a local political organization that decides who, among all potential candidates, would best represent the community's interests. Instead, individual political leaders may serve as informal mentors to those who seek elected office.

In the absence of ABC, new organizations have emerged to participate in Latino politics. One organization was launched in the mid-1990s as an outgrowth of a local Teamsters union. As noted earlier, the Teamsters Union Local 890 has had a long presence in the Salinas Valley, with food-processing and farmworker contracts dating back decades. In the 1980s the Latino-majority rank and file, led by Frank Gallegos, elected their own leaders. In 1995, the Central Coast Citizenship Project was launched by the Teamsters Local to help its members become citizens. The citizenship project soon expanded and has been instrumental in assisting thousands of Salinas-area immigrants who have become naturalized citizens.[64] The citizenship project has spawned several other organizations, including a youth group, an organization of ex-braceros, a women's group, and Voté, a membership-based Latino political action committee that combines policy work with advocacy. Voté does voter registration work and endorses candidates for local and state office as well as state propositions.

An important labor group active in Latino politics is the UFW; while it continues to organize workers, it also endorses candidates who support its members' issues and concerns. More important, it employs sophisticated electoral campaign operations using experienced local operatives who were instrumental, for example, in helping to elect prolabor candidate Fernando Armenta for Monterey County supervisor in 2000 against a well-funded Republican candidate. In the same year, they worked for the election of Simon Salinas for the Twenty-eighth Assembly seat.

Salinas's election was another milestone for the Latino community. After defeating Pizarro in the primary, Salinas won the general election against a well-funded Republican opponent. This seat had been held for the previous six years by a conservative Republican rancher, Peter Frusetta. The district spanned the tricounty region of San Benito, Monterey, and Santa Cruz and included the cities of Hollister, King City, and Watsonville, where large numbers of Latinos resided, but also rural areas where Republican voting was strong. Salinas defeated Jeff Denham by a 52 to 43 percent margin. Assembly member Salinas is the highest-ranking Latino from this region and demonstrates the growth of Latino political power in elected office.

The systemic problems of low wages, limited affordable housing, and economic control by agribusiness and tourism industries will not be solved overnight. Achieving political power and gaining control over economic resources are not the same. Finding ways to use government influence to challenge economic elites to provide better pay and working conditions and convince surrounding wealthy communities to redistribute economic resources to provide housing and badly needed social services is a new phase in a long struggle for social justice in the Salinas community.

■ Conclusion

Salinas is a case study of how a well-organized and determined community of people with popular candidates and salient issues has been effective in achieving political representation and political power in a short period of time. Through community effort, observable changes in nearly every facet of city government life have taken place. In the experience of Salinas Chicanos, local grassroots political actors have indeed been able to return greater policy benefits and resources to the community than did the previous all-white administrations.

Also, this study recognizes that movement toward political incorporation is a dynamic and complex process that ebbs and flows. The internal strife that developed within the Alisal Betterment Committee in 1993 over support for different candidates for county supervisor has not healed. The ABC has not been replaced by a comparable community organization of activists. Other community-based organizations and unions, including

LULAC, Voté, Teamsters Local 893, UFW, and the Service Employees International Union (SEIU), have stepped up their political activities. Further advances in political incorporation in the Salinas area hinge on the ability of local Mexican American political actors to continue working together on policy that benefits the Latino community. Differences among political actors over who can best represent the community will remain a sore point, but they need not overshadow the political gains made since the late 1980s. The political incorporation efforts by a diverse group of communtiy activists are a model for how to achieve political power and then expand to win a wide range of elected and appointed positions at different levels of government. Collectively, they have transformed the political landscape in the region and in doing so have taken a small step toward the broader goal of full inclusion of the U.S. Latino community.

The experience of local political activists in Salinas is not unique to this community; rather, it reflects the potential of Latino politics in similarly situated communities. Efforts to build and achieve strong political incorporation are being undertaken in countless communities around the United States where Latinos are a growing segment of the population. The efforts of Chicano activists to become community leaders and civic leaders within local governing coalitions is instructive for practitioners of Latino politics elsewhere.

■ Notes

1. California (2002a).
2. J. Steinbeck (1937a).
3. J. Steinbeck (1937b).
4. J. Steinbeck (1952).
5. J. Levy (1975); R. Taylor (1975); M. Wells (1996).
6. Salinas (1960), p. 1.
7. U.S. Bureau of the Census (1960).
8. C. Guerin-Gonzales (1994), p. 129; J. Gomez Quiñones (1994), p. 139.
9. R. Acuña (1988).
10. R. Taylor (1975), pp. 251–253.
11. C. E. Daniels (1995), pp. 392–393.
12. R. Taylor (1975), p. 259.
13. Ibid., p. 261.
14. C. E. Daniels (1995), p. 392.
15. Mike Johnston, business agent, Teamsters Local 890, personal interview (September 19, 1998).
16. "Latinos at Last Get Foot in Political Door," *Monterey Herald*, September 7, 1992, p. 2c.
17. Ibid.
18. W. Flores (1992).
19. *Salinas Californian*, February 2, 1987, p. 1.
20. Ibid.

21. *Salinas Californian*, June 3, 1987, p. 1.

22. *Salinas Californian*, July 10, 1987, p. 1.

23. *Salinas Californian*, April 22, 1988, p. 1.

24. "Latinos at Last Get Foot in Political Door," *Monterey Herald*, September 7, 1992, p. 2c.

25. W. Flores (1992).

26. Ibid.

27. *Salinas Californian*, October 12, 1988, p. 1.

28. *Salinas Californian*, November 22, 1988, p. 1.

29. *Salinas Californian*, December 7, 1988, p. 1.

30. W. Flores (1992).

31. W. Flores (1992).

32. *Salinas Californian*, May 26, 1989, p. 1.

33. *Salinas Californian*, June 5, 1989, p. 1.

34. W. Flores (1992).

35. *Register Pajaronian*, June 8, 1989, p. 1.

36. *Salinas Californian*, September 15, 1992, p. 1.

37. R. Lineberry (1977).

38. P. Peterson (1981).

39. Salinas (1991).

40. "Latinos at Last Get Foot in Political Door," *Monterey Herald*, September 7, 1992, p. 2c.

41. R. Lineberry (1977).

42. *Salinas Californian*, January 29, 1991, p. 1.

43. *Salinas Californian*, April 20, 1991, p. 1.

44. Ibid.

45. *Salinas Californian*, June 5, 1991, p. 1.

46. R. Browning, D. Marshall, and D. Tabb (1984).

47. *Salinas Californian*, June 12, 1993, p. 1.

48. *Salinas Californian*, May 6, 1993, p. 1.

49. *Salinas Californian*, October 7, 1993, p. 1.

50. Ibid.

51. *Metropolitan News-Enterprise*, October 3, 2001, p. 3.

52. R. Browning, D. Marshall, and D. Tabb (1990).

53. Salinas (1994).

54. "Latinos at Last Get Foot in Political Door," *Monterey Herald*, September 7, 1992, p. 2c.

55. Salinas (1994).

56. Ibid.

57. *Salinas Californian*, September 7, 1994, p. 1.

58. Salinas (n.d.), p. 1.

59. Salinas (1996–97).

60. *Salinas Californian*, September 29, 1993, p. 1.

61. *Coast Weekly*, January 15, 1998, p. 14.

62. *Salinas Californian*, "CHISPA Builds Dreams: Agency Celebrates 25 Years of Helping Renters Build Homes for Their Families," February 1, 2005, p. 1.

63. R. Pitnick (1998).

64. R. Crocker (2000).

8

Today's Latino
Elected Officials

N ot all electoral efforts begin for the same reasons, seek the same objectives, or accomplish the same goals. There are internal dynamics within and between ethnic Latino communities and forces external to the Latino community that influence the level and extent of political activities among Latinos. These distinctions reflect the structural limits of electoral politics, the uneven political development in states and local areas in which Latinos operate, and the dynamics of biracial and multiracial politics. These factors in turn influence the motivations of individuals to seek political office. Differences in local or state-level political structures, strength of political parties, demographics of electoral districts, and Latino candidates' individual philosophies on the role of government combine to produce a wide array of Latino politicians with distinct political agendas.

Previous chapters have summarized the history of Latino efforts to achieve political power in the United States and explored the process of political empowerment from disenfranchisement to political incorporation. In this chapter the question of political incorporation will be addressed in several ways. An overview of contemporary Latino elected officials (LEOs) will explore how they were elected to office and whether they took part in political incorporation efforts. The demographic characteristics and political views of current LEOs will be surveyed, with a view to both stages of the electoral process, the political campaign and officeholding. Themes discussed throughout this book are interwoven—how LEOs view their elections, what type of representation they provide for the Latino community, and the importance they place on delivering policy benefits for Latinos.

As discussed previously, there are at least four distinct pathways that Latinos have used to achieve electoral office. Legal challenges, demand-protest, coalition politics (including multiethnic and issue-based coalitions), and nonconfrontational individual efforts are some of the means employed by Latinos to achieve electoral office. Some of these efforts have been part of movements for political empowerment; others were separate from these efforts or even ran counter to them. The result, as discussed in Chapter 5, has been different types of candidates, different levels of political incorporation, and different types of representation.

The election of Latinos to office creates the potential for different types of representation. Hanna Pitkin posits four dimensions of representation.[1] The first level is *formal* representation, where officials are empowered to act on behalf of others by a process that enables the representative to attain more authority than those being represented. This takes place through an institutional arrangement such as an election. At the second level, *descriptive* representation, the elected representative reflects the social characteristics of the people he or she represents. This level is also important, as it provides a marker of the extent to which LEOs have achieved visible elected positions in society.

At the third level, *symbolic* representation, a representative is accepted and supported by the community that elected him or her to office. This is important to study, because LEOs often become role models in their communities. If a candidate or officeholder is identified by the community not just as a symbol of individual achievement but as a representative of the community's values and aspirations, then symbolic representation has been achieved.

A fourth level is *substantive* representation. At this level, an elected representative is expected to act "in the interests of the represented in a manner responsive to them."[2] There is a perceived close connection between the representative and the represented. The elected leader who strives to redirect resources to the community that elected her or him to office is viewed as representing the needs of the community. Constituents come to expect that the representative will fight on their behalf. Those who do not will likely have a difficult time retaining their seat.

How do Latinos in elected positions view their role? Are they merely symbolic representatives, or do they act as substantive representatives of their constituents and the broader Latino community? These are difficult questions to answer without a careful examination of the actions of individual politicians. What can be explored as well are the attitudes and views of Latino politicians.

Latino communities have historically been neglected, and government action is required to provide affordable housing, improve the quality of education, and fund social services. In some communities, Latino officials have taken steps to direct resources to Latino neighborhoods. Also, Latinos in office have prioritized more universal concerns such as economic development, support for business interests, crime reduction, environmental protection, and traffic congestion reduction. These issues are a concern within Latino communities as well as the community at large.

Previous research on Latino elected officials has been specific to certain states or national origins[3] or has analyzed political experiences of national-origin groups in specific locations,[4] as members of caucuses in legislative bodies,[5] or as members of Congress.[6] This chapter will explore the views and attitudes of Latino elected officials in diverse communities, including how LEOs view their policy priorities and their relationship with their ethnic community. To answer these questions, information will be drawn from various sources, including a nationwide mail survey of LEOs in 2000–2001[7] and in-person interviews with Latina and Latino elected officials in nine states.[8]

■ Descriptive Analysis of Latina/o Elected Officials

To begin, what are the demographic characteristics of LEOs? Are LEOs distinct from or similar to the Latino population in terms of economic status and political views? Today's generation of Latino leaders includes public officials elected and appointed to office and leaders of political and civil rights organizations, nonprofits, and corporate entities. This chapter will primarily focus on elected officials. Elected representatives have demonstrated the ability to win support at the ballot box. This requires the support of both Latino and non-Latino voters.[9]

Of all Latinos in the United States in 2000, 66 percent were of Mexican origin, 9.0 percent were Puerto Rican, and 4.0 percent were Cuban. Also, there are a growing number of Spanish-language people from the Caribbean and Central and South America. The census reported that 14.5 percent were Central and South Americans and 6.4 percent were of "other Hispanic" origins.[10] The large percentage of Latinos of Mexican descent is also reflected in the high percentage of Mexican American elected officials, due to their long history and concentration in the Southwest. The Southwest region is where the vast majority of LEOs reside. There are also relatively large numbers of Puerto Rican elected officials in the Northeast and Cuban American elected officials in south Florida, where these groups are heavily concentrated. There are now growing numbers of Dominican and other Latin American elected officials on the East Coast and too a lesser degree in the West. The election of a representative of one's own ethnicity can be considered a form of descriptive representation, and it is no coincidence in electoral districts where Latinos have a choice to elect a Latino that they do so more often than not. Ethnic identity is strong among Latino voters, reflected in recent years in the almost universal election of ethnic candidates of the predominant ethnic Latino group in an electoral district.

❏ *Party Identification and Ideology*

The National Association of Latino Elected Officials (NALEO) reported that among the LEOs for whom a partisan affiliation could be determined, 65 percent identified themselves as Democrats, 5 percent as Republican, and the remainder as Independents.[11] The party affiliation of Latino elected officials is somewhat consistent with that of the Latino population at large. Except for Cubans, most Latino ethnic groups identify more with the Democratic Party.[12] The Democratic Party has been associated with racial minorities and organized labor since the 1930s. Latinos have longtime ties with the Democratic Party, such as the Viva Kennedy Clubs in 1960, so it is not surprising that significantly more identify as Democrats than as Republicans. Most LEOs are Mexican American, and they are elected predominantly from Mexican-populated electoral districts; it is to be expected that they would identify as Democrats.

The ideological orientation of LEOs is moderately liberal, with 37 percent reporting that they are very liberal or somewhat liberal, 38 percent responding that they are "middle of the road," and only 24 percent stating that they are very conservative or somewhat conservative. Among Latinos, they identified themselves as predominantly moderate to conservative. In a survey of Latinos, 26 percent viewed themselves as liberal, 34 percent as moderate, and 34 percent as conservative.[13] This apparent difference between leaders and the Latino masses may not be as great as it appears at first glance, because most Latinos identify themselves as socially conservative but support a liberal social agenda.[14]

❏ *Culture, Language, and Educational Attainment*

Many Latinos "have been disillusioned by their attempt to enter into the embrace of the American way of life. They had to sacrifice too many aspects of their heritage: their color, ancestors, language and culture."[15] How prevalent among LEOs is one aspect of Latino culture—use of the Spanish language? Over 65 percent of LEOs reported that English was the primary language spoken in the home, 14 percent reported that Spanish was the primary language, and 19 percent stated that their household was bilingual. This indicates that while Spanish is common it is not the primary language among Latino elected officials in their homes. Among the Latino population, almost one-half (48 percent) said they spoke only Spanish at home, or more Spanish than English, while only 26 percent said they spoke only English or more English than Spanish; another 26 percent indicated they spoke both equally.[16]

The difference in the levels of use of Spanish in the home is an indication that most LEOs are not first-generation immigrants. There is a social distance between some Latino elected officials and the general populace, because many Latinos in the United States are immigrants. The quality of candidates and the level of their use of Spanish may become a campaign issue in heavily Spanish-speaking electoral districts, particularly if one or more candidates are not fluent in Spanish. In a recent city council race in Houston, Texas, a candidate's grasp of Spanish became an issue after his opponent tried to discredit him in the electoral race. However, as noted by other researchers, Spanish-language usage is highly sensitive to generational transition. According to a 2002 national survey of Latinos, Spanish-speaking persons compose 72 percent of first-generation immigrants, while most Latinos in the second generation are bilingual, and English is the predominant choice of the third generation, at 78 percent. Yet even with this long-term trend toward English-language acquisition, LEOs acknowledge the value of Spanish usage as an important part of their identity and effectiveness as political leaders. Many Latino candidates who are predominantly English speaking attend Spanish language schools to improve their conversational skills before running for office.

To understand the impact of the socialization of culture and values and socioeconomic conditions, it is important to explore the backgrounds of LEOs. Among a majority of LEOs, Spanish was the primary language spoken in the home when they were growing up. Significantly, nearly half of all LEOs were "working class with at least one fulltime working parent," while another 35 percent indicated they were "poor with unstable finances." Only 18 percent said their family was middle class, with one parent a professional or businessperson, and less than 1 percent indicated that they were from an upper-middle-class background. Even though a relatively high percentage reported that they were poor growing up, less than a quarter said that their family had received some form of government assistance. It appears that most LEOs had humble beginnings and grew up in families that relied on their own resources to survive. This also reflects the fact that many LEOs are older and grew up in an era when there were no social welfare programs for the poor.

The level of education of LEOs is higher than that of the Latino population and the U.S. population as a whole. Nearly 24 percent of all Americans have a bachelor's degree or more education; among Latinos, 11 percent had a bachelor's degree or more in 1999.[17] Of LEOs, however, 57 percent had a college degree or an advanced degree. LEOs also tend to have successful careers in business. Since most LEOS hold part-time elected office, they usually work full time or in positions that allow for flexibility. More than 50 percent of LEOs hold professional or technical jobs, and another 25 percent are managers or administrators. The occupational profile of LEOs is dramatically different from that of the Latino population as a whole, in which only 14 percent are employed in the combined category of manager and professional.[18] The concentration of Latinos with strong educational accomplishments and successful careers is an indication that most LEOs are high achievers.

❏ *Income Level of LEOs*

By and large, most elected officials in the United States are part-time representatives; only elected officials in large cities, in some state legislatures, and in Congress are full-time professional politicians. How well are LEOs compensated for their work as elected officials? Generally, part-time citizen politicians, as they are called, are not compensated very well. The average salary for part-time LEOs was only $8,355; more than 50 percent of part-timers were paid less than $5,700 per year, and 17 percent did not receive any salary at all for their work as elected representatives. However, the salaries are not the primary motivator for local elected officeholders, nor are they representative of the total income of these LEOs. The average income of part-time officials, excluding pay from the elected office, was $60,153 in 2001. This reflects the high concentration of LEOs in managerial and professional occupations, as noted above.

The average salary for full-time LEOs was $44,768 in 2001. This far exceeded the median household income for Latinos of $33,447 in 2001.[19] LEOs, then, are better educated and wealthier than the Latino community average. Those who are not full-time politicians generally hold a professional or management position outside of their political career. This is an indication that many were leaders in business or the community before winning success in the world of politics. In Texas, where state representatives are in session on a part-time basis, LEOs work as attorneys, as small business owners, or in any of several other occupations throughout most of the year. Texas state senator Leticia Van de Putte runs a family pharmacy business in addition to her duties as a legislator. This requires maintaining a constant juggling act between personal and political life and having strong staff support.[20]

❏ *Motivation to Seek Political Office*

Holding political office, while rewarding on many levels, is difficult and time consuming. What are the motivations for seeking political office, given that the financial remuneration is little or nonexistent? LEOs have strong aspirations to hold office and were usually encouraged by community leaders to seek the position. Some were dissatisfied with the performance of the incumbent. Depending on the location and the relative importance of party slates or tickets, some LEOs coordinate their election campaigns with those of like-minded candidates. Many LEOs ran as part of a slate or coalition of candidates to increase their chances of winning and to save costs.

To win a political campaign takes not only the support of voters but also the support and financial backing of crucial interest groups. What kind of support do LEOs receive in their campaigns for office? LEOs recognize the need for major stakeholders to back their candidacy, and most need the support of more than one group. LEOs view ethnic community groups, ethnic businesses, unions, as well as women's groups, environmental groups, and other organizations as part of their support base. As shown in Table 8.1, those surveyed identified personal or family members as their most important Latino community supporters, with ethnic businesses the next most influential.

They indicated that their main supporters outside the ethnic community were personal friends, businesses, and labor groups (see Table 8.2). Only a small minority of LEOs indicated that they had no support from outside the ethnic community for their election. This is a sign that minority candidates need non–minority community support in order to win elections in districts where they are not the majority population.[21]

For Latino elected officials, ethnic community support, particularly from family members, community organizations, and local businesses, was

Table 8.1   Top Ethnic Community Supporters of Candidates

Community Group	Percentage Support
Business	23.5
Labor	11.1
Women	1.2
Single issue group	1.2
Personal/family	39.5
Other groups	11.1
More than one answer	8.6
Total	100[a]

Note: a. These numbers do not exactly total 100, due to rounding and missing data.

Table 8.2   Top Non–Ethnic Community Supporters of Candidates

Community Group	Percentage Support
Business	26.1
Labor	14.5
Women	2.9
Single issue group	1.4
Personal friends	24.6
Other groups	13.0
No non-ethnic support	7.2
Total	100[a]

Note: a. These numbers do not exactly total 100, due to rounding and missing data.

a strong factor in their electoral victory. Also, Latino officeholders made the decision to run for office based more on personal motivation than on pressure from party leaders or interest groups to seek office. This reflects the strong individualized decision-making process that today's candidates use to decide to run for office. However, it is also an interactive process, with party and interest groups encouraging potential candidates. Potential candidates are sought out and encouraged to consider running. The decision to seek office may be prompted by potential supporters' indication of their willingness to back a candidate.

Beyond LEOs' individual reasons for seeking elected office, what role does the support of Latino ethnic communities play in their decision to run? More than 75 percent of LEOs say that ethnic community support is a strong inducement to run for office. When Latinos were asked in a previous study how they would vote in a race between a coethnic and an Anglo candidate, more than 77 percent said they would support the coethnic candidate.[22] More recently, a majority of Latinos indicated that it is important to work together to achieve common political goals, and 84 percent said that if various Latino groups worked together politically, Latinos would be better off.[23] The Latino community provides a strong reservoir of support for Latino candidates running for office, and candidates tap into this support during their campaigns.

❏ *Economic Resources*

Once a Latino candidate decides to seek office, how important are economic resources to achieve elected office? Surprisingly, in a recent survey most local Latino elected officials indicated that money was not the crucial factor in their election to office, and 4 percent did not raise any funds whatsoever. While the average amount of money received by local and state representatives in their most recent campaign was $39,430, more than 70 percent raised less than $20,000. The average amount raised by Latino candidates was $48,431 for full-time state and local elected positions, while the mean amount of campaign funds for part-time positions was only $31,653. The LEOs reported that financial support for their electoral campaign from their ethnic community came to 42 percent of the total amount raised, which shows that many LEOs relied on non–ethnic community supporters for the majority of the material resources for their campaign.

■ **Coalitional Politics and Latinos**

The significance of biracial coalitions was an important finding of early political incorporation theory. Today Latinos find themselves in a wide variety of electoral contexts that have produced distinct political strategies for electoral empowerment. The growing complexity and diversity of political environments in which LEOs seek office, and the individualized character of most campaigns, make it difficult to identify a dominant pathway to election. Forty-nine percent of LEOs coordinated their campaigns with like-minded candidates to win office. The candidates who coordinated their campaigns usually took part in party mailers and endorsed unions or other interest groups. It appears most Latinos candidates rely on their own initiative and their supporters within and outside the community, rather than working in concert with others, to achieve elected office.

Typically, Latino candidates win office in districts that are majority Latino. The biracial coalition theory argues that in order for racial minorities to win elected office in districts where they are less than a majority of the population, they must first build coalitions with white liberals. This generally holds true in the case of Latinos running for office because there is a high proportion of noncitizens in many Latino immigrant communities. When Latinos are the majority of the population, however, they may be less reliant on white liberal support to achieve office than would be expected by political incorporation theory. Since most LEOs represent electoral districts that are majority Latino, the lack of reliance on white liberal support may be born out of political reality rather than LEOs' choice. In electoral districts where Latinos are not the majority population, it is still rare to find Latinos holding prominent electoral offices such as in the U.S. Senate, as governor, and even big-city mayor. In 2004, Ron Gonzalez was the only Latino mayor elected in a non-majority-Latino large city, and Bill Richardson was the only Latino governor. Even Governor Richardson was elected in New Mexico, a state with a more than 40 percent Latino population and a tradition of electing Hispanos to statewide office.

■ Priorities of LEOs

Once in office, do the policy priorities of Latino elected officials change? Under 20 percent of the state and local LEOs surveyed indicated that their priorities had changed. For those who indicated they had changed their policy priorities, issues such as limited revenues, development pressures, and increased understanding of other priorities were some of the main reasons. Clearly, for those who changed their policy priorities, economics played a major role. Nevertheless, the overwhelming majority believed that they had remained focused on the issues they ran on and had not changed their policy priorities.

It is important to analyze the views of elected Latinos on important issues confronting the nation because political representatives vote on substantive policy issues. The opinions of the LEOs surveyed were consistent with their liberal ideology; the respondents were strongly in favor of increased social services, greater economic control in Latino communities, and affirmative action programs. Also there was universal support for quality education and for an increase in the numbers of Latino students attending college. In addition, ethnic studies programs in secondary and higher education received very strong support. There was only limited support for drug liberalization laws and for reducing the flow of legal immigrants (see Table 8.3).

In terms of immigration policy, a salient issue in the Latino community, LEOs were divided on the issue of limiting the number of undocumented immigrants entering the country, with almost one-half of them favoring limits. They were in favor of the active participation of noncitizens in civic and political affairs and of granting amnesty for undocumented workers already in the United States. This illustrates the strong support that most Latinos give to the rights of immigrants (see Table 8.4). The position of LEOs is consistent with the views of the Latino community. Among all registered Latino voters, about 85 percent favor granting undocumented Latin immigrants in the United States the opportunity to obtain legal status.[24]

Latino legislators are heavily concentrated in states and locales where issues of growth, development, and environment protection often clash, and they are as concerned with issues of growth, environmental preservation, and pollution controls as are non-Latinos. They believe in growth controls, alleviating traffic congestion, and addressing air and water pollution in

Table 8.3   Views of Latino Elected Officials on Contemporary Issues

Issues	Percent Answered "Very Important" or "Fairly Important"
Greater community control over your ethnic community	94.9
More ethnic studies programs in H.S. and colleges	85.0
More of your ethnic students enrolled in college	100.0
Improve quality of education	100.0
Affirmative action programs	93.8
Third party or independent party	13.2
More of your ethnic group members elected to government positions	98.1
Mass protests to achieve equality	29.3
Liberalization of drug policies	30.0
Cuts in defense spending	50.5
More attention to moral values	87.2
Greater birth control efforts	76.3
Reduce total number of legal immigrants	34.8
Limit the number of illegal immigrants	45.3
Build coalitions with others	90.3
Free or low-cost health and day care centers	96.9

Table 8.4   Responses by Latino Elected Officials on Immigration Issues

	Percentage with Yes Answers
Should noncitizens be able to participate in civic activities?	75.2
Should there be bilingual translations of government meetings?	88.8
Hiring and appointments of noncitizens to government jobs	78.8
Allow noncitizens to vote in local elections if not forbidden by law	83.1
Support H1-B visas (temporary work visas)	67.6
Amnesty for undocumented workers	83.0

their areas. They were also supportive (81 percent) of restricting development in order to preserve the environment. The opinions of LEOs on environmental issues are strongly related to the large numbers who reside and govern in small towns and rural locations. Slow growth and environmental preservation remain major issues in much of the nation, and this attitude is reflected in the views of LEOs.

■ Views on Representation of Latina/o Elected Officials

Most LEOs, even in cities where they have a numerical majority of the city council or county commission, are conscious of their role as leaders of the Latino community and seek to provide substantive representation not just for Latinos but for all the residents in their community. Latino elected officials, where the vast majority of the population is Latino, are the most conscious of the need to provide substantive representation to the ethnic community that elected them to office. Much of their effort is geared toward bringing resources to neglected neighborhoods and communities in their jurisdiction. They often fight for more affordable housing, construction of parks and provision of recreational services, and economic development projects in low-income areas to generate more jobs and community wealth. This can be controversial, as it requires either diverting resources from somewhere else or increasing resources overall.

Many LEOs take pride in being a symbol of their country of origin to members of the community, but with changing immigration patterns and the diversification of districts, they have had to adapt by becoming the representative of all races and ethnic groups. New York state senator Olga Mendez was elected from a predominantly Puerto Rican and black district in 1978. This district changed demographically over the years and now contains a large percentage of Mexican nationals. She became active in the problems of the Mexican community in her district and visited Mexico more than once to understand the conditions that draw immigrants to New York.[25]

Latino officeholders in mixed ethnic/racial districts, where no one ethnic or racial group is the majority, are more attuned to providing substantive representation to the wider community. In these electoral districts Latino officials seldom mention a Latino, Puerto Rican, Cuban, or Mexican American agenda. While almost all LEOs in these diverse districts discuss their ethnic background and the role their parents and family played in enabling them to achieve their office, they do not generally translate this into an ethnic-specific agenda. Instead, they focus their campaigns on building coalitions with like-minded groups and constituencies to win office, and they focus their policymaking on passing legislation that appeals to different constituencies. One Latino elected official remarked that LEOs consciously downplayed their ethnicity and any hint of an ethnic agenda, as others did not do so. His objective was to pass laws that benefited all his constituents. He believed that if he demanded more resources for Latinos, it would turn off his other constituents.

■ Emerging Leaders

Although LEOs are generally older than the population they serve, there are some who enter politics at an earlier age than their more experienced counterparts. They come into office in a variety of ways, such as by defeating the incumbent candidate endorsed by the political machine or by working for an incumbent and jumping into the race when the position opens up. This phenomenon of a "Gen Xers" cohort of elected officials who are young, ambitious, and not held back by their age or experience is a growing trend. In centers of Latino politics in southern California, San Antonio, and elsewhere, they are running and winning important political offices. This cohort of political actors includes Mayor Ed Garza in San Antonio, Los Angeles Council President Alex Padilla, and several in New York City. Some of them are challenging the Latino political establishment in their communities. They are highly educated, well informed on issues, and determined to make their mark on politics.

Alex Padilla was first elected to the Los Angeles City Council from the San Fernando Valley region at the age of twenty-six. After graduation, he returned from college to get involved in local politics. Believing that the Latino agenda is the American dream, he is proud of being Latino and that he "is able speak Spanish to help serve the Latino community better than it had been in the past."[26] He is now the president of the Los Angeles City Council and plays a pivotal role in the politics of the city. California Assemblyman Fabian Núñez was elected to the assembly in 2002, and in 2004 he became the state's youngest speaker of the assembly at the age of thirty-seven. He has the strong backing of organized labor and public education. In San Antonio, Texas, there are several Mexican American city council and state representatives who have won elected office at a young age. State Representative Trey Martinez Fischer is one example; he was born in 1970, obtained his master's and J.D., and returned to win a seat in the Texas House of Representatives in 2001. He continues to practice law and serves as an elected official for the west side of San Antonio. State Representative Joaquin Castro was born and raised on San Antonio's west side. He, along with his twin brother Julian (now a San Antonio city councilman), graduated from Jefferson High School in 1992, attended university, and returned to run for office and serve the community. These emerging leaders reflect a growing trend of young people becoming engaged in politics.

Another important group of LEOs is the growing cohort of Latina legislators. Many of the Latina legislators surveyed or interviewed were in their thirties and forties, but there were also several grandmothers, including former welfare recipients who got into politics as part of their community activities. Several of them had grown children and were now focusing on building their political careers. Others still had young children at home but decided to run for office to make things better for their children. In Chicago, State Representative Cynthia Soto is the first Mexican American elected on the North Side, which has historically been a predominantly Puerto Rican district. Allied with Congressman Luis Gutierrez's camp, Soto is part of a black and brown caucus in the state legislature. She views herself as part of a progressive trend in Chicago and Illinois politics and is among a growing number of women of color legislators who work together on common concerns. Most Latinas said they began as community activists and were encouraged to enter electoral politics by friends and other community activists.

Another Latina local legislator, Barbara Herrera Hill, of mixed Cuban-Mexican descent, lives in the affluent suburban community of Weston, Florida. She ran for office after she realized that the population of her community had grown to 30 percent Latino and that the perspective of the global Latino community residing in this planned community needed to be represented at the local level. Large numbers of Venezuelans, Colombians, and other Latin Americans have moved into Weston. While the issues Hill addresses as a councilperson are local in character, many of the constituents she represents are part of broader transnational networks of immigrants with business interests and real estate investments. Given the uncertainties of homeland politics, many of these Latin Americans seek the relative safety of investing in the United States. The new crop of Latina politicians represents a new generation of leaders, many of whom were born during or after the Vietnam War, came of age during the Reagan/Bush years, and became active in politics during the Clinton era.

■ Conclusion

LEOs are on average older, better educated, and more financially secure than the general Latino population. Many of them were successful professionals or businesspeople, while others were community activists, before they sought electoral office. I don't want to generalize too broadly about a diverse group of political actors who come from many parts of the country and have roots throughout the Americas. It is probably accurate to say, however, that many LEOs are ideologically somewhat more liberal than their constituents, yet in most respects they are representative of the broad masses of Latinos. LEOs as a group are not radical; most are liberal to middle of the road and integrationist. The majority of LEOs are sophisticated inside political players who are able to build consensus and work with politicians of other beliefs and races. Some continue to raise militant calls for social justice, equality, and an end to discrimination, yet they are part of a much larger political structure that limits their ability to make dramatic change. Both types of LEOs rely heavily on those outside political institutions to highlight issues and dramatize the community's concerns, according to one local politician I spoke with.

A significant portion of LEOs were raised in households where English was not the predominant language. This reflects the immigrant and working-class origins of most LEOs. Many of these individuals had strong motivation to seek elected office but did not necessarily follow the traditional electoral path, such as first becoming a party activist or working as an aide to an elected official. LEOs relied heavily on their ethnic community, particularly their friends and family, for political and financial support, yet they also built support beyond their ethnic community for electoral victories.

The campaign priorities and the policies of Latino officeholders are also divided between ethnic community concerns and universal issues. LEOs are, in general, responsive to the Latino community and appear to be conscious of acting as representatives of their constituents. Latino elected officials exhibit significant ethnic solidarity in their political behavior. LEOs of various regions and states, offices, ethnicities, and genders are committed to being substantive, not merely descriptive, representatives for the Latino community.

The theory of political incorporation posits that a large minority population combined with even a minority of liberal white voters is necessary to achieve political empowerment for historically disenfranchised groups. However, the pathway to electoral office for LEOs does not necessarily follow this model. Latinos follow the traditional political incorporation model more closely in circumstances where they are the dominant but not the majority racial group. However, under most circumstances, they have historically needed a supermajority of the Latino population in order to achieve electoral office, in which case the need for a biracial coalition was diminished.

Latino elected officials have drawn on their ethnic community for support to achieve elected office. Most of the LEOs relied on family, friends, and organized interest groups to win their campaigns. By and large their policy concerns are rooted in their immigrant origins and liberal backgrounds. In particular, members of the older generation of politicians appear to have had extremely humble beginnings, and this may drive their policy choices.

■ Notes

1. H. Pitkin (1967).
2. Ibid., p. 209.
3. J. L. Polinard et al. (1994); K. J. Meier, J. L. Polinard, and R. D. Wrinkle (2000); L. Baker, L. Camacho, and R. Salinas (1995); A. J. Nelson (1991).
4. R. Hero and K. M. Beatty (1989); J. R. Cruz (1998); D. Moreno (1997); J. Regalado (1998); R. Browning, D. Marshall, and D. Tabb (1990 and 1997); J. Jennings and M. Rivera (1984).
5. H. Pachon and L. DeSipio (1990).
6. S. Welch and J. R. Hibbing (1988); R. Hero and C. Tolbert (1995); B. Kerr and W. Miller (1997); J. W. Endersby and C. E. Menifield (2000); M. Vigil (1996 and 1997).
7. The 2000 National Directory of Latino Elected and Appointed Officials (NALEO) was used to obtain names and addresses. The survey was distributed randomly using a stratified sample that enables the researcher to divide a population into subdivisions. Names were selected at random within each state where there were Latino elected officials. For more details on the survey methodology, please contact the author.
8. The author conducted a nationwide random mail survey in 2000–2001. There were 411 surveys distributed, and 112 completed surveys were returned. This was a 28.6 percent response rate, a respectable return rate for busy elected officials, the overwhelming majority of whom serve part-time officials while holding a full-time job. The respondents included 26 responses, or 24.1 percent, from Latinas, which corresponds to the percentage of Latinas in elective office nationally. The data gathered are available from the author. There were also 42 personal interviews conducted in the summer and fall of 2001. These interviews are used throughout the book. A complete list can be found at the end of the list of references.
9. Latinos who rise to positions of leadership in predominantly Latino and other types of organizations come to power through a variety of methods. These efforts will not be explored in this text.
10. U.S. Census (2001a). As discussed previously, there was a significant undercount of several Latino groups whose members were unable to check a box that reflected their country of origin. Large growth among Dominicans, Colombians, and persons from several countries in Central America between 1990 and 2000 was not accurately reflected in the 2000 census. See Suro (2002).
11. R. Hero et al. (2000).

12. *Washington Post*, Kaiser Family Foundation, and Harvard University (2000).

13. *Washington Post*, Kaiser Family Foundation, and Harvard University (2000).

14. L. DeSipio (1996), pp. 50–55.

15. D. Abalos (1986), p. 58.

16. *Washington Post*, Kaiser Family Foundation, and Harvard University (2000), p. 65.

17. U.S. Census (1999).

18. U.S. Census (2001b).

19. U.S. Census (2001b).

20. Texas state senator L. Van de Putte, interview (2001).

21. R. Browning, D. Marshall, and D. Tabb (1984).

22. R. de la Garza (1992), p. 138.

23. *Washington Post*, Kaiser Family Foundation, and Harvard University (2000), p. 73.

24. Pew Hispanic Center and Kaiser Family Foundation (2002b), pp. 10–11.

25. New York state senator O. Mendez, interview (2001).

26. "Alex Padilla" (2001), pp. 21–24.

9

Latino Politics in the New Millennium

The aim of this book is twofold: to describe the transition by Latinos from disenfranchised outsiders to political leaders and policymakers, and to explain to what degree Latino elected officials are sensitive to ethnic community concerns and seek to deliver policy benefits to their communities. Stated another way, the story that has been presented explored the historical struggle of Latinos to overcome discriminatory barriers to full participation and to achieve political incorporation and obtain policy benefits. This book makes a contribution to the larger study of Latino politics. First, it shows through case studies the different ways Latino communities have mobilized to achieve and consolidate Latino political incorporation. Second, it explores the demographics of Latino political leaders, the pathways they used to win elective office, and their views on contemporary policy matters. Third, it has summarized the more than 150 years of struggle by Latinos to receive, in the words of the Voting Rights Act, "an equal opportunity to participate in elections and to elect a candidate of their choice." This struggle is far from over for Latinos. Discriminatory barriers have been made illegal, yet high rates of noncitizenship, low voter registration and turnout rates, combined with continuing racially polarized voting patterns, have limited Latinos' access, full participation, and election to office. Relative to the majority population, Latinos still do not have equal opportunity to participate in the electoral process.

While some argue that Latinos have entered a post–civil rights era in which they are no longer victims of the political system and no longer in need of legal protection through court-ordered boundaries, others contend that Latinos still need the protection of the Voting Rights Act and its amendments to obtain their fair share of elected positions in a society that remains bounded by racial politics. One thing that is not in dispute is the fact that Latinos continue to live in residentially segregated areas that are densely populated and have underfunded schools, and that they have lower average levels of education and income than the average American. Social struggles are still required for Latinos and other racial minorities to achieve full equality in our democracy. These battles must continue to be waged, while others in the Latino community push forward the boundaries of who can be elected and where they can be elected.

The core of majority-Latino districts that have elected Latinos should be viewed as a base, not a ceiling, for Latino electoral aspirations. The dilemma faced by Latino political strategists is how to expand the number of districts in each state where Latinos will have the opportunity to elect the representative of their choice. Should a certain percentage of majority-minority districts be broken up and district lines redrawn to create more non-Latino-maority electoral districts where Latino candidates can compete? This assumes that non-Latino voters will vote for Latinos. While there is some evidence for this in certain areas of the country, the legacy of prejudice and discrimination against Latinos still hangs heavy over the political process. As the Mexican American Legal Defense Fund (MALDEF) noted recently about one state: "Unfortunately, racially polarized voting persists in California, thus demonstrating the continued need for and enforcement of the Voting Rights Act. MALDEF's consultants have conducted preliminary racial polarization analysis of elections occurring during the decade and have found evidence of polarization, particularly in Southern California."[1]

While for the foreseeable future the preservation of existing Latino-majority districts is a necessary part of Latino efforts for equal opportunity in the political process, this should not restrict Latino attempts to win elections in areas and regions where historically they have had only a limited presence. How to hold on to existing seats and expand into new electoral districts has become a controversial issue.

■ Drawing Conclusions and Seeking Clarity from Latino Politics

Latinos have overcome enormous barriers to achieve elected office and are now institutionalized in the very structures that previously excluded them. This seeming contradiction between societal biases toward Latinos and Latino electoral successes has mainly occurred through the group efforts of Latinos to modify electoral structures to allow them to elect candidates of their choice. Before the 1980s, in most cases, only Latinos elected Latinos to office. By the 1990s, this pattern was beginning to break down, as non-Latinos in some locations began to help elect Latinos to office. The election of Latinos in diverse locations has allowed for a more systematic study of the attitudes and patterns of Latino officeholders and their policy beliefs. This chapter will suggest some tentative conclusions that can be drawn from an analysis of the history of Latino political efforts and the case studies of contemporary Latino political incorporation efforts, and it will offer some suggestions for students and activists involved in the study and practice of Latino politics.

In spite of attempts to exclude them from participating in fundamental political activities such as voting and running for office, Latinos have overcome marginalization and discriminatory practices by the dominant majority to achieve numerous political milestones. Beginning in the eighteenth and nineteenth centuries, pioneer Latino politicians became involved in American-style electoral politics. During the Jim Crow segregation era, from the late 1800s to the 1950s, nonwhites in most communities were prevented from voting, seeking office, and fully participating in the democratic process, yet Latinos remained active in political affairs, built middle-class civil rights groups, and organized labor and political activities.

Beginning in the 1960s, Latinos organized outside the mainstream political arena, built alternative organizations, and framed new political ideologies that reflected the militancy of the times. They also used legal methods and insider politics within the political parties and at the grass-roots level to have a voice in mainstream American politics. Longtime Latino ethnic groups such as Mexicans and Puerto Ricans and new immigrants from the Caribbean Islands, Central America, and South America became more engaged in domestic and homeland politics. Foreign policy in Latin America became not just an issue for U.S. foreign policy planners; now Latin American governments and their supporters and critics within the Latino Diaspora are more actively engaged. Several Latin American nations have established dual nationality provisions for their former residents who live in the United States. Remittances from Latinos to their families and towns of origin in Latin America have become a multibillion-dollar effort and are critical for the economic development of our neighbors in the Western Hemisphere.

The stakes are high in a globalized economy. With the U.S. Hispanic market already larger than all but the eleven richest countries, there is potential for economic and political influence. The interrelationships between the United States and Latin America is illustrated by recent events: the Elian Gonzalez controversy in 2000, the efforts of George W. Bush and Vicente Fox to regularize Mexican immigrants to the United States, and U.S. government involvement in the internal politics of Venezuela. The U.S. government also provided $1.3 billion in foreign aid to the Colombian government (third largest after Israel and Egypt at the time) as part of Plan Colombia in 2000.[2] Eighty percent of the aid was earmarked for the military and police, which helped fuel Colombia's long civil war whose victims are almost all civilians. The growing interrelationships among the nations and peoples of the Western Hemisphere require ongoing attention and the active involvement of the Latino community and its leadership.

■ Learning from the Incorporation Process

A few general conclusions can be drawn regarding how the process of political incorporation unfolds and how political governing coalitions are constructed at the local level. The first conclusion is that a singular major event that sparks protests and demands for change, leading to movements for political representation, is not required. In our case studies, usually several events combined to trigger a reaction leading to movements for political incorporation. In Salinas, there was not one decisive trigger event but a string of events that culminated in political incorporation.

Another conclusion that can be drawn from these case studies relates to the role of community organizations in the incorporation process. Community organizations that mobilized to achieve the inclusion of Latinos have had an important impact on the character of the political incorporation process in various places. Community-led efforts to win district elections in San Antonio, Miami-Dade County, and Salinas built a strong foundation to carry forward the demand for full political incorporation. In Los Angeles, while district elections already existed when Latinos began to seek inclusion, the struggle took the form of drawing district boundaries that enabled Latinos to have a fair chance at winning elected office. In Salinas, the strength of Latino political incorporation was due to a strong grassroots community organization, the Alisal Betterment Committee (ABC), that fought to win district elections for community representatives who would reflect the values and beliefs of the Latino community. The formation of this organization and the mobilization of the Chicano community, combined with the sophistication of Chicano community activists, were indispensable to the campaigns to win district elections.

Another conclusion that can be drawn is that a biracial coalition to achieve political incorporation is a tactic, not a strategic necessity. Where Latinos are a minority of the population, Latino politicians will continue to work with an array of allies, including labor, African Americans, Asian and Pacific Islanders, and Native Americans, to build electoral coalitions. Where Latinos are the dominant majority, in locations such as Miami and Salinas, the role of white liberals was not critical in Latinos' ascent to political leadership, and sometimes other potential allies were not evident. In Salinas, the political incorporation efforts of Latinos were carried out without strong support from the white community, yet there was a critical minority that consistently supported Latino efforts. In Miami, white liberals and the conservative Cuban American community were at odds over many issues and failed to work together. A biracial coalition was not necessary in the political incorporation efforts within either of these communities.

This finding is similar to conclusions others have drawn regarding some Latino-majority cities in the Southwest. The point is that where Latinos are the majority of voters, they are less likely to seek or need the assistance of white liberals, although they will want to work closely with whites and with other minority groups where there is agreement on policy aims and goals. This certainly was the case with the 2001 Ed Garza mayoral victory in San Antonio, where Garza won the support of both white and Mexican American voters. In many other cities, the achievement of political incorporation for Latinos and other racial minorities was based on the forging of biracial and multiracial coalitions.[3]

■ Political Incorporation and Class Interests

Another conclusion that can be drawn from the efforts of Latinos to achieve political incorporation is that governing coalitions encompass multiple class interests. Urban government involves a complex mix of influences as commercial development, labor, neighborhood, environmental, and Latino and other minority community interests seek to steer local policy. The dominant governing coalition in cities where Latinos have been electorally successful does contain Latinos, often as members of the city council and as city bureaucrats; however, a combination of factors has limited the level of policy benefits being delivered to the working poor in the Latino community. These factors include slow economic investment, systemic poverty in the Latino community produced by a low-wage labor market, and differing land use and environmental policy agendas of elected Latinos and other local elected officials. Issues such as crime reduction, public safety, and no-growth versus progrowth tend to receive the most attention and budgetary consideration in cities; meanwhile, services desperately needed in the Latino community, such as more varied employment opportunities, training for better-paying jobs, easing of school overcrowding, improved educational services, and after-school programs have received inadequate resources.

Latino political incorporation has meant, for the first time, not only the representation of Latinos in general but, more specifically, the inclusion of low-wage Latino workers and the urban poor in the dialogue in some communities. Latino worker interests are usually involved in the electoral coalition that elects Latinos to office. Previously, local governments rarely addressed labor issues. Today, these concerns are likely to be openly discussed and debated, since they relate to water issues, housing, education, and other social policies. In many cities, policies have been created that have benefited the working poor in Latino communities; these policies appear to be much stronger than those of previous governing coalitions, which were dominated exclusively by downtown business interests. For example, the city of Los Angeles passed a living-wage ordinance in 1997 after a community coalition that included numerous Latino worker organizations carried out a grassroots campaign. The ordinance requires that any contractor doing business with the city provide health benefits and pay salaries that are substantially higher than the state's current minimum wage of $6.75 per hour.

Another observation from the case studies and history of political incorporation efforts is that Latino community stakeholders and officeholders have not always acted with a common vision. The need for an ongoing community-based movement of Latinos that can articulate demands for policy equity, hold city leaders (including Latino council members) accountable for their actions, and push for a greater share of policy benefits in the future was an important lesson learned by community activists in places like San Antonio and Los Angeles. However, Latinos are not the dominant economic players in most communities, and thus they remain economically dependent on the same economic interests that have controlled local and regional politics for decades. In cities such as Salinas and San Antonio, where Latinos are the majority of the governing coalition, the Latino community must negotiate a relationship with the dominant economic forces that shape the policy agenda. In these locations, the governing coalition must deal with the dual pull of corporate influences and the need to redistribute resources to the working poor in Latino and other communities.

In Miami, where Latino business interests are quite powerful, Cuban American politicians are also brokers for the wealth and power of their community's members in the business world. Here there appears to be a more equitable relationship between race and class forces; however, this is highly unusual. In most cities, the role of Latino politicians is to negotiate policy benefits for the Latino community in the context of supporting large economic development projects. This usually involves obtaining agreements from private developers to build affordable housing, hire from the community, and fund urban education or parks and recreation areas in Latino communities as part of development efforts.

Economic interests will remain significant where there are investment opportunities. This requires that they deal with the political forces that occupy the seats of power. Economic interests must find ways to compromise to achieve their financial goals or use their economic strength to negotiate a deal most favorable to them. This is the logic of the market system. Latinos in power in local and higher levels of government should continue to leverage their political power to obtain the best possible economic deals for their communities and for others in need of community development and social services.

■ Levels of Political Incorporation and Policy Benefits

The results of these case studies indicate that the level of political incorporation is not an accurate predictor of the strength of Latino political power. The more important question is, how does political power manifest itself in the strength of policy benefits returning to local Latino communities? The level of political incorporation alone does not determine the answer to this question. Particularly in cities that use district elections, where candidates are elected from different neighborhoods with widely divergent socioeconomic conditions and issue formation, there are different types of Latino officeholders.

At least in cities with district elections, the number of Latinos on a city council does not fully explain differences in policy formation among cities. Even in cities with at-large electoral systems, the ability of Latinos to get elected stems from the support of different voter bases. This will, in turn, affect the character and type of governing coalition that is created. A 1990s study of California Latina officeholders found that almost 100 percent of them were of working-class origins and "given [this], these elected officials may introduce policy perspectives more responsive to the needs of poor and working-class people."[4]

Not only is who is elected significant, but what type of administrators are hired into key positions, such as city manager, police chief, and head of economic development, are also important in the construction of a governing coalition. Those holding these positions, in conjunction with elected officeholders, have a powerful role at the local level. They shape local policy decisions and can steer cities in a variety of directions. These usually nonelected local government leaders can provide leadership regarding key issues and direct resources to solve long-standing problems.

A final conclusion of the case studies is that in addition to the important roles of economic interests, Latino politicians, and city administrators, an ongoing, organized community-led movement of Latinos must be vigilant to ensure that policy benefits are returned to the community. The key lesson from the many political incorporation efforts is the need for the Latino community to continue to mobilize to receive its fair share of resources and highlight broader social issues *after* Latinos are elected to office. This can take the form of a well-organized interest group such as Communities Organized for Public Service (COPS) in San Antonio, Texas, that regularly meets with elected officials and holds them accountable for the stands they take on local issues. Where it is absent, there is no mechanism other than electing different political actors to keep local government accountable to the needs of the Latino community. Latino politicians, even if they have run for office on a program to implement a Latino agenda, may soon lapse into a business-as-usual mentality that is disconnected from the most pressing needs of the community. This situation existed for a time in Los Angeles, where elements of the Latino elected leadership had grown removed and insulated from the grassroots needs of their communities.[5] This is a dangerous trend and adds to cynicism in the Latino community that elections are an ineffective and counterproductive arena for democratic action.

In a representative democracy, an overreliance on the electoral arena, on elected Latino officeholders, and on achieving the maximum numbers of Latinos in office will not solve the complex problems of Latino communities. In addition to maintaining the accountability of political leaders, issue-based neighborhood organizing in Latino communities is vital to address structural inequalities. Understanding the interplay between political incorporation efforts and empowerment efforts at the grassroots level is important for the study of Latino politics.

Community initiatives usually begin as small and seemingly insignificant actions but form the basis for later large-scale changes, such as the dramatic changes in the cities we explored. These efforts are difficult to maintain, as movements ebb and flow; yet the existence and maintenance of organized interest groups, neighborhood-based organizations, community activists, and local residents can extend inclusion in a governing coalition or force changes in policies of cities as small as Salinas and as large as Los Angeles.[6] More often than not, it is these efforts that provide the spark that ultimately leads to reevaluation of public policy, institutional changes, and the election of new leaders.

■ Final Thoughts

The diversity of the political experiences of Latinos makes broad generalizations difficult. For example, the rapid rise to local political power of Cuban Americans in south Florida is due to the combination of a favorable U.S. government policy and local political and economic underdevelopment in Miami that enabled Cubans to overcome the discriminatory obstacles created by the city's Anglo establishment.[7] The Cuban experience reflects a different process of political incorporation from that of Puerto Ricans, who are citizens by decree of the U.S. government; of Mexican Americans in the Southwest and Midwest, who have suffered a much longer history of entrenched structural discrimination and social ostracism; and of recent immigrants and refugees from Central and South America, who have only recently begun to achieve electoral office.

Latinos do not share an identical political experience in this country, and no one method is adequate to study such a diverse group of people. Although Latinos have a common history of conquest and colonization, their diverse paths to political officeholding and political power reflect a multiplicity of factors—the conditions they entered as ethnic immigrants, their social and political status upon entering this new environment, and the sorts of efforts they made to change their status. For these reasons, this book did not attempt to capture the totality of Latino political experience; rather, it is a more focused exploration of how racial politics have unfolded in the post–civil rights era, where racial identities, economics, and political power have been contested in various ways. While I did analyze the political conflicts with whites in some cities and the transition of power away from those who had held it for many decades, the book did not fully explore the dynamics of black and Latino political relationships. This is an important topic that others have more fully examined.[8]

This book sought to capture the contemporary thinking of Latino elected officials. The results of the survey of Latino elected officials demonstrate that LEOs exhibit significant concern for the needs of the Latino community in their political behavior. The interviews conducted with LEOs confirmed the initial finding of the mail survey that most Latino political leaders were committed to being substantive representatives of the Latino community. They consciously sought to set policy that would benefit this community.

With Latinos achieving political office, and in some cases dominating the local political power structure, have the limitation of Latinos' collective economic fortunes and lack of economic control reduced their officeholding to window dressing, merely giving the appearance that they have gained equality with whites? It is my belief that Latino politics, as it is played out in numerous locations, has the potential to create partnerships for the economic development of Latino communities. This will not be easy, as the Latino community does not control most of the economic resources in its regions; yet the sheer number of Latino voters is forcing global economic interests to address their needs. The U.S. Hispanic market is enormous, and the Latino community has the potential to shape economics and politics in the hemisphere. Within the constraints of an unequal economic system, Latino political power can at opportune moments redirect economic resources to solve some long-standing social problems.

As the numbers of Latinos continue to grow in urban, suburban, and rural communities, different pathways to political empowerment are becoming available. There will undoubtedly be a wider variety of Latino candidates from both major parties and as independents. More important, the ongoing poverty and social inequality in many communities will require the construction of new and varied forms of social movements to respond to new conditions. As many U.S.-born Latinos move away from the barrios to the suburbs, the growth of middle-class enclaves of Latinos and the integration of Latino families into non-Latino areas will also create new challenges and new voting patterns. Furthermore, the continuing growth of anti-immigrant forces that fan racial and cultural wars will also prompt new and varied responses within the Latino and other immigrant communities. As old alliances fray, new ones may emerge.

Undoubtedly this book is but one piece of a much larger puzzle. The types of electoral districts and candidates seeking office can be explored more systematically and compared in other qualitative studies. As part of the growing body of literature on racial politics in American cities, however, this study helps to validate the development of Latino politics at the local and national level. Latino politics is still a relatively new subfield of social science investigation, and as various social theories are tested in the context of the experiences of Latinos, and in interaction with others, these theories will be enriched.

In a society as diverse as the United States, equality for all remains an elusive goal. In a nation where physical and cultural differences have been used by a dominant majority to discriminate against and marginalize groups of people, symbolic and substantive representation are necessary steps in a long process of gaining full equality for historically underrepresented groups. The political representation of people of color, however, is not exclusively the responsibility of those of that particular racial or ethnic group. The historical divisions among peoples of color in this country require continued exploration of how minority representatives act to represent their own historically underrepresented group members and others. As Melissa Williams (1998) notes, "Although representation for marginalized groups is not in itself a cure for injustice, there is good reason to believe it is at least a healing measure."[9]

■ Notes

1. MALDEF (2001).
2. G. Leech (2000).
3. R. Hero (1997), p. 257.
4. P. C. Takash (1993).
5. J. Regalado (1997).
6. R. Rosales (2000); J. Regalado (1998); J. Anner (1996); P. Medoff and H. Sklar (1994).
7. D. Moreno (1997).
8. N. Vaca (2004); E. Morales (2004); J. Jennings (1994); C. P. Henry (1980); J. Miles (1992).
9. M. Williams (1998), p. 243.

References

Abalos, David T. 1986. *Latinos in the United States: The Sacred and the Political.* Notre Dame, IN: University of Notre Dame Press.

Abramson, Michael, and the Young Lords Party. 1971. *Palante: Young Lords Party.* New York: McGraw-Hill.

Acuña, Rodolfo F. 1981. *Occupied America: A History of Chicanos.* 2nd ed. New York: Harper and Row.

———. 1988. *Occupied America: A History of Chicanos.* 3rd ed. New York: HarperCollins.

———. 1996. *Anything But Mexican: Chicanos in Contemporary Los Angeles.* New York: Verso.

"Alex Padilla." 2001. *Latino Leaders: The National Magazine of the Successful Hispanic American,* June-July, pp. 21–24.

America Online and Time Warner Foundation. 2002. Hispanic Opinion Tracker Survey (HOT). Cited in *Mobilizing the Vote: Latinos and Immigrants in the 2002 Midterm Election.* www.nclr.org.

Anders, Evan. 1982. *Boss Rule in South Texas: The Progressive Era.* Austin: University of Texas Press.

Anner, John, ed. 1996. *Beyond Identity Politics: Emerging Social Justice Movements in Communities of Color.* Boston: South End.

Avila, Joaquin G. 1997. "The Political Integration of Racial and Ethnic Minorities." Twelfth Annual Ernesto Galarza Lecture, Stanford Center for Chicano Research, Palo Alto, CA.

Ayon, David R. 2000. "Fault Lines below Latino Politicians." *Los Angeles Times,* February 6, p. M6.

Baker, Lou, Linda Camacho, and Robert Salinas. 1995. *Latino Political Representation: The 1993–94 California Latino Legislative Caucus.* Chicano/Latino Policy Project 2, no. 1. Berkeley: University of California, Institute for the Study of Social Change.

Barone, Michael, and Grant Ujifusa. 1999. *The Almanac of American Politics 2000.* Washington, DC: National Journal.

Baver, Sherrie. 1984. "Puerto Rican Politics in New York City: The Post–World War II Period." In *Puerto Rican Politics in Urban America,* edited by James Jennings and Monte Rivera. Westport, CT: Greenwood.

Bean, Frank D., and Marta Tienda. 1985. *The Hispanic Population of the United States.* New York: Russell Sage Foundation.

Berman, David R. 1998. *Arizona Politics and Government: The Quest for Autonomy, Democracy, and Development.* Lincoln: University of Nebraska Press.

Betancur, John J., and Douglas C. Gills. 1993. "Race and Class in Local Economic Development." In *Theories of Local Economic Development: Perspectives from across the Disciplines,* edited by Richard D. Bingham and Robert Mier. Newbury Park, CA: Sage.

———. 2000. "The African and Latino Coalitional Experience in Chicago under Mayor Harold Washington." In *The Collaborative City: Opportunities and Struggles for Blacks and Latinos in U.S. Cities,* edited by John J. Betancur and Douglas C. Gills. New York: Garland.

Bluestone, Barry, and Bennett Harrison. 1982. *The Deindustrialization of America.* New York: Basic Books.

Bonilla, Frank, and Walter Stafford. 2000. "African Americans and Puerto Ricans in New York: Cycles and Circles of Discrimination." In *The Collaborative City: Opportunities and Struggles for Blacks and Latinos in U.S. Cities,* edited by John J. Betancur and Douglas C. Gills. New York: Garland.

Booth, John A., and David R. Johnson. 1983. "Power and Progress in San Antonio Politics, 1836–1970." In *The Politics of San Antonio: Community, Progress, and Power,* edited by David R. Johnson, John A. Booth, and Richard J. Harris. Lincoln: University of Nebraska.

Bositis, David A. 2003. "Black Elected Officials: A Statistical Summary." Joint Center for Political and Economic Studies. http://www.jointcenter.org/publications/BEO/BEO-01.html (accessed December 17, 2003).

Boswell, Thomas D. 1994. *The Cubanization and Hispanization of Metropolitan Miami.* Miami, FL: Cuban American National Council.

Bridges, Amy. 1997. *Morning Glories: Municipal Reform in the Southwest.* Princeton, NJ: Princeton University Press.

Bridges, Amy, and Katherine Underwood. 2000. "Life after Districts." In *Minority Politics at the Millennium,* edited by Richard A. Keiser and Katherine Underwood. New York: Garland.

Bridges, Tyler. 2001. "Hard Work, Elián Issue Gave Diaz a Major Boost: From Background to Spotlight, Candidate Quickly Built Up Image." *Miami Herald,* November 14, p. 1.

Brischetto, Robert R. 1988a. "Electoral Empowerment of Texas Mexicans: The Case for Tejanos." In *Latino Empowerment: Progress, Problems, and Prospects,* edited by Roberto E. Villarreal, Norma G. Hernandez, and Howard D. Neighbor. Westport, CT: Greenwood.

———. 1988b. *The Political Empowerment of Texas Mexicans, 1974–1988.* San Antonio, TX: Southwest Voter Research Institute.

Brischetto, Robert R., Charles L. Correll, and R. Michael Stevens. 1983. "Conflict and Change in the Political Culture of San Antonio in the 1970s." In *The Politics of San Antonio: Community, Progress, and Power,* edited by David R. Johnson, John A. Booth, and Richard J. Harris. Lincoln: University of Nebraska Press.

Brischetto, Robert R., David R. Richards, Chandler Davidson, and Bernard Grofman. 1994. "Texas." In *Quiet Revolution in the South: The Impact of the Voting Rights Act, 1965–1990,* edited by Chandler Davidson and Bernard Grofman, pp. 233–70. Princeton, NJ: Princeton University Press.

Browning, Rufus P., Dale R. Marshall, and David H. Tabb. 1984. *Protest Is Not Enough: The Struggle of Blacks and Hispanics for Equality in Urban Politics.* Berkeley: University of California Press.

———, eds. 1990. *Racial Politics in American Cities*. New York: Longman.

———. 1994. "Political Incorporation and Competing Perspectives on Urban Politics." Paper delivered at the American Political Science Association annual meeting, New York City, September.

———. 1995. "Mobilization, Incorporation, and Policy." Paper delivered at the 1995 annual meeting of the American Political Science Association. Chicago.

———, eds. 1997. *Racial Politics in American Cities*. 2nd ed. New York: Longman.

———, eds. 2003. *Racial Politics in American Cities*. 3rd ed. New York: Longman.

California, State of. 2001. "Labor Market Information, Directory of California Local Area Wages: Wages from 1998–2000." CCOIS Surveys, Employment Development Department.

———. 2002a. "Labor Force Data for Sub-county Areas" (February 21). Department of Employment Development.

———. 2002b. "Revised Historical City and County Population Estimates 1991–2000 with 1990 and 2000 Census Counts" (March). Department of Finance.

California Institute of Rural Studies. 2000. "Suffering in Silence: A Report on the Health of California's Agricultural Workers." November 21.

Center for Voting and Democracy. n.d.a. "Voting Rights Act." www.fairvote.org/vra/vra.htm.

———. n.d.b. "Latinos in State Legislatures." www.fairvote.org/vra/stateleg2003.htm.

Chandler, Charles Ray. 1968. *The Mexican-American Protest Movement in Texas*. Ann Arbor, MI: University Microfilms.

Chinchilla, Norma, Nora Hamilton, and James Loucky. 1993. "Central Americans in Los Angeles: An Immigrant Community in Transition." In *In the Barrios: Latinos and the Underclass Debate*, edited by Joan Moore and Raquel Pinderhughes. New York: Russell Sage Foundation.

CNN.com. 2000. "100,000 March in Miami in Protest over Elian." April 30 (accessed May 15, 2004).

Coalition for Humane Immigrant Rights in Los Angeles (CHIRLA). n.d. http://www.chirla.org/aboutus.htm (accessed October 10, 2004).

Colburn, David R.. and Lance deHaven-Smith. 1999. *Government in the Sunshine State: Florida since Statehood*. Gainesville: University Press of Florida,.

Cole, Caroline L. 2001. "Lawrence Mayoral Race: Sullivan Follows Brother's Path." *Boston Daily Globe*, November 17. www.boston.com (accessed November 8, 2001).

Collins, Sheila D. 1986. *The Rainbow Challenge: The Jackson Campaign and the Future of U.S. Politics*. New York: Monthly Review.

Conyers, James E., and Wallace, Walter L. 1976. *Black Elected Officials: A Study of Black Americans Holding Governmental Office*. New York: Russell Sage Foundation.

Córdova, Teresa. 1999. "Harold Washington and the Rise of Latino Electoral Politics in Chicago, 1982–1987." In *Chicano Politics and Society in the Late Twentieth Century*, edited by David Montejano. Austin: University of Texas Press.

Cox, Kenneth R., and A. Mair. 1988. "Locality and Community in the Politics of Local Economic Development." *Annuals of the Association of American Geographers* 78, no. 2: 307–325.

———. 1989. "Urban Growth Machines and the Politics of Local Economic Development," *International Journal for Urban and Regional Research* 13, no. 1: 137–146.

Crocker, R. 2000. "La Raza to the Top." *Coast Weekly,* October 5, p. 1.

Cruz, Jose E. 1998. *Identity and Power: Puerto Rican Politics and the Challenge of Ethnicity*. Philadelphia: Temple University Press.

Dahl, Robert. 1961. *Who Governs? Democracy and Power in an American City*. New Haven, CT: Yale University Press.

Dallek, Robert. 1998. "Taking the Long View on Alarcón's Victory." *Los Angeles Times*. July 15, p. 7.

Daniels, Cletus E. 1995. "Cesar Chavez and the Unionization of California Farmworkers." In *Working People of California*, edited by Daniel Cornford, pp. 371–404. Berkeley: University of California Press.

Date, S. V. 2002. "Cuban Americans' Clout in Legislature Growing." *Palm Beach Post*, May 1, p. 1A.

Davidson, Chandler. 1972. *Biracial Politics: Conflict and Coalition in the Metropolitan South*. Baton Rouge: Louisiana State University Press.

Davidson, Chandler, and Bernard Grofman, eds. 1994. *Quiet Revolution in the South: The Impact of the Voting Rights Act, 1965–1990*. Princeton, NJ: Princeton University Press.

Davidson, Charles 1990. *Race and Class in New Mexico*. Princeton, NJ: Princeton University Press.

Davis, Mike. 1992. "Chicano (and Landlord) Power! Is Bell Gardens' Not-Quite-Grassroots Revolt the Future of L.A.'s Working-Class Immigrant Suburbs?" *LA Weekly*, January 10–16, p. 10.

De la Garza, Rodolfo O. 1992. "From Rhetoric to Reality: Latinos and the 1988 Election in Review." In *From Rhetoric to Reality: Latino Politics in the 1988 Elections*, edited by Rodolfo O. de la Garza and Louis DeSipio. Boulder, CO: Westview.

De la Garza, Rodolfo O., and Louis DeSipio. 1997. "Save the Baby, Change the Bathwater, and Scrub the Tub: Latino Electoral Participation after Twenty Years of Voting Rights Act Coverage." In *Pursing Power: Latinos and the Political System*, edited by F. Chris Garcia. Notre Dame, IN: University of Notre Dame Press.

———, eds. 1999. *Awash in the Mainstream: Latino Politics in the 1996 Elections*. Boulder, CO: Westview.

De la Garza, Rodolfo O., and David Vaughan. 1985. "The Political Socialization of Chicano Elites: A Generational Approach." In *The Mexican American Experience: An Interdisciplinary Anthology*, edited by Rodolfo O. de la Garza et al. Austin: University of Texas Press.

De León, Arnoldo. 1989. *Ethnicity in the Sunbelt: A History of Mexican Americans in Houston*. Houston: Mexican American Studies.

De Los Angeles Torres, Maria. 1991. "The Commission on Latino Affairs: A Case Study of Community Empowerment." In *Harold Washington and the Neighborhoods: Progressive City Government in Chicago, 1983–1987*, edited by Pierre Clavel and Wim Wiewel, pp. 165–87. New Brunswick, NJ: Rutgers University Press.

———. 1999. *In the Land of Mirrors: Cuban Exile Politics in the United States*. Ann Arbor: University of Michigan Press.

DeSipio, Louis. 1996. *Counting on the Latino Vote: Latinos as a New Electorate*. Charlottesville: University of Virginia Press.

Diehl, Kemper, and Jan Jarboe. 1985. *Cisneros: Portrait of a New American*. San Antonio, TX: Corona.

Donato, Ruben. 1987. "In Struggle: Mexican Americans in the Pajaro Valley Schools, 1900–1979." Ph.D. diss., Stanford University, Stanford, CA.

Duany, Jorge. 1998. "Reconstructing Racial Identity: Ethnicity, Color, and Class among Dominicans in the United States and Puerto Rico." *Latin American Perspectives* 25, no. 3 (May): 148–49.

Dye, Thomas R. 2001. *Politics in America*. 4th ed. Upper Saddle River, NJ: Prentice Hall.

Edsall, Thomas B. 2001. "A Political Fight to Define the Future: Latinos at Odds over California's Two New Democratic Congressional Districts." *Washington Post*, October 31, p. A8.

Endersby, James W., and Charles E. Menifield. 2000. "Representation, Ethnicity, and Congress: Black and Hispanic Representatives and Constituencies." In *Black and Multiracial Politics in America*, edited by Yvette M. Alex-Assensoh and Lawrence J. Hanks. New York: New York University Press.

Endersby, James W., and Byron E. Price. 2001. "Hispanic Representation in State and Local Governments." Paper presented at the annual meeting of the Western Political Science Association, Las Vegas, March 15–17.

Escutia, Martha, and Gloria Romero. 2001. "MALDEF's Lawsuit Is Racially Divisive." *Los Angeles Times*, November 1, p. B13.

Estrada, Leobardo F., F. Chris Garcia, Reynaldo Flores Macias, and Lionel Maldonado. 1988. "Chicanos in the United States: A History of Exploitation." In *Latinos and the Political System*, edited by F. Chris Garcia. Notre Dame, IN: University of Notre Dame Press.

Eulau, Heinz, and John C. Wahlke. 1978. *The Politics of Representation: Continuities in Theory and Practice*. Beverly Hills, CA: Sage.

Fagen, Richard R., Richard A. Brody, and T. J. O'Leary. 1968. *Cubans in Exile: Disaffection and Revolution*. Palo Alto, CA: Stanford University Press.

Fainstein, Susan S., Norman L. Fainstein, Richard C. Hill, Dennis R. Judd, and Michael P. Smith, eds. 1983. *Restructuring the City: The Political Economy of Urban Redevelopment*. New York: Longman.

Falcon, Angelo. 1984. "A History of Puerto Rican Politics in New York City: 1860s to 1945." In *Puerto Rican Politics in Urban America*, edited by James Jennings and Monte Rivera. Westport, CT: Greenwood.

———. 1988. "Black and Latino politics in New York City: Race and Ethnicity in a Changing Urban Context." *New Community* 14, no. 3 (Spring): 370–384.

———. 1992. "Puerto Ricans and the 1988 Election in New York City." In *From Rhetoric to Reality: Latino Politics in the 1988 Elections*, edited by Rodolfo O. de la Garza and Louis DeSipio. Boulder, CO: Westview.

———. 1996. "Puerto Ricans and the 1992 Presidential Election in New York." In *Ethnic Ironies: Latino Politics in the 1992 Elections*, edited by Rodolfo O. de la Garza and Louis DeSipio. Boulder, CO: Westview.

———. 1999. "Beyond La Macarena? New York City Puerto Rican, Dominican, and South American Voters in the 1996 Election." In *Awash in the Mainstream: Latino Politics in the 1996 Elections*, edited by Rodolfo O. de la Garza and Louis DeSipio. 1999. Boulder, CO: Westview.

———. 2001. "Census 2000 Misreporting of Latino Subgroups." www.prldef.org (accessed October 12, 2001).

———. 2002. "Another Response to Gregory Rodriguez." Unpublished letter, May 21.

———. 2003. "Pues, at Least We Had Hillary: Latino New York, the 2000 Election, and the Limits of Party Loyalty" (November). www.prldef.org.

Fears, Darryl. 2002. "A Diverse—and Divided—Black Community: As Foreign-Born Population Grows, Nationality Trumps Skin Color." *Washington Post*, February 24, p. A1.

Finnegan, Michael. 2001. "Latinos Blast Rep. Berman in Map Fight: Redistricting; Protesters Say Proposed Boundary Changes, Which the Congressman Backs,

Dilute Their Power." *Los Angeles Times.* September 7, p. B3.

Fitzgerald, B. 2003. "Reflections on a Glass Ceiling." *New York Times,* New Jersey ed., August 10. www.nytimes.com (accessed August 12, 2003).

Flores, Henry. 2002. "Mayor Ed Garza of San Antonio, Texas: A Cisneros Legacy." Paper presented at the Western Political Science Association, Long Beach, CA, March 22–24.

Flores, William V. 1992. "Chicano Empowerment and the Politics of At-Large Elections in California: A Tale of Two Cities." In *Chicano Empowerment and Chicano Scholarship: Proceedings of the National Association of Chicano Studies Conference 17th Annual Conference, Berkeley,* edited by Mary Romero and Cordelia Candelaria.

Flores, William V., with Rina Benmayor, eds. 1997. "Constructing Cultural Citizenship." In *Latino Cultural Citizenship: Claiming Identity, Space, and Rights.* Boston: Beacon.

Foley, Douglas E., Clarice Mota, Donald E. Post, and Ignacio Lozano. 1988. *From Peones to Politico: Class and Ethnicity in a South Texas Town, 1900–1987.* Austin: University of Texas Press.

Fraga, Luis Ricardo. 1992. "Prototype from the Midwest: Latinos in Illinois." In *From Rhetoric to Reality: Latino Politics in the 1988 Elections,* edited by Rodolfo O. de la Garza and Louis DeSipio. Boulder, CO: Westview.

Galarza, Ernesto. 1964. *Merchants of Labor: The Mexican Bracero Story.* Charlotte, NC: McNalley and Loftin.

Garcia, F. Chris. 1974a. *La Causa Politica: A Chicano Politics Reader.* Notre Dame, IN: University of Notre Dame Press.

———. 1974b. "Manitos and Chicanos in Nuevo México Politics." *Aztlán* 5, nos. 1–2: 177–188.

Garcia, F. Chris, and Paul L. Hain. 1976. *New Mexico Government.* Albuquerque: University of New Mexico Press.

Garcia, F. Chris, and Rodolfo O. de la Garza. 1977. *The Chicano Political Experience: Three Perspectives.* North Scituate, MA: Duxbury.

Garcia, Ignacio M. 1989. *United We Win: The Rise and Fall of La Raza Unida Party.* Tucson: University of Arizona Press.

———. 1997. *Chicanismo: The Forging of a Militant Ethos among Mexican Americans.* Tucson: University of Arizona Press.

———. 2000. *Viva Kennedy: Mexican Americans in Search of Camelot.* College Station: Texas A & M University Press.

Garcia, John A. 2003. *Latino Politics in America: Community, Culture, and Interests.* Lanham, MD: Rowman & Littlefield.

Garcia, Juan R., and Thomas Gelsinon. 1997. *Mexican Americans in the 1990s: Politics, Policies, and Perceptions.* Tucson: University of Arizona Press.

García, María Cristina. 1996. *Havana USA.* Berkeley: University of California Press.

Garcia, Mario T. 1989. *Mexican Americans: Leadership, Ideology, and Identity, 1930–1960.* New Haven, CT: Yale University Press.

———. 1994. *Memories of Chicano History: The Life and Narrative of Bert Corona.* Berkeley: University of California Press.

Garcia, Richard A. 1983. "The Mexican-American Mind: A Product of the 1930s." In *History, Culture, and Society: Chicano Studies in the 1980s,* edited by Mario T. Garcia et al. Ypsilanti, MI: Bilingual Press.

Gay, Claudine. 2001. *The Effect of Minority Districts and Minority Representation on Political Participation in California.* San Francisco: Public Policy Institute of California.

Gee, Robert W. 2001. "Easy Smile, Confident Stride Hide New Mayor's Story of

Struggle." *Austin American Statesman*, November 7. www.statesman (accessed November 10, 2003).

Georges, Eugenia. 1984. *New Immigrants and the Political Process: Dominicans in New York*. New York: Research Program in Inter-American Affairs.

Geron, Kim. 1998. "The Political Incorporation of Latinos: Symbolic or Substantive Changes at the Local Level?" Ph.D. manuscript, University of California Riverside.

Gimpel, James G., and Karen Kaufman. 2001. "Impossible Dream or Distant Reality? Republican Efforts to Attract Latino Voters." Backgrounder. Center for Immigration Studies (August). www.cis.org.

Gold, Mateo. 2001. "Villaraigosa Lets Others Court Latinos." *Los Angeles Times*, June, 2, p. A1.

Gomez Quiñones, Juan. 1990. *Chicano Politics: Reality and Promise, 1940–1990*. Albuquerque: University of New Mexico Press.

———. 1994. *Mexican American Labor, 1790–1990*. Albuquerque: University of New Mexico Press.

Gonzales, Manuel G. 1989. *The Hispanic Elite of the Southwest*. El Paso: Texas Western Press, University of Texas at El Paso.

———. 1999. *Mexicanos: A History of Mexicans in the United States*. Bloomington: Indiana University Press.

Gonzalez, Juan. 2000. *Harvest of Empire: A History of Latinos in America*. New York: Penguin.

Gonzalez-Pando, Miguel. 1998. *The Cuban Americans*. Westport, CT: Greenwood.

Gottleib, Catherine. 1993. "Pomona: A Voting Change Shifts Political Power." *Los Angeles Times*, July 26, p. B4.

Gould, William B., IV. 1993. *A Primer on American Labor Law*. 3rd ed. Cambridge, MA: MIT Press.

Graham, Pamela M. 1998. "The Politics of Incorporation: Dominicans in New York." *Latino Studies Journal* 9, no. 3 (Fall): 39–64.

Grassroots.org. 2002. "La Mujer Obrera: The Woman Worker."www.grass-roots.org/usa/mujer.shtml (accessed January 11, 2002).

Greenhouse, Steven. 2001. "At the End, Labor Made Little Effort for Green." *New York Times*, November 8. www.nytimes.com (accessed November 9, 2001).

Grenier, Guillermo J., and Max J. Castro. 1998. "The Emergence of an Adversarial Relation: Black-Cuban Relations in Miami, 1959–1998." In *Research in Urban Policy: Solving Urban Problems in Urban Areas Characterized by Fragmentation and Division*, edited by Fred W. Bala and Milan J. Dluchy, 7:33–55. Stamford, CT: JAI Press.

———. 2001. "Blacks and Cubans in Miami: The Negative Consequences of the Cuban Enclave on Ethnic Relations." In *Governing American Cities: Interethnic Coalitions, Competition, and Conflict*, edited by Michael Jones-Correa. New York: Russell Sage Foundation.

Grenier, Guillermo J., Fabiana Invernizzi, Linda Salup, and Jorge Schmidt. 1994. "Los Bravos de la Politica: Politics and Cubans in Miami." In *Barrio Ballots: Latino Politics in the 1990 Elections*, edited by Rodolfo O. de la Garza, Martha Menchaca, and Louis DeSipio. Boulder, CO: Westview.

Griswold del Castillo, Richard. 1990. *The Treaty of Guadalupe Hidalgo: A Legacy of Conflict*. Norman: University of Oklahoma Press.

Griswold del Castillo, Richard, and Arnoldo De León. 1996. *North to Aztlán: A History of Mexican Americans in the United States*. New York: Twayne.

Grofman, Bernard, and Chandler Davidson, eds. 1992. *Controversies in Minority*

Voting: The Voting Right Act in Perspective. Washington, DC: Brookings Institution.

Guerin-Gonzales, Camille. 1994. *Mexican Workers and American Dreams: Immigration, Repatriation, and California Farm Labor, 1900–1939.* New Brunswick, NJ: Rutgers University Press.

Guerra, Fernando J. 1991. "The Emergence of Ethnic Officeholders in California." In *Racial and Ethnic Politics in California*, edited by Bryan O. Jackson and Michael B. Preston. Berkeley, CA: Institute of Governmental Studies Press.

Guinier, Lani. 1994. *The Tyranny of the Majority: Fundamental Fairness in Representative Democracy.* New York: Free Press.

———. 1995. "The Representation of Minority Interests." In *Classifying by Race*, edited by Paul E. Peterson. Princeton, NJ: Princeton University Press.

Gutiérrez, David G. 1995. *Walls and Mirrors: Mexican Americans, Mexican Immigrants, and the Politics of Ethnicity.* Berkeley: University of California Press.

Gutierrez, Jose Angel, and Rebecca E. Dean. 2000. "Chicanas in Texas Politics." Julian Samora Research Institute Occasional Paper Series 66 (October). www.jsri.msu.edu/RandS/research/ops/oc66.html.

Guzman, Betsy. 2001. "The Hispanic Population: Census 2002 Brief." Report C2KBR/01-3 (May). U.S. Census Bureau.

Hamilton, Nora, and Norma Stoltz Chinchilla. 1991. "Central American Migration: A Framework for Analysis." *Latin American Research Review* 26, no. 1: 75–110.

Hanks, Lawrence J. 1987. *The Struggle for Black Political Empowerment in Three Georgia Counties.* Knoxville: University of Tennessee Press.

Hardy-Fanta, Carol. 1993. *Latina Politics, Latino Politics: Gender, Culture, and Political Participation in Boston.* Philadelphia: Temple University Press.

Heins, Marjorie. 1972. *Strictly Ghetto Property.* Berkeley, CA: Ramparts.

Henry, Charles P. 1980. "Black-Chicano Coalitions: Possibilities and Problems." *Western Journal of Black Studies* 4: 202–232.

Hernandez, Ramona, and Francisco L. Rivera-Batiz. 2003. "Dominicans in the United States: A Socioeconomic Profile 2000." Dominican Research Monograph, CUNY Dominican Studies Institute, October 6.

Hernandez-Gomes, Carlos. 2001. "Latino Leadership: Population Grows, but Political Power Lags." *Chicago Reporter*, September/October, p. 1.

Hero, Rodney. 1992. *Latinos and the U.S. Political System: Two-Tiered Pluralism.* Philadelphia: Temple University Press.

———. 1997. "Latinos and Politics in Denver and Pueblo, Colorado: Differences, Explanations, and the 'Steady-State' of the Struggle for Equality." In *Racial Politics in American Cities*, 2nd ed., edited by Rufus P. Browning, Dale R. Marshall, and David H. Tabb. New York: Longman.

Hero, Rodney, and Kathleen M. Beatty. 1989. "The Election of Federico Peña as Mayor of Denver: Analysis and Implications." *Social Science Quarterly* 70, no. 2 (June): 300–310.

Hero, Rodney, F. Chris Garcia, John Garcia, and Harry Pachon. 2000. "Latino Participation, Partisanship, and Office Holding." *PS: Political Science and Politics* 23, no. 3 (September): 529–34.

Hero, Rodney, and Caroline Tolbert. 1995. "Latinos and Substantive Representation in the U.S. House of Representatives: Direct, Indirect, or Nonexistent?" *American Journal of Political Science* 39 (August): 240–61.

———. 1999. "Dealing with Diversity: Racial/Ethnic Context and Policy Change." Paper presented at the annual meeting of the Western Political Science Association, Seattle, March 25–27.

Hickey, Jennifer G. 2003. "No Monopoly on Ethnicity." www.insightmag.com (accessed March 21, 2003).

Hill, Kevin V., and Dario Moreno. 2005. "Battleground Florida." In *Muted Voices: Latinos and the 2000 Elections*, edited by Rodolfo O. de la Garza and Louis DeSipio. Lanham, MD: Rowman and Littlefield.

Hill, Kim Quaile, and Kenneth R. Mladenka. *Texas Government: Politics and Economics*. 4th ed. Belmont, CA: Wadsworth.

Hirsch, Arnold R. 2001. "Harold Washington of Chicago and 'Dutch' Morial of New Orleans." In *African American Mayors: Race, Politics, and the American City*, edited by David R. Colburn and Jeffrey S. Adler. Chicago: University of Illinois Press.

Holbrook, Stett. 1999. "Land Plan Nixed: LAFCO Rejects Proposal for Watsonville Annexation." *Santa Cruz Sentinel*, August 4, p. A1.

Holmes, Jack E. 1967. *Politics in New Mexico*. Albuquerque: University of New Mexico Press.

Industrial Areas Foundation. n.d. "About IAF." www.industrialareasfoundation.org.

Ingram, David. 2000. *Group Rights: Reconciling Equality and Difference*. Lawrence: University Press of Kansas.

Izigsohn, Jose, Carlos D. Cabral, Esther Hernandez Medina, and Obed Vazquez. 1999. "Mapping Dominican Transnationalism: Narrow and Broad Transnational Practices." *Ethnic and Racial Studies* 22, no. 2, March: 316–339.

Jennings, James. 1977. *Puerto Rican Politics in New York City*. Washington, DC: University Press of America.

———. 1992. *The Politics of Black Empowerment: The Transformation of Black Activism in Urban America*. Detroit, MI: Wayne State University Press.

———, ed. 1994. *Blacks, Latinos, and Asians in Urban America: Status and Prospects for Politics and Activism*. Westport, CT: Praeger.

Jennings, James, and Monte Rivera. 1984. *Puerto Rican Politics in Urban America*. Westport, CT: Greenwood.

Johnson, David R., John A. Booth, and Richard J. Harris. 1983. *The Politics of San Antonio*. Lincoln: University of Nebraska Press.

Joint Center for Political and Economic Studies. 2001. "Number of Black Elected Officials in the United States by State and Office, January 1999." www.joint-center.org (accessed November 9, 2001).

Jones-Correa, Michael. 2001. "Under Two Flags: Duel Nationality in Latin America and Its Consequences for Naturalization in the United States." *International Migration Review* 35, no. 4 (winter): 997–1029.

Jordan, Howard. 1997. "Dominicans in New York: Getting a Slice of the Apple." *NACLA Report of the Americas* 30, no. 5 (March/April): 37–42.

Keiser, Richard A. 1990. "The Rise of a Biracial Coalition in Philadelphia." In *Racial Politics in American Cities*, edited by Rufus P. Browning, Dale R. Marshall, and David H. Tabb. New York: Longman.

Kerr, Brinck, and Will Miller. 1997. "Latino Representation: It's Direct and Indirect." *American Journal of Political Science* 41, no. 3 (July): 1066–71.

Kleist, Trina. 2000. "Old Foes, New Trust: North-South Cooperation Proved Vital to Approval of Watsonville School Site." *Santa Cruz County Sentinel*. March 19, p. A1.

Kousser, J. Morgan. 1999. *Colorblind Injustice: Minority Voting Rights and the Undoing of the Second Reconstruction*. Chapel Hill: University of North Carolina Press.

———. 2001. "The Role of Cross-Over Districts in a Fair Redistricting: Lessons from the 1990s." In *California Senate Redistricting Plan*. Submitted July 31,

2001 by MALDEF and WCVI. www.maldef.org/publications/pdf/ Senate_Plan.pdf (accessed June 9, 2003).

Kripalani, Jasmine. 2003. "Many Broward Latino Residents Still Participate in Their Home Countries' Elections but Ignore Local Politics." *Miami Herald*, September 28.

Lai, James S. 2000. "Asian Pacific Americans and the Pan-ethnic Question." In *Minority Politics at the Millennium*, edited by Richard A. Keiser and Katherine Underwood. New York: Garland.

La Mujer Obrera. n.d. www.mujerobrera.org (accessed January 9, 2004).

Latinos Issues Forum. 1998. "The Latino Vote 1998" (May). http://www.lif.org/.

Leech, Gary. 2000. "Plan Colombia: A Closer Look." Colombia Journal Online, www.colombiajournal.org/plancolombia.html (accessed January 10, 2005).

Leighley, Jan E. 2001. *Strength in Numbers? The Political Mobilization of Racial and Ethnic Minorities*. Princeton, NJ: Princeton University Press.

Lemus, Frank. 1973. *The National Roster of Spanish Surnamed Elected Officials*. Los Angeles: Atzlan Production.

Levitt, Peggy. 2001. *The Transnational Villagers*. Berkeley: University of California Press.

Levy, Jacques E. 1975. *Cesar Chavez: Autobiography of La Causa*. New York: W. W. Norton.

Lewis Mumford Center for Comparative Urban and Regional Research. 2001. "The New Latinos: Who They Are, Where They Are" (September 10). mumford1.dyndns.org/cen2000/HispanicPop/ (accessed December 3, 2003).

Libertad. 1994. "40th Anniversary of the Attack on Congress." National Committee to Free Puerto Rican Prisoners of War and Political Prisoners. www.etext.org/ Politics/Autonome.Forum/Political.Prisoners/ Puerto.Rico/libertad.spring94 (accessed January 15, 2004).

Lineberry, Robert L. 1977. *Equality in Urban Policy: The Distribution of Minority Public Services*. Sage Publications 39. New York: Sage Library of Social Research.

Logan, John, and Harvey Molotch. 1987. *Urban Fortunes: The Political Economy of Place*. Berkeley: University of California Press.

Lopez, Robert J. 1994. "Campaign's Bitter Roots Run Deep." *Los Angeles Times*, April 10, p. B19.

Los Angeles Times. 1994. Exit poll, November 10. www.latimes.com/polls (accessed November 10, 2001).

———. 1996. Exit poll, November 5.

Los Angeles Times/CNN. 1998. Exit poll, June 2.

Los Angeles Times. 2001. Exit poll 460, June 5.

Louie, Miriam Ching Yoon. 2001. *Sweatshop Warriors: Immigrant Women Take on the Global Factory*. Cambridge, MA: South End.

Lucas, Isidro. 1984. "Puerto Rican Politics in Chicago." In *Puerto Rican Politics in Urban America*, edited by James Jennings and Monte Rivera. Westport, CT: Greenwood.

Marrable, Manning. 2004. "Globalization and Racialization." *Znet*. www.zmag.org/content/showarticle.cfm?SectionID=30&ItemID.

Marquez, Benjamin. 1985. *Power and Politics in a Mexican Barrio: A Study of Mobilization Efforts and Community Power in El Paso*. New York: University Press of America.

———. 1993. *LULAC: The Evolution of a Mexican American Political Organization*. Austin: University of Texas Press.

Martinez, Oscar J. 1980. *The Chicanos of El Paso: An Assessment of Progress.* Southwestern Studies Monograph 59. El Paso: Texas Western Press, University of Texas at El Paso.

Matos Rodríguez, Félix V. 2003. "Puerto Rican Politics in New York City: A Conversation with Roberto Ramirez." *Centro: Journal of the Center for Puerto Rican Studies* 15, no. 1 (spring): 196–211.

McCormick, Joseph P., and Charles E. Jones. 1993. "The Conceptualization of Deracialization." In *Dilemmas of Black Politics: Issues of Leadership of Leadership and Strategy*, edited by Georgia A. Persons, pp. 66–84. New York: HarperCollins.

McWilliams, Carey. 1990. *North from Mexico: The Spanish-Speaking People of the United States.* New York: Greenwood.

Medoff, Peter, and Holly Sklar. 1994. *Streets of Hope: The Fall and Rise of an Urban Neighborhood.* Boston: South End.

Meier, Kenneth J., J. L. Polinard, and Robert D. Wrinkle. 2000. "Michael Giles and Mancur Olson Meet Vincent Ostrom: Jurisdiction Size and Latino Representation." *Social Science Quarterly* 81, no. 1 (March): 123–135.

Menchaca, Martha. 1995. *The Mexican Outsiders: A Community History of Marginalization and Discrimination in California.* Austin: University of Texas Press.

Menifield, Charles E. 2001a. "Hispanic Representation in State and Local Governments." In *Representation of Minority Groups in the U.S.: Implications for the Twenty-first Century*, edited by Charles E. Menifield. Lanham, MD: Austin and Winfield.

———. 2001b. "Minority Representation in the Twenty-first Century: An Introduction." In *Representation of Minority Groups in the U.S.: Implications for the Twenty-first Century*, edited by Charles E. Menifield. Lanham, MD: Austin and Winfield.

Metropolitan News-Enterprise. 2001. "Ex-Wilson Appointee, Ousted by Voters, Named to Monterey Court." October 3. www.metnews.com (accessed January 30, 2005).

Metz, David H., and Katherine Tate. 1996. "The Color of Urban Campaigns." In *Classifying by Race*, edited by Paul Peterson, pp. 262–77. Princeton, NJ: Princeton University Press.

Mexican American Legal Defense and Education Fund (MALDEF). n.d. "About Us: The Founding of MALDEF." http://www.maldef.org/about/index.htm (accessed December 8, 2001).

Migration Policy Institute. n.d. "Migration Information Source." www.migrationin-formation.org/USfocus/ (accessed November 29, 2003).

Miles, Jack. "Blacks vs. Browns." 1992. *Atlantic Monthly*, October, pp. 41–68.

Milkman, Ruth, ed. 2000. *Organizing Immigrants: The Challenge for Unions in Contemporary California.* Ithaca, NY: ILR Press and Cornell University Press.

Miller, Gary J. 1981. *Cities by Contract: The Politics of Municipal Incorporation.* Cambridge, MA: MIT Press.

Miller, Ronald F. 1987. "Our Town: Salinas, California." n.d. Oral history, April. Salinas Public Library, Special Collections Reference Room.

Mohl, Raymond A. 1989. "Ethnic Politics in Miami, 1960–1986." In *Essays on Ethnicity, Race, and the Urban South*, edited by Randell M. Miller and George E. Pozzetta. Boca Raton: Florida Atlanta University Press.

Mollenkopf, John. 1997. "New York: The Great Anomaly." In *Racial Politics in*

American Cities, 2nd ed., edited by Rufus P. Browning, Dale R. Marshall, and David H. Tabb. New York: Longman.

Montejano, David. 1987. *Anglos and Mexicans in the Making of Texas, 1837–1986*. Austin: University of Texas Press.

Monterey County. 1993. "Monterey County Economic Development Program."

———. 1999. "21st Century General Plan Update" (October 12), p. II-A-9.

Morales, Ed. 2004. "Brown like Me? Book Review." *Nation*, February 19. www.thenation.com/doc (accessed February 8, 2005).

Morales, Iris. 1998. "Palante, Siempre Palante!" In *The Puerto Rican Movement: Voices from the Diaspora*, edited by Andrés Torres and José E. Velázquez. Philadelphia: Temple University Press.

Moreno, Dario. 1996. "Cuban Americans in Miami Politics: Understanding the Cuban Model." In *The Politics of Minority Coalitions: Race, Ethnicity, and Shared Uncertainties*, edited by Wilbur C. Rich. Westport, CT: Praeger.

———. 1997. "The Cuban Model: Political Empowerment in Miami." In *Pursuing Power: Latinos in the Political System*, edited by F. Chris Garcia. Notre Dame, IN: Notre Dame University Press.

———. n.d. "The Election of the First Cuban Congresswoman." www.fiu.edu/ ~morenod/ (accessed June 15, 2001).

Moreno, Dario, Kevin Hill, and Lourdes Cue. n.d. "Racial and Partisan Voting in a Tri-ethnic City: The 1996 Dade County Mayoral Election." www.fiu.edu/~morenod/ (accessed June 15, 2001).

Moreno, Dario, and Christopher L. Warren. 1992. "The Conservative Enclave: Cubans in Florida." In *From Rhetoric to Reality: Latino Politics in the 1988 Elections*, edited by Rodolfo O. de la Garza and Louis DeSipio. Boulder, CO: Westview.

Moret, Louis F. 1998. "The Latino Political Agenda in Southern California Municipalities." D.P.A. diss., University of La Verne, California.

Munoz, Carlos, Jr. 1989. *Youth, Identity, and Power: The Chicano Movement*. London: Verso.

Munoz, Carlos, Jr., and Charles Henry. 1990. "Coalition Politics in San Antonio and Denver: The Cisneros and Peña Mayoral Campaigns." In *Racial Politics in American Cities*, edited by Rufus Browning, Dale Marshall, and David Tabb. New York; Longman.

Myrdal, Gunnar. 1944. *An American Dilemma: The Negro Problem and Modern Democracy*. New York: Harper.

National Association of Latino Elected and Appointed Officials (NALEO). 1994. *National Roster of Hispanic Elected Officials*. Los Angeles, CA: NALEO Educational Fund.

———. 1996. *National Roster of Latino Elected Officials*. Los Angeles, CA: NALEO Educational Fund.

———. 2000a. *2000 Latino: Election Handbook*. Los Angeles, CA: NALEO Educational Fund.

———. 2000b. *2000 National Directory of Latino Elected Officials*. Los Angeles, CA: NALEO Educational Fund.

———. 2001a. *National Directory of Latino Elected Officials*. Los Angeles, CA: NALEO Educational Fund.

———. 2001b. "Research Brief: The Growth of Latinos in the Nation's Congressional Districts: The 2000 Census and Latino Political Empowerment" (June). Los Angeles, CA: NALEO Educational Fund.

———. 2002. http://www.naleo.org/civic_education.htm.

————. 2003. *National Directory of Latino Elected Officials*. Los Angeles, CA: NALEO Educational Fund.

————. 2004. "Latinos Win Big on Election Night." Press release, November 3, 2004. www.naleo.org/press_releases/PR_NALEO_EDay_Win_110304.pdf (accessed November 4, 2004).

National Civic League. 1996. *Communities and the Voting Rights Act: A Guide to Compliance in These Changing Times*. Denver: Author.

Navarro, Armando. 1995. *Mexican American Youth Organization: Avant-Garde of the Chicano Movement in Texas*. Austin: University of Texas Press.

————. 1998. *The Cristal Experiment: A Chicano Struggle for Community Control*. Madison: University of Wisconsin Press.

————. 2000. *La Raza Unida Party: A Chicano Challenge to the U.S. Two-Party Dictatorship*. Philadelphia: Temple University Press.

Navarro, Carlos, and Rodolfo Acuña. 1990. "In Search of Community: A Comparative Essay on Mexicans in Los Angeles and San Antonio." In *Twentieth Century Los Angeles: Power, Promotion, and Social Conflict*, edited by Norman Klein and Martin Schiesl. Claremont, CA: Regina.

Nelson, Albert J. 1991. *Emerging Influentials in State Legislatures: Women, Blacks, and Hispanics*. New York: Praeger.

————. 1996. *Democrats under Siege in the Sunbelt Megastates: California, Florida, and Texas*. Westport, CT: Praeger.

Oliver, J. Eric. 2001. *Democracy in Suburbia*. Princeton, NJ: Princeton University Press.

Omi, Michael, and Howard Winant. 1994. *Racial Formation in the United States: From the 1960s to the 1990s*. 2nd ed. New York: Routledge.

Ong, Paul, Edna Bonacich, and Lucie Cheng. 1994. "The Political Economy of Capitalist Restructuring and New Asian Immigration." In *The New Asian Immigration in Los Angeles and Global Restructuring*, edited by Paul Ong, Edna Bonacich, and Lucie Cheng. Philadelphia: Temple University Press.

Pachon, Harry P., and Louis DeSipio. 1990. *Latino Legislators and Latino Caucuses*. Working Paper 11, IUP/SSRC Committee for Public Policy Research on Contemporary Hispanic Issues. Austin: Center for Mexican American Studies, University of Texas.

Pachon, Harry P., Lupe Sanchez, and Dennis Falcon. 1999. "California Latino Politics and the 1996 Elections: From Potential to Reality." In *Awash in the Mainstream: Latino Politics in the 1996 Elections*, edited by Rodolfo O. de la Garza and Louis DeSipio. Boulder, CO: Westview.

Padilla, Felix M. 1985. *Latino Ethnic Consciousness: The Case of Mexican Americans and Puerto Ricans in Chicago*. Notre Dame, IN: University of Notre Dame Press.

————. 1987. *Puerto Rican Chicago*. Notre Dame, IN: University of Notre Dame Press.

Pantoja, Adrian D., Ricardo Ramirez, and Gary M. Segura. 2001. "Citizens by Choice, Voters by Necessity: Patterns in Political Mobilization by Naturalized Latinos." *Political Research Quarterly* 54, no. 4 (December): 729–750.

Pantoja, Adrian D., and Gary M. Segura. 2000. "Citizens by Choice, Voters by Necessity: Patterns in Political Mobilization by Naturalized Latinos." Paper presented at the annual meeting of the Western Political Science Association, San Jose, CA, March 24–26.

Pardo, Mary. 1998. *Mexican American Women Activists: Identity and Resistance in Two Los Angeles Communities*. Philadelphia: Temple University Press.

Passel, Jeffery. 2002. "New Estimates of the Undocumented Population" (May 22). http://www.migrationinformation.org/USfocus/display.cfm?ID=19.

Pazniokas, Mark. 2001. "Perez's Crowning Moment Is at Hand." *Hartford Courant*, December 4, p. 1.

Perez y Gonzalez, Maria E. 2000. *Puerto Ricans in the United States*. Westport, CT: Greenwood.

Peterson, Paul. 1981. *City Limits*. Chicago: University of Chicago Press.

Pew Hispanic Center and Kaiser Family Foundation. 2002a. "The Latino Population and the Latino Electorate: The Numbers Differ" (October).

———. 2002b. "The 2002 National Survey of Latinos" (December).

———. 2004. "The 2004 National Survey of Latinos: Politics and Civic Participation" (July). www.pewhispanic.org (accessed October 15, 2004).

Pinderhughes, Dianne M. 1997. "An Examination of Chicago Politics for Evidence of Political Incorporation and Representation." In *Racial Politics in American Cities*, 2nd ed., edited by Rufus Browning, Dale R. Marshall, and David H. Tabb. New York: Longman.

Pitkin, Hanna. 1967. *The Concept of Representation*. Berkeley: University of California Press.

Pitnick, R. 1998. "Outside In: Latino Political Clout on the Rise in Salinas Mayoral Race." *Coast Weekly Online*, October 15. www.coastweekly.com (accessed December 18, 2001).

Pitt, Leonard. 1998. *The Decline of the Californios: The Social History of the Spanish-Speaking Californians, 1846–1890*. Berkeley: University of California Press.

Piven, Francis F., and Richard A. Cloward. 1977. *Poor People's Movements: Why They Succeed, How They Fail*. New York: Vintage.

Polinard, Jerry L., Robert D. Wrinkle, Tomas Longoria, and Norman E. Binder. 1994. *Electoral Structure and Urban Policy: The Impact on Mexican American Communities*. Armonk, NY: M. E. Sharpe.

Política Social. 2002. "Redistricting Latino Communities: Turning our Numbers into Political Power?" Newsletter of the PRLDEP Institute for Puerto Rican Policy, Policy Division of the Puerto Rican Legal Defense and Education Fund (summer).

Porter, Eduardo. 2001. "Up to 8.5 Million Immigrants Believed to Be in the U.S. Illegally." *Wall Street Journal*, August 14. Reprinted at www.deseretnews.com.

Ramakrishnan, S. Karthick, and Thomas J. Espenshade. 2001. "Immigrant Incorporation and Political Participation in the United States." *International Migration Review* 35, no. 3 (fall): 870–895.

Ramirez, Roberto R., and G. P. de la Cruz. 2002. *The Hispanic Population in the United States*, (March). Current Population Reports, U.S. Census Bureau.

Reed, Adolph, Jr. 1995. "Demobilization in the New Black Political Regime: Ideological Capitulation and Radical Failure in the Post-segregation Era." In *The Bubbling Cauldron: Race, Ethnicity, and the Urban Crisis*, edited by Michael P. Smith and Joe R. Feagin. Minneapolis: University of Minnesota Press.

Regalado, Jaime. 1988. "Latino Representation in Los Angeles." In *Latino Empowerment: Progress, Problems, and Prospects*, edited by Roberto E. Villarreal, Norma G. Hernandez, and Howard D. Neighbor. New York: Greenwood.

———. 1998. "Minority Political Incorporation in Los Angeles: A Broader Consideration." In *Racial and Ethnic Politics in California*, edited by Michael B. Preston, Bruce E. Cain, and Sandra Bass, 2: 381–409. Berkeley: Institute of Government Studies Press.

Regalado, Jaime, and Gloria Martinez. 1991. "Reapportionment and Coalition Building: A Case Study of Informal Barriers to Latino Empowerment in Los Angeles County." In *Latinos and Political Coalitions: Political Empowerment in the 1990s*, edited by Roberto E. Villarreal and Norma G. Hernandez, pp. 126–43. New York: Praeger.

Reid, Stuart. 1987. *Working with Statistics: An Introduction to Quantitative Methods for Social Scientists*. Totowa, NJ: Rowman and Littlefield.

Reinoso, Felipe. 2001. "Representative Reinoso Elected New President of the Association of Peruvian Organizations." Press release, Office of Connecticut State Representative Felipe Reinoso, 130th Assembly District, D-Bridgeport (May 31).

Renner, T., and V. De Santis. 1993. "Contemporary Patterns and Trends in Municipal Government Structures." In *Municipal Yearbook*. Washington: International City Managers' Association.

Reuter, Theodore. 1995. *The Politics of Race: African Americans and the Political System*. New York: M. E. Sharpe.

Richman, Josh. 2001. *Daily Review*, September 8, pp. C1–2.

Rodriguez, Gregory. 1996. "The Browning of California: Proposition 187 Backfires." *New Republic* 215, no. 10 (September 2): 18.

———. 2002a. "Where the Minorities Rule." *New York Times*, February 10. www.nytimes.com (accessed November 6, 2003).

———. 2002b. "Latinos: No Longer Society's Victims." *Los Angeles Times*, May 12. www.latimes.com (accessed May 15, 2002).

Rodriguez, Lori. 2001. "Sanchez's Mayoral Bid Targets Disparate Voters." *Houston Chronicle*, October 7, p. 1.

Romero, Mary. 1985. "El Paso Salt War: Mob Action or Political Struggle?" *Aztlán* 16, nos. 1–2: 119–43.

Romo, David. 2001. "Running with Ray: Is El Paso's Next Mayor a Caballero?" *Texas Observer*, April 27, pp. 1–4.

Rosales, Rodolfo. 2000. *The Illusion of Inclusion: The Untold Political Story of San Antonio*. Austin: University of Texas Press.

Rosenbaum, Robert J. 1981. *Mexicano Resistance in the Southwest: The Sacred Right of Self-Preservation*. Austin: University of Texas Press.

Ross, Karl, Jay Weaver, and Oscar Corral. 2001. "Cuban American Vote Lifts Diaz to Miami Mayor's Post." *Miami Herald*, November 14. www.herald.com (acessed November 10, 2003).

Ruiz, Vicki L. 1987. *Cannery Women, Cannery Lives: Mexican Women, Unionization, and the California Food Processing Industry, 1930–1950*. Albuquerque: University of New Mexico Press.

Sailer, Steve. 2001. "Analysis: Mexican-Americans and the Vote." United Press International, July 24. declaration.net/news.asp?docID=1886 (accessed February 8, 2005).

Salinas, City of. 1960. "Historical Sketch of Salinas." In "General Plan." Salinas: City Planning Department.

———. 1980. "Affirmative Action Plan."

———. 1988. "Housing Element." In General Plan.

———. n.d. "Affirmative Action Goals, 1990–1994."

———. 1991. "Salinas Housing Trust Fund Task Force" (April).

———. 1994. "City of Salinas 1994–2000 Affirmative Action Plan Update."

———. 1996a. "Community Awareness and Education Committee" (February).

———. 1996b. "Violent Injury Prevention Coalition, Briefing Packet" (August).

———. 1996–97. Annual Budget.

———. n.d. "Equal Employment Opportunity Plan, 2001–2005."

———. 2002. "Housing Element." General Plan (January).

Salinas Valley Chamber of Commerce. 1996. *The 1996 Business and Community Profile*. Monterey, CA: Monterey County Herald.

———. *The 2000–2001 Salinas Business and Community Profile*. Monterey, CA: Monterey County Herald.

Sampaio, Anna. 2002. "Transforming Chicana/o and Latina/o Politics: Globalization and the Formation of Transnational Resistance in the United States and Chiapas." In *Transnational Latina/o Communities: Politics, Processes, and Cultures*, edited by Carlos G. Velez-Ibanez and Anna Sampaio, with Manolo González-Estay. Lanham, MD: Rowman and Littlefield.

Sanchez, George J. 1993. *Becoming Mexican American: Ethnicity, Culture, and Identity in Chicano Los Angeles, 1900–1945*. Oxford: Oxford University Press.

Sánchez, José R. 1996. "Puerto Rican Politics in New York: Beyond "Secondhand" Theory." In *Latinos in New York: Communities in Transition*, edited by Gabriel Haslip-Vera and Sherrie L. Baver. Notre Dame, IN: University of Notre Dame Press.

———. 2000. "*Bailando con el Monstruo:* Lessons on Power from the Puerto Rican Community." Paper presented at the annual meeting of the American Political Science Association, Washington, DC, August 31–September 3.

Sánchez Korrol, Virginia E. 1994. *From Colonia to Community: The History of Puerto Ricans in New York City*. Berkeley: University of California Press.

Sanders, Haywood T. 1979. "Government Structure in American Cities." In *The Municipal Yearbook*. Washington: International City Managers' Association.

Schiffrin, Andrew. 1984. "The Story of Measure J—Santa Cruz County's Growth Management Program." Regional Exchange: A Quarterly Publication of People for Open Space, February, p. 1.

Scott, Steve. 2000. "Competing for the New Majority Vote." *California Journal* 41, no. 1 (January): 16–23.

Segura, Gary M., Dennis Falcon, and Harry Pachon. 1997. "Dynamics of Latino Partisanship in California, Immigration, Issue Salience, and Their Implications." *Harvard Journal of Hispanic Policy* 10: 62–80.

Sekul, Joseph D. 1983. "Communities Organized for Public Service: Citizen Power and Public Policy in San Antonio." In *The Politics of San Antonio: Community, Progress, and Power*, edited by David R. Johnson, John A. Booth, and Richard J. Harris. Lincoln: University of Nebraska Press.

Sena, Gilbert Louis. 1973. "The Politics of New Mexico, 1960–1972." M.A. thesis, California State University, Fullerton.

Shockley, John Staples. 1974. *Chicano Revolt in a Texas Town*. Notre Dame, IN: University of Notre Dame Press.

Sierra, Christine Marie. 2000. "Hispanics and the Political Process." In *Hispanics in the United States: An Agenda for the Twenty-first Century*, edited by Pastora San Juan Cafferty and David W. Engstrom. New Brunswick, NJ: Transaction.

Sierra, Christine Marie, and Adaljiza Sosa Riddell. 1994. "Chicanas as Political Actors: Rare Literature, Complex Practice." In *The Challenge to Racial Stratification: National Political Science Review*, vol. 4, edited by Matthew Holden Jr. New Brunswick, NJ: Transaction.

Skelton, George. 2001. "Latino Impact Felt through Labor Movement." *Los Angeles Times*, June 14, pp. 2–10.

Smith, Adam C. 2003. "Alex Penelas Confronts a Tough Critic: His Own Party." *St. Petersburg Times*, August 31. www.sptimes.com (accessed September 12, 2003).

Smith, Robert C. 1990a. "From Insurgency toward Inclusion: The Jackson

Campaigns of 1984 and 1988." In *The Social and Political Implications of the 1984 Jesse Jackson Presidential Campaign*, edited by Lorenzo Morris. New York: Praeger.

———. 1990b. "Recent Elections and Black Politics: The Maturation or Death of Black Politics?" *PS: Political Science and Politics* 22 (June): 160–62.

Smith, Zackary A. 1996. *Politics and Public Policy in Arizona*. 2nd ed. Westport, CT: Praeger.

Sonenshein, Raphael J. 1993. *Politics in Black and White: Race and Power in Los Angeles*. Princeton, NJ: Princeton University Press.

———. 1997."Post Incorporation Politics in Los Angeles." In *Racial Politics in American Cities*, 2nd ed., edited by Rufus P. Browning, Dale R. Marshall, and David H. Tabb. New York: Longman.

Sosa Riddell, Adaljiza. 1974. "Chicanas and el Movimiento." *Aztlán* 5: 155–165.

Sosa Riddell, Adaljiza, and Robert Aguallo Jr. 1979. "A Case of Chicano Politics: Parlier, California." *Aztlán* 9: 1–22.

Southwest Voter Registration and Education Project. 1984. *Analysis of the Hispanic Vote in 1984 Presidential Elections*. San Antonio, TX: Author.

———. n.d. "About SVREP." www.svrep.com/aboutsvrep/fact_sheet.html (accessed January 5, 2004).

———. n.d. "10-4 Campaign." ww.svrep.org/10_4_campaign/10_4_campaign.html (accessed December 15, 2003).

Starks, Robert T., and Michael B. Preston. 1990. "Harold Washington and the Politics of Reform in Chicago, 1983–1987." In *Racial Politics in American Cities*, edited by Rufus P Browning, Dale R. Marshall, and David H. Tabb. New York: Longman.

Steinbeck, John. 1937a. *Tortilla Flats*. New York: Modern Library.

———. 1937b. *Of Mice and Men*. New York: Collier.

———. 1952. *East of Eden*. New York: Viking.

Stepnick, Alex, Guillermo Grenier, Max Castro, and Marvin Dunn. 1993. *This Land Is Our Land: Immigrants and Power in Miami*. Berkeley: University of California Press.

Stinchcombe, Arthur L. 1987. *Constructing Social Theories*. Chicago: University of Chicago Press.

Stone, Clarence N. 1989. *Regime Politics: Governing Atlanta, 1946–1989*. Lawrence: University Press of Kansas.

Stone, Clarence N., and Heywood Saunders, eds. 1987. *Politics of Urban Development*. Lawrence: University Press of Kansas.

Suárez-Orozco, Marcelo M., and Mariela M. Páez. 2002. Introduction to *Latinos Remaking America*, edited by M. M. Suárez-Orozco and M. M. Páez. Berkeley: University of California Press.

Suro, Roberto. 1998. *Strangers among Us: How Latino Immigration Is Transforming America*. New York: Alfred A. Knopf.

———. 2002. "Counting the Other Hispanics: How Many Colombians, Dominicans, Ecuadorians, Guatemalans, and Salvadorans Are There in the U.S.?" Pew Hispanic Center. www.pewhispanic.org.

Swain, Carol M. 1993. *Black Faces, Black Interests: The Representation of African Americans in Congress*. Cambridge, MA: Harvard University Press.

Takash, Paula Cruz. 1990. "A Crisis of Democracy: Community Responses to the Latinization of a California Town Dependent on Immigrant Labor." Ph.D. diss., University of California, Berkeley.

———. 1993. "Breaking Barriers to Representation: Chicana/Latina Elected Officials in California." *Urban Anthropology* 22, no. 3–4 (fall-winter):

325–360.

Takash, Paula Cruz, and Joaquin Avila. 1989. "Latino Political Participation in Rural California." Working Paper 8 (February), Working Group on Farm Labor and Rural Poverty. Davis: California Institute for Rural Studies.

Taylor, Ronald B. 1975. *Chavez and the Farm Workers*. Boston: Beacon.

"Tejano Politics." n.d. *Handbook of Texas Online*. www.tsha.utexa.edu/handbook/online/ (accessed August 22, 2002).

Texas Civil Liberties Union. 1938. "San Antonio: The Cradle of Texas Liberty and Its Coffin?" Document 13. http://womhist.binghamton.edu/pecan/doc13.htm (accessed January 4, 2004).

Therrien, Melissa, and Roberto R. Ramirez. 2001."The Hispanic Population in the United States: Population Characteristics." Report P30-535 (March). Current Population Reports, U.S. Census Bureau.

Tijerina, Andrés. 1994. *Tejanos and Texas under the Mexican Flag, 1821–1836*. College Station: Texas A & M University Press.

Tocqueville, Alexis de. 1956. *Democracy in America*. New York: Mentor/Penguin.

Tolbert, Caroline, and Rodney Hero. 1996. "Race/Ethnicity and Direct Democracy: An Analysis of California's Illegal Immigrant Initiative." *Journal of Politics* 58, no. 3 (August): 806–18.

Tomas Rivera Policy Institute. 2001. "2001 Post-election Analysis: LA Mayoral Race." wwww.trpi.org/Mayoral2001.html (accessed July 2, 2001).

Torres, Andres, and Jose E. Velazquez, eds. 1998. *The Puerto Rican Movement: Voices from the Diaspora*. Philadelphia: Temple University Press.

Travis, Toni-Michelle. 1990. "Boston: The Unfinished Agenda." In *Racial Politics in American Cities*, edited by Rufus P. Browning, Dale R. Marshall, and David H. Tabb. New York: Longman.

Trejo, Jennifer. 2001. "WCVI Analysis Shows Split among Non-Hispanic White Voters." *La Prensa* 12, no. 51 (June 24): 1a.

Underwood, Katherine. 1997a. "Pioneering Minority Representation: Edward Roybal and the Los Angeles City Council, 1949–1962." *Pacific Historical Review* 66, no. 3 (August): 399–425.

———. 1997b. "Ethnicity Is Not Enough: Latino-Led Multiracial Coalitions in Los Angeles." *Urban Affairs Review* 33, no. 1 (September): 3.

United Farm Workers of America (UFW). n.d. "The Rise of the UFW." www.ufw.org (accessed April 12, 2002).

U.S. Bureau of Labor Statistics. 2000. "Salinas Metropolitan Statistical Area, 2000 Metropolitan Area Occupational Employment and Wage Estimates: Occupational Employment Data." U.S. Department of Labor. www.bls.gov (accessed March 21, 2002).

U.S. Bureau of the Census. 1910. "Population." Vol. 1, table 28. Washington, DC: U.S. Government Printing Office.

———. 1930. "Population." Vol. 1, table 13. Washington, DC: U.S. Government Printing Office.

———. 1940. "Population." Washington, DC: U.S. Government Printing Office.

———. 1960. "Census of Population and Housing Summary." Washington, DC: U.S. Government Printing Office.

———. 1970. "Census of Population and Housing Summary." Washington, DC: U.S. Government Printing Office.

———. 1980. "Census of Population and Housing Summary." Washington, DC: U.S. Government Printing Office.

———. 1990. "Census of Population and Housing Summary." Washington, DC: U.S. Government Printing Office.

———. 1992. "Popularly Elected Officials: Census of Governments." Washington, DC: U.S. Government Printing Office.

———. 1997. Current Population Survey (March).

———. 1999. Current Population Survey (March).

———. 2000a. "Census 2000 Summary File 1." Miami-Dade County, Florida.

———. 2000b. "Household Income, Per Capita Income, and Persons Below Poverty." Census of Population and Housing, Demographic Profile.

———. 2000c. "Voting and Registration in the Election of November 1998" (August).

———. 2001a. "The Hispanic Population in the United States: Population Characteristics, March 2000." Current Population Survey (CPS).

———. 2001b. "The Hispanic Population: 2000, Percent of Population for One or More Races" (September).

———. 2002. "Voting and Registration in the Election of November 2000: Population Characteristics" (February). Current Population Survey (CPS).

———. 2004. "We the People: Hispanics in the United States: Census 2000 Special Reports" (December).

U.S. Department of Justice. n.d. "About Language Minorities Voting Rights." www.usdoj.gov/crt/voting/sec_203/activ_203.htm.

U.S. Library of Congress. n.d. "Hispanic Americans in Congress." http://lcweb.loc.gov/rr/hispanic/congress/menendez.html (accessed January 9, 2004).

———. n.d. "Hispanic Americans in Congress, 1822–1995." http://lcweb.loc.gov/rr/hispanic/congress/geog.html.

Vaca, Nicolás C. 2004. *The Presumed Alliance: The Unspoken Conflict between Latinos and Blacks and What It Means for America*. New York: HarperCollins.

Valdes, Daniel T. 1971. *A Political History of New Mexico, Stressing new Sources, Offering Startling New Interpretations*. Book 1, *Political Growth*.

Valle, Victor M., and Rodolfo D. Torres. 2000. *Latino Metropolis*. Globalization and Community Series 7. Minneapolis: University of Minnesota Press.

Vargas, Arturo. 1999–2000. "A Decade in Review." *Harvard Journal of Hispanic Policy* 11: 3–7

Velázquez, José E. 1998. "Coming Full Circle: The Puerto Rican Socialist Party, U.S. Branch." In *The Puerto Rican Movement: Voices from the Diaspora*, edited by Andrés Torres and José E. Velázquez. Philadelphia: Temple University Press.

Vigil, Maurillo E. 1978. *Chicano Politics*. Washington DC: University Press of America.

———. 1980. *Los Patrones: Profiles of Hispanic Political Leaders in New Mexico History*. New York: University Press of America.

———. 1985. *The Hispanics of New Mexico: Essays on History and Culture*. Bristol, IN: Wyndham Hall.

———. 1987. *Hispanics in American Politics: The Search for Political Power*. New York: University Press of America.

———. 1996. *Hispanics in Congress: A Historical and Political Survey*. New York: University Press of America.

———. 1997. "Hispanics in the 103rd Congress: The 1990 Census, Reapportionment, Redistricting, and the 1992 Election." *In Pursuing Power: Latinos and the Political System*, edited by F. Chris Garcia. Notre Dame, IN: University of Notre Dame Press.

———. 2000. "The Ethnic Organization as an Instrument of Political and Social Change: MALDEF, a Case Study." In *En Aquel Entonces: Readings in Mexican American History*, edited by Manuel G. Gonzales and Cynthia M. Gonzales. Bloomington: Indiana University Press.

Villarreal, Roberto E., Norma G. Hernandez, and Howard D. Neighbor, eds. 1988. *Latino Empowerment: Progress, Problems, and Prospects*. Westport, CT: Greenwood.

Voter News Service. 2000. "VNS Election Day Exit Polls, November 8."

Warren, Christopher L., and Dario V. Moreno. 2003. "Power without a Program: Hispanic Incorporation in Miami." In *Racial Politics in American Cities*, 3rd ed., edited by Rufus P. Browning, Dale R. Marshall, and David H. Tabb. New York: Longman.

Washington Post, Henry J. Kaiser Family Foundation, and Harvard University. 2000. "National Survey on Latinos in America." www.kff.org/content/2000/3023/ (accessed November 7, 2001).

Weiss, Eric M. 2001. "Call Him Señor Alcalde: Perez Sweeps to Overwhelming Victory as First Hispanic Mayor." *Hartford Courant*, November 7, p. A1.

Welch, Susan, and John R. Hibbing. 1988. "Hispanic Representation in the U.S. Congress." In *Latinos and the Political System*, edited by F. Chris Garcia. Notre Dame, IN: University of Notre Dame Press.

Wells, Miriam J. 1996. *Strawberry Fields: Politics, Class, and Work in California Agriculture*. Ithica, NY: Cornell University Press.

Whitby, Kenny J. 1997. *The Color of Representation: Congressional Behavior and Black Interests*. Ann Arbor: University of Michigan Press.

William C. Velásquez Institute. 1997. The 1996 California Latino Vote. Special issue of *Southwest Voter Research Notes* 10, no. 2 (spring).

———. 2000a. *Special Edition: The 2000 Latino Vote in California* 1, no. 3 (winter). www.WCVI.org.

———. 2000b. *Special Edition: The 2000 Latino Vote in Texas* 1, no. 4 (winter). www.WCVI.org.

———. 2000c. "U.S. Latinos Cast Record Number of Votes." Press release. November 15.

———. 2002. Texas exit poll (November). www.wcvi.org (accessed January 30, 2005).

———. 2004(a). "More than 7.6 Million Latino Vote in Presidential Race." Press release. November 4.

———. 2004(b) "The 2004 WCVI National Latino election Day Exit Poll." Dr. Henry Flores, St Mary's University, www.wcvi.org/latino_voter_research/polls/national/2004/flores.html(accessed January 28, 2005).

Williams, John. 2001."Ground Effort Put Brown over Top." *Houston Chronicle*, December 3, p. 1.

Williams, Melissa S. 1998. *Voice, Trust, and Memory: Marginalized Groups and the Failings of Liberal Representation*. Princeton, NJ: Princeton University Press.

Wilson, Robert H. 1997. *Public Policy and Community*. Austin: University of Texas Press.

Zars, Belle. 2001. "Ed Garza Takes the Pot: The Mayor Is San Antonio's New Favorite Son." *Texas Observer Online*, September 28.

Zucker, Norman L., and Naomi Flink Zucker. 1996. *Desperate Crossing: Seeking Refuge in America*. New York: M. E. Sharpe.

■ Interviews with Elected Officials

All interviews were conducted in person, unless indicated otherwise.
Amador, Augusto. Newark City Council member. July 16, 2001.

Armenta, Fernando. Monterey County (CA) supervisor. January 16, 2002.

Armijo, Armando. Albuquerque City councilor. June 27, 2001.

Barrera, Enrique. San Antonio City Council member. June 21, 2001.

Betancourt, Annie. State representative, District 116, FL. July 11, 2001.

Bower, Matti. Miami Beach Council member. July 11, 2001.

Briones, Dolores. El Paso County judge. June 25, 2001.

Caballero, Anna. Mayor, Salinas, CA. December 21, 2001.

Cabrera, Ralph. City of Coral Gables Council member. Coral Gables, FL. July 6, 2001 (phone interview).

Cedillo, Gilbert. California state representative. August 12 (phone interview) and September 5 (in person).

Chacon, Alicia. Former El Paso County judge. June 25, 2001.

Devers, Marcos. Lawrence (MA) Council member. July 21, 2001.

Diaz, Joe. Mayor, Sweetwater, FL. July 12, 2001.

Gallegos, Steve. Bernalillo county commissioner. June 27, 2001 (phone interview).

Garcia, Jesus. Former Illinois state senator and Chicago alderman. July 25, 2001.

Gonzalez, Efrain. New York state senator. July 15, 2001 (phone interview).

Gonzalez, Minnie. Connecticut state representative. July 19, 2001.

Granato, Jesse. City of Chicago alderman. July 24, 2001.

Herrera Hill, Barbara. City of Weston Council member, Weston, FL. July 13, 2001.

Linares, Guillermo. New York City Council member, July 16, 2001.

Lujan, Louis. La Puente (CA) Council member. August 13, 2001.

Maldonado, Roberto. Cook County commissioner. July 24, 2001.

Martinez, Lydia. Connecticut state representative. July 19, 2001.

Martinez Fischer, Trey. Texas state representative. June 20, 2001.

Mendez, Olga. New York state senator. July 18–19, 2001 (two phone interviews).

Mendoza, Susana. Illinois state representative. July 27, 2001.

Munoz, Rick. City of Chicago alderman. July 25, 2001.

Pacheco, Robert. California State Assembly representative. August 13, 2001.

Padilla, Alex. Los Angeles City Council member and president. August 13, 2001.

Perez, Bobby. San Antonio City Council member. June 21, 2001.

Phares, Ana Ventura. Watsonville (CA) Council member. November 15, 2001.

Rivera, Cheryl. Massachusetts state representative, July 20, 2001 (phone interview).

Rodriguez, Rose. El Paso City Council member. June 25, 2001.

Sanchez, Bernadette. New Mexico state senator. June 27, 2001 (phone interview).

Sanchez, Ken. Bernalillo county commissioner. June 28, 2001.

Sanchez, Orlando. City of Houston Council member at large, Houston, Texas. June 19, 2001.

Smith, Jose. Miami Beach Council member. July 11, 2001.

Solario, Jose. Santa Ana (CA) Council member. August 14, 2001.

Soto, Cynthia. Illinois state representative. July 27, 2001.

Van de Putte, Leticia. Texas state senator. June 22, 2001.

Vasquez, Gabriel. City of Houston Council member, Houston, Texas. June 18, 2001.

Vega, Mariano. Jersey City Council member. July 18, 2001.

Villarreal, Michael. Texas state representative. June 21, 2001.

Index

Acosta, Ralph, 73
Affirmative action, California's elimination of, 102, 181
African American elected officials: compared to LEOs, 7; deracialization strategy and, 130
African American–Latino coalitions, 9, 71–76, 130
Alarcón, Richard, 154
Alatorre, Richard, 46, 151, 152–153
Alatorre, Soledad, 48
Alianza Federal de Pueblos Libres, 44–45
Alisal Betterment Committee, 174, 186
Anaya, Toney, 69
Anglo, defined, 3
Apodaca, Jerry, 69
Armenta, Fernando, 174, 186
ASPIRA, 51
August 29th Movement, 48
Austin, Texas: 2001 mayoral elections in, 122–123

Badillo, Herman, 52, 69, 75
Barrios, Jarrett, 84
Bautista, Maria, 76
Becerra, Xavier, 154, 155, 157
Berman, Howard, 131–132
Berrios, Jose, 67
Berriozábal, Maria, 148–149
Betancourt, Annie, 144
Bilingual education, attacks on, 102, 104

Bosch, Juan, 55
Boston, multiracial political coalition in, 73
Bracero Program, 29, 37, 43, 164, 165
Bradley, Tom, 151
Briones, Dolores, 83
Bush, George W., 104, 105, 106

Caballero, Anna, 174–175, 184, 185
Caballero, Ray, 121
California: anti–affirmative action law in, 181; anti-immigrant ballot proposition in, 84–86; at-large elections in, 109; Chicano-majority city councils in, 50; Latina officeholders in, 211; Latino voter turnout in, 101–102, 103; Proposition 187 in, 84–85, 86; racialized voting patterns in, 128–129, 206; redistricting plan of 2000, 131–132. *See also* Los Angeles/Los Angeles County; Salinas Valley
Californios: defined, 3; governance and political participation of, 20, 22–23, 25
Carter, Jimmy, 51
Castro, Joaquin, 201
Cedillo, Gil, 74
Central American immigrant(s): citizenship for, 87, 98; grassroots political organizing of, 60; political participation of, 87; as political

About the Book

An untold story of the last decade is the rapid ascent to electoral office of Latinos nationwide, who now hold more than five thousand elected positions. *Latino Political Power* provides a comprehensive and accessible introduction to Latino politics from the early 20th century to the present.

The purpose of the book is twofold: to capture the transition of Latinos from disenfranchised outsiders to political leaders, and to observe the relationship between those leaders and their ethnic communities. Geron tackles a number of key questions: Who is running for office? How are they elected? How does ethnicity variously shape the politics of candidates and the priorities they pursue once in office? He also addresses commonalities and differences among Latinos based on location, gender, party affiliation, and ethnic ties. Students will come away from the rich case studies and nationwide survey data with a broad understanding of contemporary Latino political behavior.

Kim Geron is assistant professor of political science at California State University, East Bay.